SM 2724RAG
19(fre)

B 48899

Utility and Rights

Utility
and
Rights

R. G. Frey, Editor

Basil Blackwell

Copyright © 1984 by the University of Minnesota

First published 1985
Basil Blackwell Limited
108 Cowley Road, Oxford OX4 1JF, England

British Library Cataloguing in Publication Data

Utility and rights.
  1. Ethics
  I. Frey, Raymond
  170   BJ1012
    ISBN 0-631-13713-0

Printed in the United States of America

Contents

Preface

No matter looms larger or promises to be of more importance for moral and political (and so legal) philosophy than the clash beween utilitarianism and the theory of rights. For what is being fought over is the absolutely fundamental issue of the nature of the theoretical structure that will underpin these areas and so form the basis of approach to more particular, substantive questions. Is that structure to be, as so much work in the recent past has assumed, utility- or welfare-based? Or is it to be, as critics of utilitarianism increasingly insist, rights-based?

This is a volume of essays on various aspects of this controversy. It looks at the foundations, nature, and theory of moral rights; it looks at the role of rights in utilitarianism, at whether there can be an utilitarian theory of moral rights, and so at the clash between claims of justice and welfare; it looks at different parts of rights-theory and utilitarianism, and subjects them to careful scrutiny and analysis; it looks at natural rights, at the rights that figure in contractualism, and at rights in the law; it looks at property rights, their analysis, and role in utilitarianism; it looks at how certain moral theories seek to accommodate rights and at what failure in this regard implies for their adequacy; and it looks at the whole question of the centrality and importance of rights for moral theory. In a word, the book covers most of the ground of rights-theory, as well as the clash between rights-theory and utilitarianism. Accordingly, it should be of interest, not only to those specifically involved in the quest for a satisfactory utilitarianism and to those specifically concerned to use moral rights in order to reject utilitarianism once and for all as an adequate normative ethical theory, but also, in view of the importance accorded moral rights by recent moral and political theorists and of the fact that many of the most fundamental questions in these areas arise in connection with the clash between individual rights and social welfare, to anyone interested in contemporary moral and political theory.

The book aims to make a difference to present debate; it differs in several crucial respects, therefore, from the usual collection. The essays are not surveys of past or present positions on rights or descriptive pieces illustrating different strains or movements in the literature or detached compilations of basic ideas and distinctions that those positions and that literature make manifest; they are not presented as and do not amount to a set of readings designed to acquaint the uninitiated with the present 'state of the art' in moral and political theory; and they are not addressed to novices in philosophy. Rather, the essays are sophisticated studies on rights, at times building upon and molding, at others taking issue with and rejecting earlier work in the area; they are argumentative wholes, committed in outlook, often with a sharp cutting edge, by individuals very much a part of present controversies; and they are pieces by and for philosophers, though students and others with a grounding in moral and/or political theory will find them accessible.

Of the eleven essays included, eight are published here for the first time, and a ninth (my own) is so altered and expanded as to constitute a fresh paper; of the remaining two, one (by Joseph Raz) appears here more or less contemporaneously with its appearance elsewhere, and the other (by Charles Fried) is a revised version of a paper from a legal journal. As a glance at the list of the contributors will show, I am the only unknown; the others are among the most prominent moral, political, and legal philosophers of the day.

The volume, then, is a collection of new essays by prominent figures on some of the most important themes in moral and political theory.

My introduction does not attempt to summarize the essays, but rather focuses upon one way uneasiness with utilitarianism can lead some to rights-theory. My concern is with the particular uneasiness in question, to do with the place of persons in utilitarianism and with what causes it; thus, I want to sketch one way rights-theory can seem the answer to alleged inadequacies in utilitarianism. The emphasis, I must stress, is not upon whether these inadequacies are genuine or can be repaired, but upon how the perception of them can make rights-theory seem the natural alternative to utilitarianism.

Finally, it is with great sadness that I record the death of one of this volume's contributors, J. L. Mackie. John took a keen interest in the book, and I know he was looking forward to its publication and to the appearance of his exchange with Dick Hare. Happily, John's essay, one of his last pieces, is entirely characteristic, and it is particularly fitting that it should appear with a rejoinder by Dick. For these two, in their seminar in Oxford, brought moral philosophy alive to numerous students and professionals, and it is nice to be able to give in print some indication of what those weekly sessions were like and so to mark the passing of an important stimulus to philosophy. With John's tragic death, all of us have lost a good philosopher, and some of us, a good friend.

R. G. F.
Oxford

Utility and Rights

Introduction: Utilitarianism and Persons

R. G. Frey

One of the central worries over utilitarianism that prompts some to turn to rights-theory has to do with the protection accorded persons in an unconstrained utilitarianism. Rights are typically postulated in order to protect persons and their vital interests, and recourse to them can seem natural as persons and their interests are perceived to come under threat from utilitarianism. The important point to critics is not that such threats are possible but that they seem endemic to, an inescapable part of, utilitarianism. This perception of utilitarianism as antipathetic to the protection of persons and their vital interests is nowhere more acutely apparent, I suspect, than over the utilitarian explanation of the wrongness of killing, and I want to show how rights-theory can seem to critics of this explanation the natural alternative.

(Whether anyone has ever held a wholly unconstrained utilitarianism where persons are at issue is not the point here; my concern is with utilitarianism prior to constraints being built into it. Nor shall I bother with the niceties involved in determining who or what is a person; I shall assume that, whatever view of persons one holds, ordinary, adult humans are persons.)[1]

I

During the 1960s and 1970s, the removal of the alleged defects of classical or act-utilitarianism spurred the extraordinary proliferation in types and versions of rule-utilitarianism and utilitarian generalization. Part of the motivation behind these developments was the conviction that, if only we continued to explore different types and versions of utilitarianism, eventually we should work out a theory that met many of the objections to and contained few of the defects in classical utilitarianism.

3

Then, with the objections met and defects purged, the theory would be put forward as a satisfactory utilitarianism and, if it perhaps met certain other requirements, as an adequate normative ethical theory. In fact, however, the new theories did not prove very satisfactory, and soon the sustained attack upon them—that they were open to the old objections or gave rise to new ones, that they 'collapsed' into act-utilitarianism or were 'extensionally equivalent' to it—ended their brief dominance of theoretical discussion of utilitarianism. Today, it remains true that, when utilitarianism is criticized, it is almost always classical utilitarianism that critics have in mind. This is true of rights-theorists; as we shall see, however, their central worry can be generalized to include any utilitarianism having a consequence component. (I put the matter this way to allow for innovations in utilitarian theory.)

There is nothing which is 'utilitarianism' *per se*: the term refers not to a single theory but to a cluster of theories that are variations on a theme, the components of which can be distinguished. This theme, taken here to revolve around acts (as opposed, say, to lives, policies, decisions, or rational choice), involves (at least) four components: (i) the consequence component, to the effect that the rightness or wrongness of acts is tied in some way to (the production of) good and bad consequences; (ii) the value conponent, to the effect that the goodness or badness of consequences is to be evaluated by means of some standard of intrinsic goodness; (iii) the range component, to the effect that it is the acts consequences as affecting everyone and not just the agent himself that are to be considered in determining rightness; and (iv) a principle of utility, to the effect that one should seek to maximize that which the adopted standard of goodness identifies as intrinsically good.

Classical utilitarianism is the view that acts are right or wrong solely in virtue of the goodness or badness of their consequences. It possesses the four components. First, its consequence component is consequentialism, or the view that acts are right or wrong solely in virtue of their consequences. A consequence component of this sort is strong, since consequences alone determine rightness. Second, different species of classical utilitarianism can be generated through employing different standards of goodness, at least one of which is required in any such species, in order to be able to evaluate consequences. The distinction between hedonistic and ideal standards requires further distinctions within each camp, but, on the whole, contemporary writers have rejected hedonism, adopted an ideal standard of goodness, and maintained that a number of things are good-in-themselves. This last is not unimportant, since, to both camps, the standard of goodness adopted is a standard of intrinsic goodness. The two camps have also agreed over the identity of those things that are intrinsically good, namely, certain cognitive states or states of mind or consciousness, collectively referred to as 'pleasure', 'happiness', etc. In recent years, however, numerous writers have moved away from a mental-state view of utility and value, on the ground that it is too confining to restrict utility to a concern with states of mind, to an interest-satisfaction view, in which 'interests' is a generic term covering a multiplicity of desires or preferences. Thus, construed as I have done here, preference-utilitarianism is classical utilitarianism with an expanded value theory. Third, the range component in classical utilitarianism covers all persons affected by the act, and it covers them equally, to the degree that they are affected. Not every theory that contains the consequence and value components of classical utilitarianism is utilitarian in character: the only major difference between ethical egoism and classical utilitarianism is that the egoist is concerned with maximizing utility in his own case, and only consequences that affect him bear upon the rightness and wrongness of acts. Finally, in addition to providing the means by which acts' consequences are evaluated, some standard of intrinsic goodness is necessary to the application of the principle of utility. An abstract formulation of the principle, such as 'Always maximize net utility' cannot be applied in the absence of some interpretation of utility, since one would not know what to maximize. Such an interpretation is applied by a standard of intrinsic goodness, and a concrete and applicable formulation of the principle, such as 'Always maximize net desire-satisfaction', thereby becomes possible. The term 'utility', then, is a blanket term, to be filled in by whatever standard of goodness is adopted. The principle, moreover, is a maximizing one, enjoining its adherents to maximize in the world that which their value-theory is focused around, and it is applied directly to individual acts.

Consequentialism and utilitarianism are distinct. One may be a consequentialist without being a utilitarian, as with ethical egoists, and one may be a utilitarian without being a consequentialist, as with rule-utilitarians and adherents to the different forms of utilitarian generalization, all of whom specifically reject the view that acts are right or wrong solely in virtue of their consequences. Nor is consequentialism to be identified with classical utilitarianism: any act-utilitarianism requires a standard of goodness by which to evaluate consequences and in terms of which to formulate its principle of utility; and different act-utilitarianisms are generated, even though they all are consequentialist in character, through the adoption of different standards of goodness.

Among the many issues surrounding consequentialism, a distinction may be drawn between (i) those that arise in connection with consequentialism independently of its inclusion within classical utilitarianism and (ii) those that arise in connection with classical utilitarianism as a result of its inclusion of consequentialism. The former are such that any consequentialist, utilitarian or otherwise, would have to consider; they pertain, for example, to the defense of consequentialism against rival accounts of what makes right acts right. Among the latter group of issues are those, for example, that center around the nature, place, and weight of moral and social rules within a classical utilitarianism. (Included among the issues that fall under this latter group are those to do with moral rights, since it is not clear what the cash value of moral rights are or what cutting edge they have in a rigorously consequentialist ethic.)

Now nearly everyone thinks, special circumstances apart, that it is wrong to kill persons; the problem, of course, is to say why it is wrong. The classical utilitarian can say why: an act of killing a person is wrong because of its consequences.

II

Classical utilitarians, who are to be understood in this section as having a conception of utility formulated around pleasure/pain (or some other mental-state view of utility and value), have always had difficulty persuading others of their case over why it is wrong to kill persons. The surface reasons for this are readily apparent.

First, armed essentially with only the argument from side effects (in which by 'side effects' is meant any and all of the consequences of an act of killing, as they affect people other than the person killed), classical utilitarians possess no direct reason against killing. To many, the use of a consequentialist account of rightness in the case of killing has seemed to produce an odd result, since it makes it appear that what is wrong with killing someone is, and can only be, the negative effects upon others of killing him. This, it is suggested, so jars with our intuitions about killing and the destruction of persons, intuitions which demand that the wrongness of killing be more intimately connected with the person destroyed, as to cast severe doubt upon the classical utilitarian's case over killing. Second, what reason classical utilitarians do have against killing is completely at the mercy of whether killing actually produces negative side effects. If, for example, such side effects do not arise or can be neutralized, then the argument from side effects provides no reason at all against killing. Third, though it is a relatively safe generalization that killing produces numerous and serious negative side effects and an equally safe generalization that there is on the whole little we can do to prevent such effects arising or to neutralize them once they have arisen, these are nevertheless generalizations about contingent matters of fact; in a particular case, they may not apply. (Critics, of course, try to assist this process by artificially devising cases, often of a bizarre or fantastic nature, in which these generalizations are wholly inapplicable.) Fourth, not only can the argument from side effects on occasion provide no reason against killing, but it can also on occasion provide a positive reason for killing. If instead of negative side effects an act of killing were to produce positive side effects, if, that is, there were to be a net gain in pleasure over pain, then, leaving aside any attempts to build constraints into the theory, that would provide a classical utilitarian with a reason for killing the person in question.

(These surface reasons for worry are perfectly compatible with acknowledging that the argument from side effects does carry weight. The side effects of killing are usually both numerous and serious, and very few of us are likely simply to dismiss them as irrelevant in deciding upon the rightness of what was done. Looked at in this way, the above worries arise as the result of resting *everything* upon side effects.)

In addition to these surface reasons for disquiet with the classical utilitarian's explanation of the wrongness of killing, there are several deeper ones. I call them 'deeper' because they reveal something of the nature of classical utilitarianism's view of persons, a view that seems at odds with the more intimate link between persons and killing which critics think our intuitions over the wrongness of killing demand.

Replaceability

On those occasions when the argument from side effects cannot be brought to bear against killing, classical utilitarians are not without a further argument. They can and do still claim that, special circumstances apart, killing diminishes the amount of pleasure in the world, something that, given their value-theory and their concern with the maximization of pleasure, they are bound to regard as objectionable.

Quite apart from the fact that this claim about diminution in pleasure seems likely to appeal, as an explanation of the wrongness of killing, only to someone already tempted by classical utilitarianism, it commits the classical utilitarian to the replaceability argument. If what matters is the loss in total pleasure in the world, then if the person killed were replaced by another, whose life was roughly commensurate in terms of pleasure, the loss in total pleasure would be made good; and if the loss were made good, then, of course, killing that person would not be wrong. Plainly, so long as replacement remains possible, that is, leaving aside constraints, so long as we can create new life of a roughly commensurate level of pleasure to the life we take, the wrongness of killing vanishes. The replaceability argument, therefore, effectively licenses killing, and not even confirmed, classical utilitarians seem likely actually to welcome its embrace.

The fact that people are replaceable in an unconstrained classical utilitarianism points up three things about persons in the theory. First, persons matter in the theory primarily because they are the vessels or receptacles of pleasure. What is important is the total amount of pleasure in the world, and what importance persons have derives from this and consists in their being the containers or bearers of pleasure. In the appropriate sense, one container is as good as another, and the destruction of one is made good by replacing it with another. Accordingly, though it is persons who have pleasure, what is centrally of value is the pleasure they have; that I am I and you are you, each of us autonomous persons in our own right, with our own individuality and interests, matters only derivatively, at best. Second, while killing is the destruction of autonomous persons, with their own individuality and interests, the classical position, with its value-theory focused around pleasure/pain (or for some other mental-state view of value), treats this destruction as a loss in value because of the loss of pleasure involved. That is, its value-theory effectively separates the person from the pleasure a person has; and since it is pleasure that is of value, the amount of pleasure becomes the crucial fact for the theory. Third, as the replaceability argument makes very clear, it is the total amount of pleasure in the world that the classical utilitarian is ultimately concerned with, and this total is to be determined by summing pleasures across persons. With a value-theory that effectively separates pleasure from persons, summing or aggregating pleasures is a person-neutral exercise; it is the adding up of elements of value without regard, leaving aside constraints, as to who has them. Thus, replacement is possible because, since it is the totality of pleasure that matters and summing pleasures is person-neutral, who has what pleasure is of no consequence; a replacement person will do as well as the person killed, so long as the sums work out.

Utilitarian Sacrifice

The argument from side effects can provide a reason for killing when killing produces positive rather than negative side effects or a net gain in pleasure over pain. Since these side effects and gain do not accrue to the person killed but to others, we have a trade-off, between one person's life and the loss in pleasure this represents, and positive side effects for others and the compensating gain in pleasure these represent.

Today, of course, when numerous people support killing in cases of abortion, euthanasia, infanticide, suicide, a just war, capital punishment, and so on, the complete inviolability of persons is no longer so widely maintained; resistance to the present trade-off, therefore, is not likely on this score to be so widespread as it once was. Nevertheless, many people worry about the case; and what worries them is that it is one of killing one person to benefit others, an instance of the more general, classical utilitarian phenomenon of diminishing one person's pleasure in order to produce a greater increase in the pleasure of others.

This diminution of one person's pleasure in order to produce a greater increase in the pleasure of others, which we might call utilitarian sacrifice, also points up three things of interest here about unconstrained classical utilitarianism. First, since what centrally matters in the theory is the amount of pleasure in the world, not its distribution, if that amount can be increased by utilitarian sacrifice, then that is what the theory licenses. Second, utilitarian sacrifice is systematic. By this, I mean that, in the unconstrained theory, there is no person who in principle is beyond the scope of utilitarian sacrifice, no set of interests the pleasure from which cannot be sacrificed to the production of greater pleasure in others, no part of a person's life that is so private or personal or vital as to elude potential sacrifice. Third, in the unconstrained theory, utilitarian sacrifice is without a cutoff point. It will justify massive as well as small drops in a person's pleasure; it will justify one or many such drops; and there is no point below which, provided a further diminution in pleasure remains possible, its claim of justification cannot in principle reach.

This sacrifice of one person for another cannot be brought to an end, in the unconstrained theory, by appeal to the alleged, inherent worth of each individual, autonomous person. As we have seen, the worth of persons is derivative from their status as the receptacles or bearers of pleasure; individual persons matter, then, but not in such a way that precludes their sacrifice, so long as there is in others an offsetting gain in pleasure.

Thus, if utilitarian sacrifice can increase the amount of pleasure in the world, it, too, can justify killing; far from providing a barrier against killing, it, just as the replaceability argument, licenses it.

Value-Reductionism

While a constraint that has the effect of justifying the utilitarian sacrifice of a life or vital interests only in cases of nonmarginal increases in pleasure can be built into a classical utilitarianism, those bothered by such sacrifice do not typically point to the amount of pleasure lost or gained; indeed, they do not point to anything whatever to do with pleasure. Some claim about the inherent value of life, however, is not so easily accommodated by classical utilitarianism. With its value-theory focused around pleasure (or some other mental-state view of utility and value), it is forced to construe the value of life in terms of a life's actualities and potentialities for pleasure, and this is but an instance of what might be called its value-reductionism.

Value-reductionism encapsulates the classical utilitarian's implicit endorsement of four theses: the things we treat as having value can be ranked and ordered in terms of the amount of pleasure they (actually/potentially) give; the pleasure these things give can be placed upon a single scale of measurement; this scale of measurement is person-neutral, capable of having the pleasures of different persons placed upon it, and intensity-sensitive, capable of capturing the different levels of pleasure that these things produce in different people; and the position of these things on the scale determines their relative value and so their relative ordering. Both replacement and utilitarian sacrifice in part rely upon these theses, and it is obvious that they are integral to the whole enterprise of trade-offs in pleasures between persons.[2]

These theses in turn point up three things about an unconstrained classical utilitarianism, regarded now in the context of sacrifice and trade-offs. First, the theory is, without refinement, inimical to some claim that there are incommensurable values (such as human life). In the present case, such a claim would amount to the view either that there are values that cannot be expressed on a scale (or a single scale) of pleasure or that, though values can be so expressed, there is in fact no such (or single such) scale. Quite what these claims amount to or how they would be defended is not to the point here; but it is as well to be aware that, depending upon the answers to these questions, massive numbers of laymen would reject these claims, even where human life is concerned. At least, human life is frequently traded off against other values, as, for example, numerous medical cases illustrate. Second, classical utilitarianism, as a theory about trade-offs, applies prudential reasoning to social contexts. Just as an individual person weighs, balances, and trades off his pleasures against each other, so the classical utilitarian weighs, balances, and trades off the pleasures of different persons, depending upon where these pleasures fall on the scale of measurement and so upon the degree of gain over loss involved in particular cases. In this regard, utilitarian reasoning treats the pleasures of different persons, expressed on the scale of measurement, in the way that a single individual treats different pleasures of his own. Third, since the summing or aggregation of pleasures is person-neutral, since the scale of measurement for pleasures is person-neutral, since one person's gain in pleasure can offset another person's loss, and since there is no cutoff point to such sacrifice, the protection of persons and their vital interests seems perpetually at risk. Since utilitarian reasoning can justify trade-offs and utilitarian sacrifice whenever contingencies so dictate, and since there are no person-relative principles that bar utilitarian sacrifice of persons and their vital interests within the unconstrained theory, there seems no way to deflect the risk to persons. And constraints that might deflect the risk, for example, that a life is of inherent worth irrespective of its pleasure or capacity for pleasure, that life is an incommensurable value and so beyond the compass of utilitarian trade-offs, that this or that person-relative principle could secure persons and their vital interests from such trade-offs, do not obviously form part of the classical theory.

In short, far from providing a persuasive case over the wrongness of killing, classical utilitarianism, critics will urge, seems perpetually to place persons and their vital interests at risk, a risk that will be realized if the contingencies fall out one way rather than another. The security that people feel through the protection of persons and their interests seems at best, therefore, a fortuitous outcome of how the contingencies fall out. Accordingly, worry by critics about the classical utilitarian's explanation of the wrongness of killing seems likely to persist.

III

Most utilitarians today distinguish between classical and desire- or preference-utilitarianism, the latter, as we have seen, with a conception of utility formulated around the satisfaction of desires and preferences; and a great many go on to embrace preference-utilitarianism, in order to distance themselves from a mental-state view of utility and value and so to open up the scope of their (value-theory and, therefore, overall) theory. Whether or not these individuals specifically opt for preference-utilitarianism with the case of killing in mind, the theory does supply additional leverage in the attempt to explain the wrongness of killing. (Once again, I am concerned with the theory prior to constraints being built into it.)

Preference-utilitarianism provides a direct reason against killing. The theory is concerned with the maximization of the satisfaction of desires, and this draws attention to the fact that, quite apart from side effects and a diminution in pleasure in the world, there are all of a person's future-related desires to be considered, including his very powerful desire to go on living, all of which will be frustrated if the person is killed. This, in turn, provides a direct reason for not killing him. Indeed, if we bear in mind that almost all of us have numerous future-related desires, often of great strength, and have among our very most powerful desires the desire to go on living, then preference-utilitarianism provides a rather weighty, direct reason against killing.

Instances of preference-utilitarianism providing no reason at all against killing would have to be of a particular order. The person would have to lack any and all future-related desires, including the desire to go on living; and though one can artificially devise cases in which all such desires are absent, they are most unlikely to be in the vast preponderance of cases in real life.

For preference-utilitarianism to provide, in the same way that the argument from side effects does, a positive reason for killing, it would not be enough that a person desire not to go on living; he would also have to desire this to such a degree that its strength exceeded the combined strengths of all of his other, future-related desires. He would also have to appreciate, should the desire not to go on living come upon him, that the satisfaction of this desire would preclude having any further desires, with respect to himself, his family, or whatever, while recognizing that the variety and multiplicity of a person's desires, and their satisfaction, are what give a person's life (and, through it, often the lives of others) the texture and richness it possesses. (I leave aside any talk of rational desires and their incorporation into preference-utilitarianism, which would certainly arise at this point.) Of course, a person's desires might fall out in the way envisaged here, in which case preference-utilitarianism would provide a reason for killing; but they are unlikely to do so in the vast preponderance of cases. And when they do so fall out, when a person desires not to go on living, when this desire is of a strength to exceed the combined strength of all of his other future-related desires, and when the person fully appreciates the effect of the satisfaction of this desire with respect to any further desires on this part (and to the desires of other people), then the morality of killing him may well strike many as a much more open question than it does when killing him will produce merely positive side effects or a net gain in pleasure.

Preference-utilitarianism arguably bars the replacement of persons. A person's (future-related desires and) desire to go on living will be thwarted if he is killed, and the creation of another person neither undoes nor offsets this loss in satisfaction that his death produces. A person's desire for continued life is not satisfied through his death and the creation of another person; hence, his death inflicts a loss that another's creation cannot make good.

While utilitarian sacrifice will still be possible, preference-utilitarianism places an obstacle in its way that concern with a mere net gain in pleasure cannot. Most people have powerful, future-related desires; in particular, most people's desire to go on living is among the strongest they have, and it typically increases in strength when one's life is endangered. Thus, utilitarian sacrifice is going to be possible only if the overall gain in satisfaction of desires is substantial enough to offset the sizable loss in satisfaction in the person sacrificed.

An unconstrained preference-utilitarianism, then, may well appeal to some of those left unpersuaded by the classical utilitarian account of the wrongness of killing. Nevertheless, it, too, has provoked concern, and, in part, for some of the same reasons classical utilitarianism has. Rather than translate earlier remarks into the present idiom, however, I shall turn to several reasons for concern specifically to do with preference-utilitarianism.

It may well be that one has already to be a utilitarian of sorts in order to find the preference-utilitarian account of the wrongness of killing—that it thwarts a person's desires—acceptable and even, perhaps, plausible. To be sure, thwarting a person's desires is typically a concomitant of killing him, but that it should be the explanation of the wrongness of killing him might well only occur to someone already leaning in the direction of preference-utilitarianism.

Though preference-utilitarianism does provide a direct reason against killing, it provides a reason grounded in the effective separation of a person from his desires. It is loss in desire-satisfaction that centrally matters, not the autonomous person who is, so to speak, the bearer of that (loss in) satisfaction. To many, then, preference-utilitarianism will be seen as not providing a direct reason against killing of the right sort, a sort that locates the wrongness of killing in the attack upon the autonomous person and not in the contingent fact of the particular degree of desire-satisfaction that person has.

In the unconstrained theory, there is no way of discounting desires. If what matters, if what is to be maximized, is desire-satisfaction, then the fact that the Jew desires to live and the Nazi desires to kill him must be reckoned with; there is nothing in the unconstrained theory about either ignoring or devaluing desires (i) that are from this particular source or have that particular character, (ii) that most would find deeply repugnant, or (iii) that most see as issuing from a condition of incomplete information or misinformation. The switch from actual and/or future desires to rational ones, of course, may help to discount certain desires that we should wish to see discounted; but there is no *a priori* reason why only those desires most of us would find 'morally appropriate' would turn out to be rational.

In the unconstrained theory, there is no way of disregarding desires. The theory is one of maximization of desire-satisfaction, and, without constraints, it takes desires when and where it finds them; that is, it seeks to maximize the satisfaction of the desires of those in and affected by the situation. But this seems in turn to allow a rather broad compass to the desires to be taken into account. If you and your neighbor are discussing whether to erect a chain fence between your properties, which he is against and you favor, and if I, another resident but with no adjoining property, make known to you both my strong desire that chain fences not be erected in the neighborhood and so the loss in satisfaction I am likely to suffer if my desire is thwarted, then my desire and my loss in desire-satisfaction may not obviously be disregarded. Suppose, therefore, you and your wife are trying to decide about an abortion: if you know your neighbor opposes abortions and strongly desires that they not be performed, and if you know as well that he typically suffers loss in satisfaction when (he finds out that) this desire is thwarted by members of the community, then because he is affected by your decision it is not obvious his desire in the matter can be disregarded. Even if a weighting mechanism were introduced, so that your desires would count more than your neighbor's in the matter, it would not follow that his desires could be disregarded.

A person's desire to go on living is not incommensurable with the desires of other parties for that person's death. However strongly a person desires to go on living, this desire is commensurable with other desires, including the desires of other parties; its strength may enable it to prevail at first, but in principle, since it is commensurable, it can cease to prevail through the combined strength of the countervailing desires of others. Whether or not it does cease to prevail is a contingent matter, and the rightness of killing the person, therefore, is a function of how this matter of fact turns out.

Replacement is barred only to the extent that a person has future-related desires, including the desire to go on living, and the weight of other persons' countervailing desires does not exceed the weight of his own. Again, while it is true that utilitarian sacrifice has a further hurdle to overcome in the case of preference-utilitarianism, since there is the person's desire to go on living to consider, this hurdle is overcome when the preponderance of this person's desire is eroded through others coming strongly to desire his demise. And if the case is one of sacrificing him or his vital interests in order to confer increased benefits upon others, the strength of the desires allied against him may well exceed the strength of his own desires.

With the preference-utilitarian account of the wrongness of killing, therefore, critics are unlikely to find much improvement on classical util-itarianism, and three things in particular stand out in this regard. First, though the theory seems to move in the right direction by coming up with a direct reason against killing, that reason effectively separates a person from his desires and focuses not upon the attack on the autonomous person but upon the loss in desire-satisfaction. This separa-tion in turn not only allows (the strength of) his desires to be placed upon a person-neutral scale but also, in the unconstrained theory, seem-ingly places the wrongness of killing beyond some explanation depen-dent upon the employment of person-relative principles. It is the loss in desire-satisfaction that centrally explains the wrongness of killing. Second, though the theory does interpose desires into the discussion over killing, these do not pose, for the reasons given, a strong enough barrier to killing. Third, what might enable them to pose a strong enough barrier—for example, the use of a person-relative principle that treats a person's desire to go on living as virtually sacrosanct, the claim that a person's desire to go on living is incommensurable with the desires of other people for that person's death, and the use of some device that discounts, disregards, and neutralizes the desires of others in cases of utilitarian sacrifice involving life and vital interests—is not ob-viously part of the theory.

IV

The problem for classical and preference-utilitarians is that an explana-tion of the wrongness of killing in terms of negative side effects, diminu-tion in pleasure, and frustration of desires just does not seem to provide the intimate link to the destruction of individual, valuable, autonomous persons that, critics will urge, our intuitions demand. Indeed, both classical and preference-utilitarians separate persons from the pleasures (or mental states) and desires that persons have, and employ a value-theory that exploits this separation, to the seeming detriment of in-dividual, autonomous persons. In a word, then, these theories, critics will maintain, are not sufficiently person-relative, and protective of per-sons and their vital interests, to accommodate our intuitions over killing.

The question obviously arises of whether a series of constraints can-not make utilitarianism sufficiently person-relative to solve the problem and so of whether constrained versions of classical or preference-utilitar-ianism can still the disquiet over killing to which unconstrained versions apparently give rise. This is much too large an issue to take up here, but we do not need to take it up in order to appreciate the unenviable posi-tion in which critics will see the utilitarian as placed. There are three dimensions, from the point of view of critics, to this position of unenviableness.

First, if the constraints employed move to meet the sorts of worries outlined earlier, then they seem likely to inject into utilitarianism features at odds with the character of that theory. Thus, the utilitarian has, on utilitarian grounds, in order to construct an adequate explanation of the wrongness of killing, to inject person-relative principles into a theory that is quintessentially person-neutral; incommensurable values into a theory that is paradigmatically a theory of trade-offs; devices that limit or bar replacement, utilitarian sacrifice, and trade-offs into a theory that is at bottom about these very sorts of things; and so on. To try to render one's theory person-relative by injecting features into it that run against the grain of that theory seems unlikely to bolster confidence in its eventual success in accounting for the wrongness of killing, quite apart from the fact that, unless the constraints used are severe enough, worry will not only persist about the utilitarian's views on killing but will also arise over whether the basic theory may not reassert itself over the constraints built into it. For, to critics, the basic theory will be seen as pulling in one direction and the constraints in another, and unless the constraints are strong enough, unless they more or less completely bar utilitarian reasoning in particular cases, the theory may reassert itself and so license replacement, utilitarian sacrifice, and trade-offs involving the loss of life or vital interests in one person for the enhancement of others.

If, on the other hand, the constraints to be employed do not move to meet the sorts of worries outlined earlier, then it seems unlikely, critics will urge, that the utilitarian will ever effectively still the disquiet to which utilitarian accounts of the wrongness of killing give rise. A person-neutral theory, unless constrained, is going to give results sharply at odds with intuitions over killing that exemplify and are grounded in person-relative considerations.

Second, if the constraints employed are quite severe in constraining utilitarianism; if, that is, they are sufficiently severe to make a person-neutral theory person-relative, with principles that radically limit or bar, over persons and their vital interests, replacement, utilitarian sacrifice, trade-offs involving the loss of life or vital interests in one person for the enhancement of others, and the application of utilitarian reasoning to particular cases; then the question arises of the cash value of being a utilitarian. If the net effect of constraints is to make of the utilitarian's practice what the practice of, say, a rights-theorist with person-relative principles is, then it is not clear what one gains by being a utilitarian, particularly, it will be urged, when the whole problem here stems in the

first place from inadequacies in the utilitarian's account of the wrongness of killing.

Third, to take a person-neutral theory and then try to constrain it in
such a way and to a degree as to make it yield over the wrongness of
killing what person-relative theories yield straightforwardly seems a
rather peculiar and cumbersome way of constructing an adequate explanation of the wrongness of killing. There is, as we have seen, a question about the suitability of the materials the utilitarian is trying to mold
into such an explanation; but even assuming that through experimenta-
tion with constraints he were to succeed in constructing this explanation, he has chosen an indirect and cumbersome way of doing so. To
critics, the utilitarian's enterprise here is a bit like a person with a round
hole and two pegs, one round, one square, one of which must be put
through the hole; even if by a good deal of carving the unsuitable square
peg could be made adequate to the task, the person in taking up the
square peg would be setting about the task in so indirect and cumbersome a way as virtually to preclude it from selection. In the case of killing, if in order to give anything like an acceptable explanation of the
wrongness of killing the utilitarian must constrain his theory in
whatever ways and to whatever degree is necessary to enable it to capture the person-relative character of our intuitions, then has he not, in
proceeding, and even if eventually successful, effectively chosen the
square peg?

But will the employment of constraints upon utilitarianism suffice to
the task? Critics, I think, will be pessimistic, but their pessimism here
is not traced to the unenviableness of the position in which utilitarians
find themselves. It runs to a deeper source.

Can any theory with a consequence component, whether or not that
component is consequentialism, provide an adequate account of the
wrongness of killing? The point is not that few people think side effects,
diminution in pleasure, or the frustration of desires comprise such an account; it is rather that any view of rightness and wrongness that links
them to consequences, whether directly or indirectly, wholly or partly,
moves us away from the person-centered exercise of, so to speak, looking at the autonomous person killed to the person-neutral exercise of
trying to determine whether the world is a better or worse place, with
more or less net pleasure or desire-satisfaction or whatever, as a result
of the killing. A consequence component links rightness and wrongness
with subsequent states of the world, and this link, because it compels
a theory to provide as the explanation of the wrongness of killing some
person-neutral description of the state of the world subsequent to action, puts an obstacle in the way of constructing a satisfactory explana-

tion. For killing then has to be looked at in terms of how the world is, how much pleasure or desire-satisfaction or whatever it contains, how it stands as the result of action; and this is already for a theory to distance itself from the person-relative character of our intuitions over killing. Thus, it is not that classical and preference-utilitarianism come up with the wrong terms in which to describe the world; it is the demand for such a description in the first place that critics will see as the problem, as if it could constitute the explanation we seek. And any theory whatever that exemplifies the utilitarian theme to the extent of possessing a consequence component would seem to demand just such a description.

V

As I noted at the outset, moral rights are typically postulated in order to protect persons and their vital interests, and their need must seem all the stronger as threats to persons and their interests arise in utilitarianism. Inevitably, then, the more the protection of persons and their vital interests seem called into question by utilitarianism, the more attractive rights-theory seems bound to appear. The case of killing has been used here to show how weak that protection can apparently be.

Room for rights-theory, then, is created by the alleged shortcomings of utilitarianism in protecting persons and their interests. It does not follow, of course, that rights-theory itself is guaranteed to provide an adequate explanation of the wrongness of killing; but it does, critics will maintain, assemble materials for this task that do not share the deficiencies that render ill-suited the materials assembled by the utilitarian. It seems natural, in other words, to see a person-relative theory as supplying over killing what a person-neutral theory with a consequential account of rightness arguably cannot and so natural to see rights as suitable materials out of which to construct an adequate explanation of the wrongness of killing.

I have not, of course, looked at what utilitarians, including myself, make of all this emphasis upon persons and their vital interests or how they might accommodate it within their theories; rather, I have tried to show how such emphasis can seem the natural outgrowth of and response to what appears to be the status of persons in utilitarianism.

NOTES

1. This paper is indebted to H. L. A. Hart's excellent article "Between Utility and Rights," in *The Idea of Freedom,* ed. A. Ryan (Oxford: Oxford University Press, 1979); to

James Griffin's equally excellent "Bentham and Modern Utilitarianism," *Revue International de Philosophie* 141 (1982), and other, unpublished papers of his; to Jonathan Glover's *Causing Death and Saving Lives* (Middlesex: Penguin Books, 1975); to Peter Singer's *Practical Ethics* (Cambridge: Cambridge University Press, 1979); and to numerous discussions with Griffin, L. W. Sumner, R. M. Hare, and the late J. L. Mackie.

2. This and the next paragraph draw directly from Griffin's "Bentham and Modern Utilitarianism."

1

Rights Denaturalized

L. W. Sumner

Like the arms race, the rhetoric of rights is out of control. In the liberal democracies of the West, public issues, whatever their nature, are coming to be increasingly perceived as conflicts of rights. In order to remain competitive in the political marketplace, interest groups have had to resort to more and more exotic rights-claims; a casual survey of recent controversies yields, for instance, the right of parents to raise their children in an environment free of pornography, the right of embryos not to be frozen and stored, and the right of all of us to be (have been?) conceived by sexual means. The resulting inflation of rights-rhetoric threatens to devalue the notion of a right. If we are to continue to take rights seriously we must impose some control on the proliferation of rights-claims. The needed control is a standard that will enable us to sort authentic from inauthentic rights. A standard of authenticity, in turn, must be grounded in a moral theory. Thus if we are to continue to take rights seriously we must contain them within the framework of an independently plausible moral theory.

There is no shortage of candidates; rights can, apparently, be built into the framework of any of our currently dominant moral theories. Historically, the most influential rights-theories have belonged to the natural-rights tradition. The identifying mark of such theories is the claim that the existence of some set of fundamental rights is implied by or consonant with the natural order. In order to find a place for rights, however, a theory need not endorse this claim. Thus, for example, contractarian and utilitarian moral theories appear to be capable of grounding rights in utility, individual or collective. This strategy of controlling rights by appeal to utility is intrinsically attractive, since utility is an intrinsically attractive foundation for a moral theory. But the strategy would be more attractive still if we had reason to believe that natural-rights theories are incapable of yielding a standard of authenticity for rights. This paper aims to provide that reason.[1]

1. The Nature of Natural Rights

What makes a right a natural right? There is no agreed answer to this question in the natural-rights tradition. Within that tradition the existence of natural rights—or "the rights of man" or, more commonly nowadays, human rights—has been affirmed both in political rhetoric and in political theory. Rhetorical assertions of such rights have usually taken the form of declarations or manifestos in the service of some political cause. These documents are not remembered chiefly for their philosophical profundity. Declarations and manifestos seldom offer a grounding for their catalogs of rights, and they never offer an account of what makes a right a natural right.

What then of natural-rights theories? Their history may be usefully divided into its classical era—the seventeenth century, culminating in the work of Locke—and its modern era—the period following the Second World War in which philosophical interest in natural rights has shown a marked revival. Unfortunately, neither era yields an account of the nature of natural rights that is both explicit and agreed. While the classical theories appear to share a common understanding of what it is for a right (or a duty, or a law) to be natural, this understanding is too tacit and undeveloped to serve our purposes. The modern era, by contrast, features a great many discussions of the nature of natural rights but yields no consensus. There is no agreement, for instance, concerning whether natural rights are alienable, prescriptible, forfeitable, defeasible, or self-evident. Furthermore, it is a curiosity of the modern debate that only scant attention has been given to the question of what makes such rights *natural*.

There is no alternative therefore to constructing our own account. Since our eventual aim is to show that natural-rights theories are defective *by their very nature*, we must be careful not to beg the question against them by characterizing their nature in some idiosyncratic or deviant way. We will therefore require our account to satisfy two criteria. The first is that it be as faithful as possible to what is commonly understood as the natural-rights tradition. Since there is no agreement within that tradition concerning some of the features of natural rights, we cannot require that every condition that we impose be universally accepted. But we can, and will, require that each condition be at least widely accepted. When the tradition appears to be deeply divided, we will attempt to acknowledge the division by making room for both sides.

The second criterion is that our account should mark some important line of division between different types of moral theory. Natural-rights theories appear to constitute one of the main options open to us in constructing a general normative theory of morals and politics. An account of the nature of such theories should therefore reveal the deep differences between them and their principal rivals.

We will count as a natural-rights theory any moral theory that satisfies the following four conditions: (1) it contains some rights, (2) it treats its rights as morally basic, (3) it ties possession of its rights to possession of some natural property, and (4) it accepts some form of realist moral epistemology. Each of these conditions requires explication.

The first condition is conceptual: a natural-rights theory must affirm the existence of some moral rights and thus must employ some conception of a right. This may seem so obvious as to be scarcely worth stating; it is in any case entailed by each of the second and third conditions. The point of stating this first condition separately lies less in what it requires than in what it permits. All natural-rights theories must employ some conception of a right, but they need not all employ the same conception. At least two rival conceptions can be easily discovered in the theories of the modern era. Because the first of them has been inherited from the classical theories we will call it the classical conception. To have a right in this sense is to have some aspect of one's good or well-being protected by some set of duties borne by other agents. A right on the classical conception is a Hohfeldian claim.[2] Because the second conception is unique to modern theories we will call it the modern conception. To have a right in this sense is to have one's autonomous control over some domain protected by some set of duties borne by other agents, which duties are themselves subject to the control of the right-holder. A right on the modern conception is a bundle of Hohfeldian liberties, claims, powers, and immunities. The differences between the classical and modern conceptions may be illustrated by the example of the right to life. On the classical conception my life is treated as a good whose preservation requires moral protection. Because other agents are the principal threats to my life, the first line of protection is to impose on those agents the duty to preserve my life. But I too may threaten my life. The second line of protection, therefore, is to impose on me the like duty to preserve my life (whether I wish to or not), and also to deny me the power to waive or annul the protective duty borne to me by others. The net result is that I am the passive beneficiary of a network of life-preserving duties belonging both to myself and to others; my life is secured at the cost of my autonomy. On the modern conception, by contrast, my autonomous control over my life is treated as a good whose preservation requires moral protection. That control consists in my freedom to decide for myself whether my life is to be preserved; it therefore excludes any duty on my part to preserve it. Because other agents are the principal threats to my autonomy, the first line of protection is to impose on those agents the duty to preserve my autonomy. These duties would however limit my autonomy if I lacked the power to waive or annul them when I choose to do so. The second line of protection, therefore, is to confer this power on me and to secure its exercise against the like powers of others. The net result is that I am the active manager of a network of autonomy-preserving liberties and powers belonging to me, and duties and disabilities belonging to others; my autonomy is secured at the possible cost of my life.

The classical conception of a right thus ranks such first-order goods as life over such second-order goods as autonomy, while the modern conception inverts this ranking. The two conceptions flow from radically different views of the individual's moral freedom to choose his/her fate, for better or worse. This duality in the concept of a right complicates the characterization of what is to count as a natural-rights theory. Are we to stipulate a conception of a right or make room for both conceptions? Our criteria for an adequate characterization yield conflicting results in this case. The distinction between the two conceptions is deep and important, and thus the line of division between classical and modern theories is deep and important. Since the modern conception of a right is now dominant in the natural-rights tradition, it would be quite legitimate to mark this line of division by stipulating that a natural-rights theory must employ that conception and finding some other label for theories employing the classical conception.[3] If we were to pursue this policy, however, we would be forced to evict from the natural-rights tradition many theories, both classical and contemporary, that are commonly regarded as belonging to that tradition.[4] Since this step would inevitably arouse the suspicion that the notion of a natural-rights theory was being defined in some special and provocative manner, we will instead treat this as one respect in which the natural-rights tradition is divided: while it once possessed a uniform conception of a right, it no longer does so. The classical/modern duality will complicate our account somewhat, but it will not hamper it significantly since it will turn out that theories employing both conceptions suffer from essentially the same defects.

The second condition is structural: a natural-rights theory must treat its rights as morally basic.[5] Every rights-theory will assign some set of moral rights to some set of individuals. Let us assume that any such

assignment will be stated in a principle of the following form: all and only individuals who have property P have right R. Call such a principle
a rights-principle. Every rights-theory will locate some set of rights-
principles at some level in its structure. What is distinctive about a
natural-rights theory is that it locates its set of rights-principles at the
most basic level of its structure and that it locates no other moral principles at that level. Let us say that one principle grounds another if it
provides a justification for that other. Then a principle is basic in a moral
theory if it is grounded by no other moral principle in the theory. A
theory treats rights as morally basic if all of its basic principles are rights-
principles. The moral base of such a theory may contain either a single
rights-principle or a plurality of independent rights-principles, but it
may not contain any other sort of moral principle.

The intuitive idea behind this condition is that we should think of a
moral theory as an ordered set of principles, each of which employs
some moral category. Within any theory some of these principles will be
fundamental while others will be derivable from them. The entire theory
may in turn be supported by some nonmoral foundation. Then a theory
is a natural-rights theory only if rights are the moral category fundamental to the theory, thus only if the theory's base consists exclusively of
rights-principles. There are, therefore, various ways in which a theory
can fail this second condition. One is for the theory to contain no basic
principles; it might, for instance, contain several principles each of
which partially grounds each of the others. If such a moral structure is
possible, then a theory with that structure could not be a natural-rights
theory.

A more realistic possibility, perhaps, is that a theory will treat one or
more nonrights-principles as morally basic. In order to explore this possibility further we need two distinctions: between moral principles and
nonmoral principles and, within the former class, between rights-
principles and nonrights-principles. We need the first distinction
because this condition stipulates that rights must be *morally* basic in a
theory. This prohibits supporting rights-principles by means of some
further (nonrights) moral principle, but it does not prohibit supporting
them by means of some further nonmoral principle or argument. If the
distinction between moral and nonmoral principles is unclear, then the
distinction between the moral base of a theory and its nonmoral foundation will also be unclear. We need the second distinction, on the other
hand, because the condition stipulates that *rights* must be morally basic
in a theory.

It would be difficult and time-consuming to construct a satisfactory
account of either distinction. We will therefore proceed instead by

stipulating three sorts of principle that will count as moral principles. The first two sorts affirm the existence of moral rights (rights-principles) or of moral duties (duty-principles).[6] The third sort affirm the existence of moral goods (principles of the good). For our purposes a good will simply be any state of affairs whose promotion counts in favor of an action but is a matter neither of right nor of duty.

We will assume that if a moral theory has an assignable base then that base must consist of some assortment of rights, duties, and goods. (If this assumption is too restrictive, our argument will not be affected.) If a theory's base consists only of rights then the theory is right-based, if only of duties then it is duty-based, if only of goods then it is good-based.[7] These three sorts of theory all treat one moral category as basic, deriving the others from it (if they appear in the theory at all). But mixed theories, whose base consists of principles of different sorts, are also possible. The second condition requires that a natural-rights theory be right-based. A theory may, then, fail to be right-based in any of the following ways: (1) it may have no assignable base at all, (2) it may be either duty-based or good-based, or (3) it may be mixed.

The third condition concerns one element in the rights-principles basic to a theory. Assume again that each such principle takes the form: all and only individuals who have property P have right R. Possession of P is thus both necessary and sufficient for possession of R. P need not of course be what we would ordinarily think of as a single property; it may be a conjunction or disjunction of such properties. And different rights might be tied to different properties. Call the property P that is tied to some particular right R the *criterion* for R. The criterion for a right determines the distribution of that right: the class of beings who possess the right.

The criterion for a natural right must be a natural property. A natural-rights theory must assign its basic rights to individuals in virtue of their possession of some natural property. But what makes a property natural? Two requirements are obvious. First, possession of the property by an individual must be empirically ascertainable. Thus supernatural properties such as having a soul or being one of the chosen people are excluded. Second, possession of the property by an individual must require the existence of no particular institution or convention.[8] Thus conventional properties such as citizenship or knighthood are excluded. A natural property must be both empirical and nonconventional; obvious examples are height, blood type, race, and species.

To these two requirements we must add a third. Some properties while logically independent of the existence of social institutions or conventions are nonetheless causally dependent on such institutions or conventions. Power and education are obvious examples. It would be contrary to the spirit of a natural-rights theory to tie possession of basic rights to any property too closely dependent on conventional arrangements. This third requirement is much less clear-cut than the first two. There are few personal characteristics that are utterly immune to social influence. But some characteristics are less immune than others, and those that are too dependent on social conventions cannot serve as criteria for natural rights.

The intuitive idea behind this third condition is that fundamental moral rights should not be distributed on the basis of morally irrelevant characteristics. But we should note that a criterion may be both natural and morally irrelevant. A theory that assigns rights to individuals on the basis of their race or species is a bad rights-theory, but it is a bad *natural-rights* theory.

The fourth condition concerns a theory's method of supporting its basic rights-principles. The requirement that these principles be basic ensures that they cannot be grounded in any further moral principles. There appear to be two models available for the process of grounding basic principles in some nonmoral principles or arguments. On the realist model basic principles are thought of as making claims about the world; grounding them is then the process of showing these claims to be true, that is, accurate representations of the way the world is. The affirmation that individuals have some particular basic right is an assertion of a matter of fact, to be confirmed or disconfirmed by the usual means of evidence and argument. Rights are objective moral facts. The nonrealist model, by contrast, denies the existence of objective moral facts and thus denies that moral principles can be verified by checking them against the facts. The truth of such principles is not discovered but constructed or invented; grounding them is the process of showing that they would, or could, issue from some specified decision procedure. Some moral theories can adopt either model of justification. But natural-rights theories, since they treat moral rights as natural facts, are committed to the realist model.[9] They must therefore consider their basic principles to reflect fundamental features of an independent moral order.

This fourth condition completes our sketch of the nature of natural rights. A natural-rights theory is any moral theory that assigns some set of basic rights to individuals in virtue of their possession of some natural property and that treats the existence of these rights as a matter of fact. A natural right is a right that is basic within such a theory. Because there is no agreement nowadays about the nature of natural rights, this characterization of a natural-rights theory excludes some theories that are nonetheless claimed by their proponents to belong to the tradition.[10]

However, it includes most theories, classical and modern, that are usually counted as natural-rights theories. In any case, since it identifies one distinctive and influential way of attempting to provide a standard of authenticity for rights, it is an interesting question whether it can succeed.

2. The Conceptual Challenge

In order to test its success we will reconstruct and develop some criticisms that were directed against natural rights by Bentham nearly two centuries ago. Implacable, and often intemperate, opposition to natural rights was one of the constants in Bentham's long career.[11] However, he had many different grounds for this opposition, some of which are much more important than others. We may begin by dividing these grounds into two broad categories: the conceptual and the moral. The distinction is suggested by one of Bentham's typically pungent dismissals of natural rights: "The assertion of such rights, absurd in logic, is pernicious in morals."[12] We will concern ourselves for the moment only with Bentham's reasons for thinking natural rights absurd in logic, postponing until the next section their alleged subversion of our moral thinking.

As his accusation of logical absurdity suggests, Bentham believed not just that there were as a matter of fact no natural rights but that there could be no such things; the very idea of a natural right is "a contradiction in terms."[13] Furthermore, the incoherence of natural rights does not lie in some further property, such as imprescriptibility, which such rights might be claimed to possess; natural and imprescriptible rights may be "nonsense upon stilts" but natural rights *tout court* are still "simple nonsense."[14] It was the idea that rights could be natural that Bentham regarded as absurd.

His main argument in support of this allegation runs roughly as follows: (1) there can be no rights without laws; (2) there can be no natural moral laws; therefore (3) there can be no natural rights. Bentham was led to his first premise by his assumption of what we have called the classical conception of a right: roughly speaking, to have a right in Bentham's view is to be the beneficiary of some duty borne by others. The concept of a right thus analytically includes that of a duty. But a duty for Bentham is inconceivable apart from some law that imposes the duty. Thus the argument to the first premise runs roughly as follows: there can be no rights without duties; there can be no duties without laws; therefore, there can be no rights without laws. It is evident that this argument is not weakened if we replace the classical conception of a right by its modern counterpart. It will then run roughly as follows: there can be no rights without both duties and powers; there can be no duties or powers without laws; therefore, there can be no rights without laws. Indeed, if anything the argument is strengthened by this substitution (a matter to which we will return below).

The premise that there can be no rights without laws is not contentious. Theorists who affirm the existence of natural rights tend also to affirm the existence of natural laws that confer those rights. To the extent that the natural-rights tradition is closely affiliated to the natural-law tradition, it accepts the claim that the existence of (natural) rights depends upon the existence of (natural) laws.

Bentham was led to the second premise of his main argument by his concept of a law. According to Bentham a law is (roughly speaking) an expression of the will of a sovereign concerning the conduct of his subjects.[15] The concept of a law thus analytically includes that of a legislator. The argument to the second premise then runs roughly as follows: there can be no laws without a legislator; natural moral laws have no legislator; therefore, there can be no natural moral laws. This argument is unsatisfactory as it stands because of its reliance on Bentham's volitional account of the existence conditions for a law. More recent positivists have provided ample reason for abandoning this account in favor of a much more complex and plausible analysis in which (roughly speaking) the existence of a law is a matter of its validity within a legal system, and the existence of the legal system as a whole is a matter of its being sustained by social practices of compliance with and acceptance of rules on the part of those to whom the rules apply.[16] However, the substitution of this improved account does not weaken the argument to the second premise. It will now run as follows: there can be no laws whose existence is independent of conventional social practices of compliance and acceptance; the existence of natural moral laws is supposed to be independent of all such practices; therefore, there can be no natural moral laws.

The argument, however, is still inadequate because of its confinement of the notion of law (and thus also of duty and right) to the rules of municipal legal systems. Bentham plainly regarded these rules as the paradigm cases of laws. But he sometimes went further, declaring that municipal laws were the only real laws.[17] From this he drew the inevitable conclusion, which he was fond of repeating, that legal rights were the only real rights.[18] But this conclusion is a wild exaggeration. There is no analytical obstacle in the way of treating the rule systems of nonlegal institutions as sources of duties and rights. In his more careful moments Bentham was aware of this fact, for he regarded as meaningful talk of the duties (and therefore rights) created by the rules of a society's positive morality. Bentham therefore had no good reason to support his second premise by means of the assumption that the only genuine laws are the rules of a municipal legal system. But again the argument is not weakened by the deletion of this assumption. It will now run as follows: there can be no rules capable of creating rights whose existence is independent of conventional social practices of compliance and acceptance; the existence of natural moral rules is supposed to be independent of all such practices; therefore, there can be no natural moral rules. And the main argument will now run: (1) there can be no rights without rules; (2) there can be no natural moral rules; therefore (3) there can be no natural rights.

The premise that there can be no natural moral rules is contentious. Bentham's argument to this premise makes it easy to locate the point of contention. Natural-rights theorists agree that the existence of natural moral rules (or laws) is not dependent on any actual conventional practices; the law of nature is not a conventional rule system. Thus the keystone of Bentham's case against natural rights is the thesis that there are no nonconventional rule systems capable of creating rights. Bentham provided little or no explicit argument in support of this thesis; it appeared to him to be so obviously true that it needed merely to be pointed out. But the thesis appeared so obvious to Bentham because it was so strongly supported by a positivist account of the existence conditions for conventional rule systems. In this sense the needed support for the thesis is to be found in Bentham's lifework.

Before showing how the thesis can be defended, we need to be clear about its meaning. It does not claim that there are no nonconventional rule systems. The rules of arithmetic certainly constitute a system and are almost certainly nonconventional. Instead, the thesis claims that there are no nonconventional rule systems *capable of creating rights*. Nor does the thesis claim that there are no moral rights. Instead it claims, or rather implies, that there are no *natural* moral rights. Finally, the thesis does not claim that there are no natural laws. It is, as it must be, compatible with the existence of natural causal laws. Instead it claims that there are no natural *normative* laws—no laws, that is, capable of creating rights.

Defense of the thesis begins by demanding existence conditions for natural rights. Existence conditions for a right are conditions both necessary and sufficient for the existence of the right. The criterion for a natural right is that natural property in virtue of which an individual possesses the right. As we saw in the previous section, the criterion for a given right can (trivially) be built into a rights-principle: an individual has (natural) right R if and only if he/she has (natural) property P. It might be tempting to treat such a principle as providing the existence conditions for the right: having property P is necessary and sufficient for having right R. But this, of course, would be a mistake. If P is the criterion for R then having P is indeed necessary for having R, but it cannot be sufficient. If it were sufficient then the individual's having P would, all by itself, entail that he/she also has R. But plainly it does not entail this, all by itself. The criterion for a right must be supplemented by some further background conditions in order to yield a complete set of existence conditions for the right.

The same is true for conventional rights. A conventional rule system may confer some right R upon individuals in virtue of their possession of some natural property P. In that case P is the criterion for R, and we may say, as a kind of shorthand, that having P is sufficient for having R. But this would be merely a shorthand. Strictly speaking, having P is necessary for having R but it is not sufficient. The existence of the appropriate rule system containing the appropriate rule is also necessary. Possession by an individual of the criterion for a given conventional right must be supplemented by further background conditions in order to yield a complete set of existence conditions for the right.

In the case of a conventional right we know what these background conditions are. In order for an individual to possess R in virtue of possessing P, some rule must exist that applies to that individual and that confers R upon everyone who has P. In order for such a rule to exist it must be valid within some existing rule system. And in order for such a rule system to exist it must be sustained by conventional practices of compliance and acceptance on the part of the appropriate persons. A full set of existence conditions for a particular conventional right possessed by a particular individual must include both the background conditions for the right (which will include its criterion) and a statement that the individual possesses that criterion.

We know how to fill in the background conditions for the existence of conventional rights because these rights are conventional. Natural rights are not conventional. We should not, therefore, expect the same story to be told about their background conditions. But we should expect *some* story to be told which is the analog for natural rights of the story available for conventional rights. What could this story be? In order for a particular individual to have a particular natural right what *else* must be the case besides his/her possession of the natural property that is the criterion for that right? Bentham's thesis amounts to the claim that there is no story that can be told here—no further background conditions for the existence of natural rights—precisely because such rights are not conventional.

The thesis still needs to be supported. The needed support is provided by the concept of a right. On both the classical and the modern conception the existence of a right analytically includes the existence of a duty. On the modern conception it additionally includes the existence of a power. The notion of a duty is necessarily normative: that is, to have a duty, imposed by some rule system, to act in a certain way is necessarily to have a reason, relative to that rule system, for acting in that way. We will summarize this by saying that duties have *normative force* in the rule system that creates them. A power is, then, the ability to alter or control some duty with normative force. On the classical conception an account of the existence conditions for rights must be capable of explaining how individuals can have duties with normative force. On the modern conception it must additionally be capable of explaining how individuals can have the ability to alter or control such duties.

In the case of a conventional right the needed explanations are provided by the background conditions for the existence of the right. Consider the case of a legal right. Individuals have legal duties in virtue of the fact that rules requiring or prohibiting acts apply to them and are valid within the legal system—which is to say that they have issued from some source recognized as possessing the authority to create such rules. The existence of powers to alter these duties can be explained in the same way. The normative force of legal rules—their ability to impose duties and confer powers—is fully accounted for by reference to their status within a legal system sustained by the appropriate conventional practices. Once we know that the system exists, that the rule is valid within it, that the rule applies to a particular individual, that it requires or prohibits some act—once we know all of these things we need nothing more in order to explain how it can be that the individual has a duty.[19] The same sort of account will equally explain the existence of a power. When duties and powers, and therefore also rights, are conventional we can fully explain their normativity. Thus where conventional rule systems are concerned we can attach sense to the normative vocabulary of duties, powers, and rights—and therefore also of laws, in the normative rather than the causal sense.

There seems to be no analogous account available to us in the case of natural duties, powers, rights, or laws. We cannot appeal in their case to these anchoring notions of validity or authority. Natural laws do not issue from any authoritative source—this is precisely what makes them natural. But in that case how could we ever begin to explain how they can impose duties or confer powers, indeed, how they can be *laws* in the normative sense? The naturalness of natural laws seems to exclude their being laws, and thus the naturalness of natural rights seems to exclude their being rights.[20]

Natural rights are supposed to be moral rights, and thus the normative force that we must be able to explain in their case is moral force. A duty to act in a certain way has moral force if its possession by an agent provides that agent with a moral reason for acting in that way. A right has moral force on the classical conception if its possession by an agent entails that some other agents have a duty with moral force. A right has moral force on the modern conception if its possession by an agent additionally entails that the agent has the ability to alter or control this duty. The claim that moral rights are natural—that they are conferred by natural laws—is intended to explain their moral force. But it now appears to be incompatible with that force. No attempt has of course been made here to show that no rights have moral force, or that there can be no moral rights. We have been concerned only with one possible explanation of the apparent moral force of rights. This explanation cannot succeed but others, for all we know, may fare better.

The reconstruction that has been offered here of Bentham's case against natural rights is an impossibility argument. In the preceding section natural-rights theories were characterized in terms of four conditions. What the argument has shown is that no theory can satisfy all four conditions. In particular, no theory can be both right-based in its moral structure and realist in its moral method. In virtue of being right-based a theory both commits itself to the existence of rights with moral force and denies itself the option of deriving the moral force of these rights from some further, and deeper, moral principles. In virtue of being realist a theory commits itself to treating its rights as moral facts. A theory that is both right-based and realist is led inevitably to postulate the existence of laws that are both natural and normative. If there can be no such laws, then there can be no moral theory that is both right-based and realist.

In fact the argument establishes a broader result. If there can be no laws both natural and normative, then there can be no theory that is either right-based or duty-based in its moral structure and realist in its moral method. The argument thus strikes against both natural-rights theories and what we may call natural-duty theories—that is, against all forms of natural-law theory. Its main message is that deontic elements such as duties and rights cannot be basic moral facts; if there are any such facts they must be of a different character. The existence of moral facts—the truth of moral realism—is not here at stake. The questions raised by the realism controversy are too deep and difficult to be resolved here. Thus we do not know whether there are any moral facts. We also do not know whether there are any moral duties or rights. Thus we do not know whether any duties or rights are moral facts. But we do know that no duties or rights are *basic* moral facts.

Despite the fact that the argument strikes against any form of natural-law theory, it particularly threatens a natural-rights theory that employs the modern conception of a right. Suppose that it were possible to explain the moral force of natural duties. This would suffice to establish the coherence of natural-duty theories, and possibly also of natural-rights theories employing the classical conception of a right.[21] But it would not suffice to establish the coherence of natural-rights theories employing the modern conception. Natural rights in the modern sense require not only natural duties but also natural powers. It could be the case that there are natural duties but, because agents lack the ability to alter or control these duties, no natural powers. Indeed the fact that the duties would be natural suggests that agents would lack the ability to alter or control them. A natural duty would be a natural fact created by a natural law. The ability to alter or control such facts at will would amount to a magical power over nature.[22] Natural-rights theories that employ the modern conception of a right thus suffer from a special impediment that is not shared by natural-duty theories or by classical natural-rights theories. Because Bentham accepted the classical conception of a right, his original argument was in effect aimed only at the latter two sorts of theory; it did not trouble itself over the existence of natural powers. When the argument was reformulated earlier in terms of the modern conception it was noted that it was thereby strengthened. We can now see wherein this strengthening consisted.

3. The Moral Challenge

We noted earlier that Bentham's objections to natural rights divided into two categories. Having explored his reasons for thinking such rights "absurd in logic" we turn now to the allegation that they are "pernicious in morals." Of course if the conceptual challenge is successful, then there can be no natural rights and the question of their role in our moral thinking does not arise. We shall, therefore, suppose that the conceptual challenge is not conclusive, thus that a coherent natural-rights theory can be constructed. Our question now is whether such a theory could do any useful moral work.

As in the case of his conceptual arguments, some of Bentham's moral objections to natural rights are more important than others. Bentham believed that any attempt to derive moral or political conclusions from premises about individual rights was mischievous, but some of the alleged mischiefs stem from features that are not essential to natural rights. We must remember that for Bentham appeals to such rights in the service of political causes were more than abstract possibilities. Twice during his lifetime a major revolution was defended on just these grounds. The documents that occasioned Bentham's fulminations against natural rights were the rights declarations issued in defense of those revolutions. In the case of the Declaration of Independence, Bentham eventually became reconciled to, indeed a champion of, the resulting United States of America—though he continued to believe that it had been built on bad arguments.[23] But when he responded to the French Declaration of the Rights of Man and the Citizen he was animated by horror at the violence that the revolution in France had unleashed. Keeping this violence in mind will help us to understand why Bentham came to regard natural rights as the language of anarchists and terrorists.

Even in his calmer and more reflective moments, however, Bentham regarded appeals to natural rights as dangerous. In support of this belief he made an important distinction. The claim that natural rights impose moral constraints on conventional social arrangements may be interpreted in two quite different ways. On the first interpretation these rights limit what governments may do—what it is permissible for them to do. On the second interpretation these rights limit what governments can do—what it is possible for them to do. The two interpretations diverge in their account of what has happened, or failed to happen, when a government has ostensibly enacted a law that infringes some natural right. On the first interpretation, which results from combining a natural-rights theory with legal positivism, the government has enacted an unjust law. On the second interpretation, which results from combining a natural-rights theory with what we may call legal moralism, the government has enacted no valid law at all.

Consider first the coalition of natural rights and legal positivism. On this view some set of rights serves as a standard of the justice of laws but not of their legal validity. Bentham agreed that some moral standard was necessary but regarded rights as the wrong one. One of his reasons for rejecting rights as the standard stemmed from some special features of the rights declarations with which he was familiar.[24] It was common for the rights in these declarations both to be characterized in a very simple and sweeping manner, and to be treated as indefeasible or absolute. One common example was the right to liberty. As Bentham never tired of pointing out, every law that imposes a duty necessarily limits the liberty of those who will bear that duty. It follows that if everyone possesses a right to liberty that is both unlimited and indefeasible, a government may enact no such laws at all, which is to say that it may not govern. Since natural rights are not by nature either simple or indefeasible, this problem does not stem from their nature. On the other hand, it is also not easily remedied. If we retain the indefeasibility of rights but characterize them more carefully, then they may indeed leave spaces that a government may fill with legislation. But the absolute constraints that they impose are still likely to be too rigid to adapt to complex and fluctuating social and political circumstances. Thus any set of rights, however carefully drafted, will probably prove awkward if held to be indefeasible. On the other hand, if we treat rights as defeasible then we must face the question of what will suffice to override them. Some justification will then be needed for holding that nothing can override a right except another right. If any other consideration is admitted as justifying infringement of a right, however, then our background moral theory has ceased to be a natural-rights theory.

These difficulties will of course equally afflict the account that combines natural rights and legal moralism. But this combination also produces its own special mischief.[25] Bentham believed, as do most of us, that the fact that a law is unjust is not by itself sufficient justification for refusing to comply with it. In deciding whether to comply with an unjust law we must also take into account the alternative courses of action open to us, the likely consequences of our disobedience, and so on. There is thus no direct inference from the injustice of a law to the justifiability of defying it. Combining a natural-rights theory with legal moralism, however, threatens to license just this inference. On such a view an ostensible law that infringes a natural right is in fact no law at all. Doing what the law forbids, or refusing to do what it requires, is not therefore illegal. But then there is no disobedience that needs to be justified. Natural rights plus legal moralism thus appear to provide a simple and direct justification for disobeying, or rather disregarding, unjust "laws." It was chiefly for this reason that Bentham regarded such rights as anarchical.

We have not yet, however, reached Bentham's deepest and most important moral objection to appeals to natural rights in political argument, an objection that applies with equal force to either the positivist or the moralist interpretation of those appeals. The objection is best stated as a contrast between appeals to rights and appeals to Bentham's preferred standard, namely utility. The question whether a particular law promotes the general welfare is an empirical one and is thus in principle decidable. Utility therefore can provide a determinate standard of moral assessment. However, the question whether a particular law infringes natural rights is not an empirical one and is thus in principle undecidable. Natural rights therefore cannot provide a determinate standard of moral assessment.

Thus stated, the argument is defective in many respects. For our purposes the most important defect is that it constructs a misleading comparison between natural-rights and utilitarian moral theories. These two types of theories may be regarded as structural analogs, each partitionable into base and superstructure. The moral base of a theory contains its basic principles; its superstructure contains those items (principles, rules, etc.) that are derived from its basic principles. The moral base of a natural-rights theory consists of some set of rights-principles. The moral base of a utilitarian theory consists of some principle of utility. We must now distinguish between arguments to and arguments from a theory's moral base. Arguments to basic principles are attempts to show that the principles are correct or that acceptance of them is reasonable. Both rights-principles and principles of utility must be supported by some such arguments if we are to have any reason to acknowledge them as a standard of moral assessment. The question whether a set of rights should serve as such a standard does not appear to be an empirical one, but neither does the question whether utility should serve as such a standard. Arguments from basic principles are attempts to show that the principles support conclusions about particular cases. Both rights-principles and principles of utility must support some such arguments if we are to be able to employ them as a standard of moral assessment. The question whether a particular law promotes the general welfare does appear to be an empirical one, but so does the question whether the law infringes a particular right. Appeals to rights as a standard of moral assessment thus appear to be analogous in every respect to appeals to utility.

Bentham's argument that appeals to natural rights, unlike appeals to utility, are undecidable does indeed confuse the separate issues of arguments to and arguments from basic principles. But the main point of his objection can be directed specifically at the former issue. Bentham could concede that once a determinate set of basic rights has been assumed then the question whether a particular law infringes any of these rights is decidable. Having conceded this, he could however continue to maintain that arguments to a determinate set of basic rights are undecidable. And Bentham certainly believed that such arguments *are* undecidable, thus that there is no way of showing *which* set of rights should serve as the standard of moral assessment.[26] The selection of any particular set of rights is entirely arbitrary because rationally unsupportable; the language of natural rights is "from the beginning to the end so much flat assertion."[27] Bentham is of course committed to the additional claim that the selection of a particular principle of utility is not arbitrary because rationally supportable. We cannot decide here whether this claim is justified. But we can ask whether there are any special difficulties involved in arguing to basic rights principles.

At this point it will help to remind ourselves of the demand we are making of a moral theory. Our problem is the population explosion of rights-claims. This explosion can be controlled only by a determinate standard that will enable us to distinguish between justified and unjustified claims, and thus between authentic and inauthentic rights. Such a standard can in turn be supplied only by a moral theory. Thus any moral theory that makes room for rights—any rights-theory—must provide the needed standard. A rights-theory will authenticate all and only those rights that are derivable from its basic principles; those principles thus serve as its ultimate control over the proliferation of rights-claims. Two sorts of control are possible. Rights-claims are externally controlled if they are tested by means of basic principles that are not themselves rights-principles. In that case rights constitute a derivative but not a basic moral category. Rights-claims are internally controlled if they are tested by means of basic rights-principles. In that case rights constitute both a derivative and a basic moral category.

A natural-rights theory is committed to the internal control of rights-claims by basic rights-principles. It is obvious that this strategy can succeed only if there is in turn some control over the proliferation of basic rights-principles, thus some standard for distinguishing between authentic and inauthentic basic rights. Since these rights are basic they cannot be authenticated by any further, deeper moral principles. A natural-rights theory must therefore look beyond morality for a standard of authenticity for basic rights.

A set of basic rights will supply a determinate standard for assessing rights-claims only if it is itself determinate. What then is necessary for a set of rights to be determinate? For any right, moral or conventional, we may distinguish three dimensions. The first is the *scope* of the right—the class of beings who are holders of that right. As we have seen, once the background conditions for the existence of a right are in place, then its scope is determined by its criterion. The scope of a right has been completely specified when the class of individuals has been enumerated who are the exclusive holders of the right. The second dimension is the *content* of the right—what it is a right to do or to have done. On the classical conception a right is simply a claim or set of claims. On the modern conception it is a bundle of liberties, claims, powers, and immunities. In either case the content of a right has been completely specified when the contents of its constituent elements have been completely specified. Finally, the third dimension is the *strength* of the right—its tendency to override or be overriden by competing moral considerations. The strength of a right has been completely specified when its weight has been given relative to every moral consideration with which it may compete.

A right is determinate only when its scope, content, and strength have all been completely specified. A set of rights is determinate only when all of its members are determinate. Only a set of determinate basic rights can provide a determinate standard of authenticity for rights-claims. A natural-rights theory must look to nature to determine selection of a set of basic rights. But it seems unlikely that nature is up to this task. We must be careful not to ask too much here. The ideal of arguing to some unique set of perfectly determinate rights is doubtless unattainable. But if a theory is to rebut the charge of arbitrariness then it must determine at least the broad outlines of its rights, and it must also provide some procedure for settling their finer details, within reasonable limits of accuracy, when it is important for us to do so. The problem for a natural-rights theory is that appeals to nature are unlikely to satisfy even these minimal demands.

An argument from nature to rights will move from empirical premises describing natural facts to rights-principles. The ambition of a natural-rights theory is to select that set of rights-principles that is most consonant with the natural facts. But *which* natural facts? To begin with, how do we decide *whose* nature is relevant? The answer within the natural-rights tradition has usually been *human* nature, but how can we know that only our nature is relevant before we know which beings have rights? How then can the scope of rights be determined by an appeal to nature? And if we do restrict our attention to human nature, which aspects of our nature are the relevant ones? We are beings capable of choice—do we therefore have a right to be free? We are also beings with subsistence needs—do we therefore have a right to the necessaries of life? If we have both rights, how does our nature determine which is to take precedence when they conflict? How in general can we distinguish between the relevant and the irrelevant aspects of our nature without presupposing a particular outcome for the argument? The problem here is not that no arguments are possible from natural facts to rights. The problem is that too many such arguments are possible and that there seems no way to arbitrate among them by further appeals to the facts. But if this is so then nature underdetermines selection of a set of basic rights and thus provides an ineffectual control over the proliferation of rights-principles.

There is a general problem about arguments from nature to morality; such arguments are usually either inconclusive or circular. This is a problem that confronts any moral theory that accepts a realist epistemology. But the problem is particularly acute for arguments directly from nature to rights. Some moral categories, such as the good, appear to have a better fit with natural facts than do others. Deontic categories, such as duties, fit less well since their conceptual home is artificial rule systems. And rights, especially on the modern conception, fit least well of all since their complexity provides too many dimensions to be determined by the facts. But that means that among moral theories that share a commitment to moral realism, natural-rights theories are the least likely to provide a determinate standard of authenticity for rights-claims.

These appear to be the sorts of considerations that led Bentham to claim that the language of natural rights was "so much flat assertion." Like the conceptual challenge, the moral challenge is an impossibility argument. The conceptual argument attempted to show that no theory could be both right-based and realist. The moral argument has attempted to show that no theory that is both right-based and realist can yield a determinate standard for authenticating rights. Both arguments therefore converge on the same result: a rights-theory must give up either a right-based moral structure or a realist moral method (or both).

4. Unnatural Rights

The result of our discussion is paradoxical: the very theories that have taken rights most seriously are incapable of showing that rights should be taken seriously. Our purpose has been entirely negative, namely, to delete one category of theories from our list of potential rights-theories. The need remains for an independently plausible moral theory capable of yielding a standard of authenticity for rights. No attempt will be made here to enumerate all of the remaining candidates, but it is worth pointing out why two of them appear to be particularly promising.

We characterized a natural-rights theory as satisfying four conditions: it must contain rights, it must treat its rights as morally basic, it must provide a natural criterion for rights, and it must accept a realist moral epistemology. The first of these conditions must be satisfied by any rights-theory and the third must be satisfied by any adequate rights-theory, but no adequate theory can satisfy both the second and fourth. A rights-theory that violates the second condition will locate its rights at a derivative rather than a basic level in its moral structure. A rights-theory that violates the fourth condition will ground rights by means of some nonrealist methodology. The two options are importantly different. The first may leave intact the moral method of a natural-rights theory but clears rights out of its moral base. If we continue our earlier assumption, such a theory must populate its moral base with duties, goods, or some combination of these. But natural duties are only marginally more intelligible or determinate than natural rights. The only viable option therefore is a theory whose moral base consists of some set of goods that serve as external controls over rights. A utilitarian rights-theory is one such theory, distinguished by the fact that the good to which it appeals is the maximization of collective utility. The second option may leave intact the moral base of a natural-rights theory but it rejects its moral method. In its place it adopts some nonrealist moral epistemology whose central feature is that basic moral principles are not discovered but invented. A contractarian rights-theory is one such theory, distinguished by the fact that the method to which it appeals is a bargaining process among agents, each of whom is attempting to maximize individual utility.

Theories that ground rights in utility, individual or collective, are not the only alternatives that survive the demise of natural-rights theories. Furthermore, we cannot know in advance whether such theories will succeed in imposing effective controls on rights. But we do know in advance that such theories possess resources that could enable them to avoid the difficulties that were fatal for natural-rights theories. To the extent that utilitarian and contractarian moral theories are independently plausible, they merit further exploration as frameworks for moral rights.

NOTES

1. Work on this paper was supported by a Killam Research Fellowship from the Canada Council and a research grant from the Social Sciences and Humanities Research Council of Canada. Versions of it were read at Rice University, the University of Western Ontario, the University of Ottawa, Queen's University, the University of Bristol, and Oxford. I am grateful to members of those audiences, as well as colleagues who read earlier drafts, for their many helpful comments and criticisms.

2. Wesley Newcomb Hohfeld, *Fundamental Legal Conceptions as Applied in Judicial Reasoning*, ed. Walter Wheeler Cook (New Haven and London: Yale University Press, 1966).

3. Contemporary libertarians are the most obvious examples of natural-rights theorists who employ the modern conception of a right. However, this conception is quite compatible with nonlibertarian rights.

4. A recent theory that would be excluded is that defended in John Finnis, *Natural Law and Natural Rights* (Oxford: Clarendon Press, 1980). On the other hand, a characterization of the tradition that is weak enough to include both libertarian rights-theories and Finnis's theory is too uninformative to be very useful.

5. For a standard discussion which urges that natural rights are morally basic, see

Stuart M. Brown, Jr., "Inalienable Rights," *The Philosophical review* 64 (April 1955).

6. On the modern conception of a right the distinction between rights-principles and duty-principles, and thus between right-based and duty-based theories, is perfectly clear. It is less clear on the classical conception, though it is still possible to hold that at least some duties entail no rights, thus that at least some duty principles are not also rights-principles.

7. For a similar, but not identical, classification, see Ronald Dworkin, *Taking Rights Seriously* (London: Duckworth, 1978), pp. 169ff.

8. This requirement that the criterion for a natural right be nonconventional appears to lie behind the common assertion that possession of such rights is not conditional upon any special status or transaction. See, for example, Margaret Macdonald, "Natural Rights," *Proceedings of the Aristotelian Society* 47 (1946–47); and H. L. A. Hart, "Are There Any Natural Rights?" *The Philosophical Review* 64 (April 1955).

9. As has been recognized by many commentators. See, for instance, Macdonald, "Natural Rights."

10. E.g., Gilbert Harman, "Moral Relativism as a Foundation for Natural Rights," *Journal of Libertarian Studies* 4 (Fall 1980).

11. See H. L. A. Hart, *Essays on Bentham: Jurisprudence and Political Theory* (Oxford: Clarendon Press, 1980), ch. 3. For an account of Bentham's arguments against natural rights, which is different in some respects from mine, see *ibid.*, ch. 4.

12. *The Works of Jeremy Bentham*, published under the superintendence of John Bowring (Edinburgh, 1838–43), III:221. Henceforth references to the *Works* will be given in the form *Works* III:221.

13. *Jeremy Bentham's Economic Writings*, ed. W. Stark (London: George Allen & Unwin, 1952–54), I:334.

14. *Works* II:501.

15. For the full account, see *Of Laws in General*, ed. H. L. A. Hart (London: Athlone Press, 1970).

16. See H. L. A. Hart, *The Concept of Law* (Oxford: Clarendon Press, 1975); and Joseph Raz, *The Concept of a Legal System*, 2d ed. (Oxford: Clarendon Press, 1980), and *The Authority of Law* (Oxford: Clarendon Press, 1979).

17. For example, in *A Comment on the Commentaries*, ed. J. H. Burns and H. L. A. Hart (London: Athlone Press, 1977), pp. 7ff.

18. *Works* II:500, 523; III:218–21; *Economic Writings*, I:324.

19. Bentham believed that we do need something more, namely a sanction; see Hart, *Essays on Bentham*, ch. 6.

20. My arguments here resemble in some respects those in G. E. M. Anscombe, "Modern Moral Philosophy," *Philosophy* 33 (January 1958), and Alasdair MacIntyre, *After Virtue* (London: Duckworth, 1981), ch. 5.

21. This latter group of theories would still need to explain what it is for a duty to be owed to a particular person, namely, the holder of the correlative right.

22. It is a commonplace that some moral rights—for instance, those created by contracts—carry with them the power to alter or control the duties owed to the right-holder. But these are precisely *not* the sorts of rights that have been thought to be natural.

23. See Hart, *Essays on Bentham*, ch. 3.

24. *Works* II:496ff.

25. *Works* II:494–95, 500, 511. See also Hart, *Essays on Bentham*, pp. 81–82.

26. See, for example, his treatment of the law of nature in the *Introduction to the Principles of Morals and Legislation*, ed. J. H. Burns and H. L. A. Hart (London: Athlone Press, 1970), pp. 21–25.

27. *Economic Writings*, I:335.

2

Right-Based Moralities

Joseph Raz

Any moral theory allows for the existence of rights if it regards the interests of some individuals to be sufficient for holding others to be subject to duties. Some writers on morality and politics have in recent years
revived the Lockean tradition of regarding rights as the foundation of
political morality or even of morality generally. R. M. Dworkin has suggested that 'political theories differ from one another . . . not simply in
the particular goals, rights, and duties each sets out, but also in the way
each connects the goals, rights, and duties it employs. . . . It seems
reasonable to suppose that any particular theory will give ultimate pride
of place to just one of these concepts; it will take some overriding goal,
or some set of fundamental rights, or some set of transcendent duties,
as fundamental, and show other goals, rights, and duties as subordinate
and derivative'.[1] Dworkin expressed the view that political morality is
right-based. J. L. Mackie, adopting this classification, applied it to moral
theories generally and claimed that morality is right-based (or rather that
we should invent one that is).[2]

My purpose in this article is to suggest that morality is not right-
based. I do not propose to urge the view that it is either duty-based or
goal-based. My suggestion will be that among its fundamental precepts
are to be found values, rights, and duties. I shall present considerations
that tend to undermine the rights view of morality and, in combination,
to support a pluralistic understanding of the foundation of morality.
These considerations do not amount to proof. Some of them need not
apply to all right-based moralities, and they all presuppose certain moral
views for which I shall not argue here.

We are to envisage a moral theory the fundamental principles of
which state that certain individuals have certain rights. They are its fun-

damental principles for, first, their justification does not presuppose any other moral principles, and, secondly, all valid moral views derive from them (with the addition of premises that do not by themselves yield any moral conclusions). Is any moral theory of this kind valid? Or, if you prefer, does a correct or sound morality have this structure? To simplify the discussion I will endorse at once the humanistic principle which claims that the explanation and justification of the goodness or badness of anything derives ultimately from its contribution, actual or possible, to human life and its quality.

Humanism, thus conceived, is not a moral theory. It merely sets a necessary condition to the acceptability of moral theories, a condition that can be satisfied by many different moral theories. Nor are all humanists committed to the view that all human life is of ultimate moral value. Their only commitment is that if some human life has no value or if some lives have more intrinsic value than others, this is in virtue of the quality of those lives. Our goal is, therefore, to examine the plausibility of the view that morality is based on fundamental principles assigning rights to some or all human beings.

1. Some Preliminary Doubts

'X has a right' means that, other things being equal, an aspect of X's well-being (his or her interest) is a sufficient reason for holding some other person(s) to be under a duty. I have argued at some length for this conception of rights elsewhere.[3] Though the definition differs from others in various respects, it is firmly placed within one major tradition of understanding rights that is often called the beneficiary view of rights. As such it seems congenial to a humanistic rights-based approach to morality. It would fit well with a view that regards the interests of people as the only ultimate value. The protection and promotion of such human interests through the rights of people could be said to be what morality is all about.

But is it? The following sections will suggest that right-based moralities are impoverished moral theories and are unlikely to provide adequate foundation for an acceptable humanistic morality. The purpose of the present section is to introduce those critical reflections by explaining the respects in which rights-based moralities could be considered to be impoverished. They all stem from the fact that rights are the grounds of duties and nothing more. A right-based morality is a morality of rights and duties. Many moral views presuppose that there is more to morality than rights and duties and precepts that can be derived from them. Consider the following three examples in order to illustrate the ways in which right-based moralities can be thought to be impoverished.

(1) Though several moral philosophers use 'ought' and 'duty' interchangeably, many moral views presuppose a distinction between what one ought to do and what it is one's duty to do. The common view is that one ought to do that which one has a duty to do, but that one does not always have a duty to do that which one ought. Thus, while I ought to allow my neighbor who locked himself out of his house to use my phone, I have no duty to do so. On the other hand, since I have promised my neighbor to saw off this week a branch overhanging a corner in his garden, I have a duty to do so. It is sometimes supposed that the difference is simply that there is greater reason to do that which one has a duty to do than to do that which one ought but has no duty to do. If this were so, then the difference between ought and duty presents no difficulty to the rights-theorists, for they may claim that they merely use 'duty' as equivalent to 'ought' and can use 'strong duty' as equivalent to the normal 'duty'. The two examples above refute the suggestion that the difference between one's duties and what one simply ought to do is in the weight of the supporting reason since there probably is more reason to let my locked-out neighbor use my phone than to saw off the branch this week rather than next week. This is so even if one takes account of the harm my breaking my promise does to the reliability and credibility of promises between neighbors or in general. Duties are not reasons for action of a great weight. They are a special kind of requirements for action.[4] Right-based moralities consist of rights and those special requirements that we call duties.

They do not allow for the moral significance of ordinary reasons for action. It is easy to see that this point is deeply embedded in our understanding of rights and is not an arbitrary result of my definition of rights. Most people will agree, for example, that I ought to give other people information that it is in their interest to have. It is, however, generally thought that they have no right that I should do so and therefore that I have no duty to give them the information. Rights are tied to duties. Reasons for action that do not amount to duties escape the notice of a right-based morality.

(2) A second respect in which right-based moralities are impoverished is in not allowing for the moral significance of supererogation. Acts are supererogatory if their performance is praiseworthy and yet it is not morally wrong to omit them. There is no obligation to act in a supererogatory way. Indeed supererogation is identified with action beyond the call of duty.[5] Right-based moralities cannot account for the nature of supererogation and its role in moral life.

(3) Finally, right-based moralities cannot allow intrinsic moral value to virtue and the pursuit of excellence. Again the reason is much the same as before. None of the commonly recognized virtues and morally significant forms of excellence consist in discharging one's duties or being disposed to do so. Honesty is a virtue that is particularly closely tied to the duty not to deceive, yet even it is not exhausted by compliance with the duty. The exemplary honest person is one who does more than his duty to make sure that his behavior does not mislead others. He acts honestly out of certain motives; and he holds certain appropriate beliefs regarding interpersonal communications, beliefs that display themselves in appropriate attitudes that he possesses.

Rights-theorists may reply to all three examples that their views do not bar them from accommodating, in a derivative role, ordinary moral reasons for action, supererogation, and moral excellence in their moral theories. This is true, but is no reply to the objections, which are not that right-based theories cannot make room for these notions at all, but rather that they cannot allow them their true moral significance. Let me explain.

Any moral theory that allows for the existence of duties must allow for the existence of reasons that are not duties. This is a result of the fact that rights and duties are not transitive regarding the means they require. Reasons for action transfer their force to the means by which their realization is facilitated. If I have a reason to bring you a glass of water, then I have a reason to go to the kitchen to fetch a glass and fill it with water. But even if I have a duty to be in London at noon, it does not follow that I have a duty to take the ten o'clock train, even though it will bring me to London by noon.[6] Rights are like duties in this respect. The fact that you have a right that I be in London at noon does not entail that you have a right that I shall take the ten o'clock train. Needless to say, one has reason to take steps to discharge one's duties. Therefore, any moral theory that allows for the existence of duties must allow for the existence of ordinary reasons for duty-holders to take action to discharge their duties. Right-based theories allow for ordinary moral reasons of a derivative kind. This does not however avoid the objections, which are that ordinary reasons are no less important and central to moral thinking than duties.

Similarly with virtue. Right-based theories can regard the cultivation of certain dispositions as instrumentally valuable if they predispose individuals to do their duty. They may even approve of individuals' cultivating such dispositions for what they erroneously believe is their intrinsic value. But right-based theories (like utilitarian theories) cannot allow personal characteristics that are virtuous or morally praiseworthy to be judged intrinsically desirable and cultivated for their own sake. It is less clear to me what room there might be for supererogation within right-based theories. They can allow for a near relation, that is, a special category of duties performance of which requires exceptional personal qualities such that their performance deserves praise and failure to discharge them, though wrong, is excusable. Despite this palliative, the objection remains that supererogation in its proper sense, which involves action beyond the call of duty, is not recognized in right-based theories.

The preceding discussion was meant to illustrate and explain the ways in which right-based theories are impoverished. It has not established that the impoverishment involves any real moral loss. To show that is the aim of the rest of this article.

2. Rights and Individualism

Right-based moral theories are usually individualistic moral theories. There is as little agreement about the sense in which a moral outlook is or is not a form of individualism as there is on the sense of any other '-ism'. My explanation of moral individualism is therefore necessarily stipulative in part. My hope is that it captures an important element traditionally associated with individualism and a most important difference between humanistic moralities.[7] A moral theory will be said to be individualistic if it is a humanistic morality that does not recognize any intrinsic value in any collective good. In other words, individualistic moralities are humanistic moralities which hold that collective goods have instrumental value only.

Before we explore the connection between right-based theories and individualism, a few further remarks on the nature of moral individualism will be in order. A good is a public good in a certain society if and only if the distribution of its benefits in that society is not subject to voluntary control by anyone other than each potential beneficiary controlling his share of the benefits. I shall distinguish between contingent and inherent public goods.[8] Water supply in a certain town may be a public good if the water pipe network does not allow for the switching off of individual households. But it is only contingently a public good, as it is possible to change the supply system to enable control over distribution. Clean air is similarly a contingent public good. In this case we do not have the technology to control air distribution. But the limitation of our technological ability in this respect is only a contingent one.

General beneficial features of a society are inherently public goods. It is a public good, and inherently one that this society is a tolerant society, that it is an educated society, that it is infused with a sense of respect for human beings, etc. Living in a society with these characteristics is generally of benefit to individuals. These benefits are not to be confused with the benefit of having friends or acquaintances who are tolerant, educated, etc. One's friends can voluntarily control the distribution of the benefits of their friendship. The benefits I have in mind are the more diffuse ones deriving from the general character of the society to which one belongs. Different people benefit from the good qualities of the society to different degrees. But the degree to which they benefit depends on their character, interests, and dispositions, and cannot be directly controlled by others. (Usually they themselves have only partial and imperfect control over these factors.) Naturally one can exclude individuals from benefiting from such goods by excluding them from the society to which they pertain. But that does not affect the character of the goods as public goods that depend on nonexclusivity of enjoyment among members of the society in which they are public goods. I shall call inherent public goods 'collective goods'.

For obvious reasons economists have concerned themselves mostly with contingent public goods and those are mostly only of instrumental value: Clean air is important for one's health, and so on. If any public goods are intrinsically valuable, then some of the collective goods are the most likely candidates. Commitment to a humanistic morality, however, often inclines people to believe that even collective goods can only be instrumentally valuable. Living in a tolerant society, for example, is thought good because it spares one the pain of petty-minded social persecution and the fear of it, and enables one to have a happier life by enabling one to develop freely one's inclinations and tastes. To suggest otherwise, to suggest that living in a tolerant society is good independently of its consequences, that it is intrinsically good, is, in their opinion, to reject humanism; for it amounts to asserting the intrinsic value of something that is not human life or its quality.

To understand why such misgivings are misplaced and to explain why humanism is compatible with holding some collective goods to be intrinsically valuable, a brief sketch of a few more distinctions may prove helpful. Something is instrumentally good if its value derives from the value of its consequences or from the fact that it makes certain consequences more likely, or that it can contribute to producing certain consequences. Something is intrinsically good or valuable if it is valuable independently of the value of its actual or probable consequences, and not on account of any consequences it can be used to produce or of consequences to the production of which it can contribute. We need to distinguish among the intrinsically valuable things three different categories: those things are valuable in themselves or valuable *per se* if their existence is valuable irrespective of what else exists. Things are constituent goods if they are elements of what is good in itself which contribute to its value, that is, elements but for which a situation that is good in itself would be less valuable. Both goods in themselves and constituent goods are intrinsically good. So are ultimate goods or values. The aspects of a good in itself which are of ultimate value are those that explain and justify the judgment that it is good in itself, and which are such that their own value need not be explained or be justified by reference to other values. The relation of ultimate values to intrinsic values that are not ultimate is an explanatory or justificatory one. Ultimate values are referred to in explaining the value of nonultimate goods.

I hope that consideration of the following example will help explain these distinctions and show that humanism is compatible with the view that collective goods have intrinsic value. Consider the value of works of art. I mean their value not to their creators, but to their public. No doubt their value is many-sided. Owning works of art could be a sound investment, studying them could be a way of acquiring prestige, or knowledge of human psychology, and so on almost indefinitely. However, let us concentrate exclusively on their value to their public as works of art (rather than as a means of acquiring prestige or knowledge, etc.). One view of their value holds it to be intrinsic. Watching and contemplating works of art are valuable activities and a life that includes them is enriched because of them. If the life thus enriched is intrinsically good, then the existence of works of art is equally an intrinsic good. It is a constituent of the good that is a life including the experiencing of works of art. Let me refer to such a life as a life with art. The point is of course that one cannot experience works of art unless they exist. The value of the experience is in its being an experience of art. The experience cannot be explained except by reference to a belief in the existence of its object, and its value depends on that belief being true. On this view the existence of works of art is intrinsically valuable.

Such a view is compatible with humanism since the explanation of the intrinsic value of art is in its relation to the quality of life with art. A life with art is a good in itself; the existence of works of art is a constituent good; and the quality of life with art that explains its value is the ultimate good. All three are intrinsic goods.

The value of art is interpreted differently by classical utilitarians, who regard it as instrumentally valuable inasmuch as it may cause valuable sensations or emotions in an individual. The classical utilitarians interpret these sensations and emotions as capable of being caused in some other way and therefore as only contingently connected with the works of art that are therefore merely instrumentally valuable.

The existence of works of art is not a collective good. My aim so far has been to show that humanism is consistent with holding that not only life and its quality are intrinsically valuable. Hence, regarding collective goods as intrinsically valuable is compatible with a commitment to humanism. It is in principle also compatible with the view that morality is rights-based. Nevertheless right-based moral theories tend to be individualistic and to deny the intrinsic value of collective goods. The reason is not far to seek. Consider collective goods such as living in a beautiful town, which is economically prosperous, and in a society tolerant and cultured. Living in such an environment is in the interest of each of the inhabitants: it is more agreeable to live in such a society, whatever one's personal circumstances, than to live in one that lacks these attributes. But the fact that it is in my interest to live in such a society is not normally considered sufficient to establish that I have a right to live in such a society. The common view is that my interest that my society shall be of this character is a reason to develop it in such a direction, but that the existence of such a reason is not enough to show that I have a right that my society shall have this character. This is explicable on the definition of rights offered above, according to which a right is a sufficient ground for holding another to have a duty. It is the common view that my interest in living in a prosperous, cultured, and tolerant society and in a beautiful environment is not enough to impose a duty on anyone to make my society and environment so. It does not follow that no one has such duties. I am inclined to say that the government has a duty to achieve all those goals or at least to try to do so. But its duty is not grounded in my interest alone. It is based on my interest and on the interests of everyone else, together with the fact that governments are special institutions whose proper functions and (normative) powers are limited.

Nothing in this section shows that right-based moralities must be individualistic. But its argument explains that it is not accidental that right-based theories have been and are likely to be individualistic. Given some widely accepted views of the kinds of consideration that establish one person's duty to another, it is unlikely that individuals have basic rights to collective goods. If, for example, others' duty to me is confined to not violating my integrity as a person and to providing me with basic needs, then I have no right to collective goods as my interest in them is not among my basic needs for survival. Generally, since the maintenance of a collective good affects the life and imposes constraints on the activities of the bulk of the population, it is difficult to imagine a successful argument imposing a duty to provide a collective good that is based on the interest of one individual.

3. Autonomy and Rights

Is there anything wrong with moral individualism? Are any collective goods intrinsically desirable? I will suggest that some collective goods are intrinsically desirable if personal autonomy is intrinsically desirable. If this is so, then right-based theories cannot account for the desirability of autonomy. This conclusion is of great interest to the contemporary debate, since some rights-theories tend to emphasize the importance and value of personal autonomy. J. L. Mackie, for example, suggests that the fundamental right is, roughly speaking, a right to liberty: 'If we assume that, from the point of view of the morality we are constructing, what matters in human life is activity, but diverse activities determined by successive choices, we shall . . . take as central the right of persons progressively to choose how they shall live'.[9] Though he does not explicitly refer to autonomy, he seems to regard his invented morality as right-based because he maintains that only a right-based morality can express the fundamental value of autonomy. D. A. J. Richards, though not committed to the view that morality is right-based, seems to think that our concern for person autonomy requires a commitment to at least some fundamental rights.[10] Exploring the relations between the ideal of personal autonomy and the rights protecting personal autonomy is of interest for all those who care about personal autonomy, whether or not they are inclined to endorse the view that morality is right-based.

For the purpose of the present argument only one aspect of the ideal of personal autonomy need concern us.[11] An autonomous person is one who is the author of his own life. His life is his own making. The autonomous person's life is marked not only by what it is, but also by what it might have been and by the way it became what it is. A person is autonomous only if he has a variety of acceptable options available for him to choose from and his life became as it is through his choice of some of these options. A person who has never had any significant choice, or was not aware of it, or never exercised choice in significant matters but simply drifted through life, is not an autonomous person.

It should be clear from these observations that autonomy is here construed as a kind of achievement. To this sense of autonomy corresponds another, according to which autonomy is the capacity to achieve the autonomous life. In this sense a person is autonomous if he can become the author of his own life, that is, if he can be autonomous in the first and primary sense. By the second sense of autonomy a person is autonomous if the conditions of autonomous life obtain. Those are partly to do with the state of the individual concerned (that he is of sound mind, capable of rational thought and action, etc.) and partly to do with the circumstances of his life (especially that he has a sufficient number of significant options available to him at different stages of his life).

This distinction between an autonomous life as an achievement and a capacity for autonomy that is its precondition would not look quite the same to a supporter of a rights view of autonomy. He cannot claim that rights are justified because they protect autonomy. This would be to justify them instrumentally. He has to maintain that autonomy is constituted of rights and nothing else: the autonomous life is a life within unviolated rights. Unviolated rights create or protect opportunities. What one makes of them is left undetermined by the sheer existence of the rights. Therefore in terms of my distinction this would be to maintain that a capacity for autonomy guarantees that one's life is autonomous, that is, that no use or neglect of that capacity can make the life of those who have it more or less autonomous. There are serious objections to this view. But none of my arguments here depends on maintaining that autonomy is more than the life of a person with a certain capacity.

If having an autonomous life is an ultimate value, then having a sufficient number of acceptable alternative options is of intrinsic value, for it is constitutive of an autonomous life that it is lived in circumstances in which acceptable alternatives are present. The alternatives must be acceptable if the life is autonomous. A person whose every major decision was coerced, extracted from him by threats to his life or that of his children, has not had an autonomous life. Similar considerations apply to a person who has spent his whole life fighting starvation and disease, and has had no opportunity to accomplish anything other than to stay alive (imagine a person abandoned defenseless on an uninhabited island infested with deadly insects, where food is very scarce, and who just managed to stay alive). I shall not try to analyze what choices are acceptable. All that concerns us is that the ideal of personal autonomy (whose realization is clearly a matter of degree) requires not merely the presence of options but of acceptable ones.

The existence of many options consists in part in the existence of certain social conditions. One cannot have an option to be a barrister, a surgeon, or a psychiatrist in a society in which those professions, and the institutions their existence presupposes, do not exist. While this will be readily acknowledged, it is sometimes overlooked that the same is true of the options of being an architect or of getting married. It is true that one need not live in a society at all to design buildings regularly or to cohabit with another person. But doing so is not the same as being an architect or being married. An architect is one who belongs to a socially recognized profession. In many countries an homosexual can cohabit with, but cannot be married to his homosexual partner, since to be married is to partake of a socially (and legally) recognized and regulated type of relationship. Homosexuals cannot do that if their society does not recognize and regulate a pattern of relationship that could apply to them. They can imitate some other recognized relationships. But essentially they have to develop their relations as they go along and do not have the option of benefiting from existing social frameworks.

At least some of the social conditions that constitute such options are collective goods. The existence of a society with a legal profession or with recognized homosexual marriages is a collective good, for the distribution of its benefits is not voluntarily controlled by anyone other than the potential beneficiary. In a society in which such opportunities exist and make it possible for individuals to have autonomous life, their existence is intrinsically valuable. The ideal of personal autonomy entails, therefore, that collective goods are at least sometimes intrinsically valuable. I think that it entails much more than that. Commonly accepted views about humans as essentially social animals and equally common views about which options are worthwhile in life (for it is a condition of a life being autonomous that the available options include an adequate range of worthy opportunities) yield the conclusion that many collective goods are intrinsically good. At the very least, living in a society, which is a collective good, is on this view intrinsically good.

What conclusions is one to draw from these reflections (assuming they are sound) concerning the relation between rights and autonomy? In a way the most important one is that the ideal of personal autonomy is incompatible with moral individualism. Some may proceed to claim that morality is nevertheless right-based, but that since one of the fundamental rights is a right to autonomy it follows that there are rights to collective goods. Others may resist the idea that I have a right that my society shall continue to exist, and a right that it shall have architects and surgeons and monogamous marriages. My interest in being autonomous shows that it is in my interest to live in a society in which all those and many other options are available. But it is not enough by itself to justify holding others to be duty bound to make sure that my society shall offer all these options. Given that the existence of these options is intrinsically valuable, they would conclude that morality includes fundamental values or ideals as well as fundamental rights.

It is inevitable that the existence or absence of collective goods affects the lives of many individuals. This makes it unlikely that a successful argument can be found to establish an individual's right to a collective good. It also helps explain why writers who belong to the rights tradition regard fundamental human rights as including rights to individuated goods only. Yassir Arafat, being a Palestinian, has an interest in Palestinian self-determination. Furthermore, it is his interest, in combination with that of other Palestinians, which justifies the claim that there is a right to the self-determination of the Palestinian people. But because the right rests on the interests of many and because Arafat's interest by itself does not justify it, it is not his right, but the right of the Palestinian people as a group. It is important to realize that there need not be an actual conflict of interests to establish the insufficiency of an individual's interest as a foundation of an individual right to a collective good. Palestinian self-determination may be against the interests of some Israelis and Jordanians. The preservation of the historical and aesthetic character of Oxford may happen not to conflict with anyone's interest. Even if that is so I do not have a right to this result, despite my undoubted strong interest in it. The reason is plain. A right is a ground for a duty of another. A duty exists only if it would defeat certain conflicting considerations, were they to exist. The absence of actual conflict is not enough to justify a claim of a right. For this reason one may indeed be doubtful of the possibility of a justification for a fundamental individual right to a collective good. Given the intrinsic desirability of some collective goods, it is reasonable to conclude that morality is not right-based.

I will not consider the possibility that there are fundamental collective or group rights. A collective right exists when the following three conditions are met: first, it exists because the interests of human beings justify holding some person(s) to be subject to a duty. Secondly, the interests in question are the interests of individuals as members of a group in a public good and the right is a right to that public good because it serves their interest as members of the group. Thirdly, the interest of no single member of that group in that public good is sufficient by itself to justify holding another person to be subject to a duty.

The first condition is required for collective rights to be consistent with humanism. The other two conditions distinguish a collective right from a set of individual rights. The most frequently invoked collective right, the right to self-determination, exemplifies the three features. It is valued because of the contribution of self-determination to the well-being of individual members of the oppressed group. Self-determination is not merely a public good but a collective one. Finally, though many individual members of the group have an interest in the self-determination of their group, the interest of any one of them is an inadequate ground for holding others to be duty bound to satisfy that interest. The right rests on the cumulative interests of many individuals. (This explains why though the existence of the right does not depend on the size of the group, its weight or strength does.)

The same features are displayed by other collective rights. Consider, for example, the right of the British public to know how Britain was led into the Falkland War. It is a right for information to be made public, and therefore for a public good. It is held to be a collective right by those who think that it cannot be justified just on the basis of the interests of a single member of the public, but that it can be justified on the ground that the interests of many are at stake.

If this is so, then though a right-based morality including fundamental collective rights is richer than one that does not include them, it is still open to all the objections made in the text.

More important is the conclusion that if autonomy is an ultimate value, then it affects wide-ranging aspects of social practices and institutions. It would be wrong to postulate a right against coercion, for example, as a right to autonomy and to claim that it defeats, because of its importance, all, or almost all, other considerations. Many rights contribute to making autonomy possible, but no short list of concrete rights is sufficient for this purpose. Almost all major social decisions and many of the considerations both for and against each one of them bear on the possibility of personal autonomy, either instrumentally or inherently. If there is a right to autonomy, then its effect on political action and institutions is very different from what we are often led to believe.

4. Rights and Duties

The considerations advanced above are intended to suggest that apart from some rights, one finds other values at the foundations of morality. In passing I have referred to the possibility that governments have duties that do not derive from the rights of individual human beings. The possibility that there are duties that do not correspond to any rights is allowed for by the definition of rights, and is generally acknowledged by legal and political theorists. Yet the view that such duties must ultimately derive from fundamental rights or at least be based on the interests of people other than those subject to the duties has become sufficiently widespread that it is important to explain why it is rational to expect that there are fundamental moral duties that do not derive solely from the rights and interests of their potential beneficiaries, or that have no potential beneficiaries at all. I shall briefly discuss two cases purporting to show that some duties require noninstrumental justification, that is, that their existence is of intrinsic, even if not necessarily of ultimate, value. The cases will also show that there are duties that do not derive from anyone's rights.

Both cases are designed to show how one particularly troublesome objection to the possibility of noninstrumental duties can be met. Let me, therefore, begin by stating the objection. Suppose it was said that people have a duty to behave in a certain way because failing to do so is wicked or just plain morally wrong. The claim may then be made that that can be so only if there is some independent reason for objecting to that action. Otherwise there is no way of explaining why there is a duty to behave in this way rather than in any other. It would seem to follow that if an action is wrong because it is a breach of duty, then there must be a reason (other than the fact that the action is wrong) to justify the existence of the duty. That reason is bound to be that the duty is necessary to avoid infringing someone's rights or to prevent harm or to refrain from jeopardizing some value. If so, then the duty is instrumentally justified. But how else can it be justified? In what way can the order of justification be reversed, justifying the duty not to act in a certain way by the wrongfulness of the action without proceeding to explain the wrongfulness of this action, rather than any other, by reference to the fact that it harms values or violates rights?

A first step towards meeting the objection is to suggest that there might be an instrumental reason to act in that way but one that does not establish a duty so to act. The instrumental reason explains why it is a duty to act in this way rather than some other way. But as the instrumental reason does not establish a duty, the existence of the duty is intrinsically valuable. The flaw with this argument, if that is what it is, is that its premises are compatible with another possibility as well, namely, that the duty is not justified. One has still to find some noninstrumental justification that, added to the instrumental one, establishes the duty. Still the first step is helpful, since I believe that often the justification of intrinsic duties includes an instrumental component.[12] Let me now turn to my two cases of intrinsic duties.

For the purposes of the first example I shall assume that there is a duty among friends that obliges a person to compensate his friend if his action harmed the friend, even though the harm was not caused through any fault of his. Normally our responsibility to make good harm we cause to others depends on fault or on special responsibility. Friends have a no-fault obligation to each other, though normally they do not have to provide full compensation. Evidently the fact that compensating someone is likely to benefit him is an instrumental reason for doing so. That reason is not enough to establish an obligation to compensate or else everyone would have an obligation to compensate everyone else for any loss or harm he causes. Yet this instrumental reason provides an essential component in the noninstrumental justification of the duty to compensate friends for harm done to them. The other elements in the justification turn on the nature of friendship. Friendships entail a special concern for the welfare of the friend, concern for his welfare over and above the concern required of us towards other human beings generally. That concern manifests itself in many ways. But its expression is particularly urgent when we are the cause of harm to our friends. The urgency is not because then their need is greatest—it may not be. Nor is it because their need is our fault—for it need not be. The duty to friends we are considering results from the natural cultural convention to regard unsolicited acts of compensation for harm one causes, even without fault, as particularly expressive of one's concern for the welfare of the compensated person (if he is one's friend or not). Because such action expresses concern and because friendship is in part the expression of concern, one has a duty to compensate one's friend for harm caused. Since friendship consists in part in such duties, the existence of the duty is intrinsically justified if the desirability of friendship itself is, as I shall assume without argument, intrinsically justified. By recognizing and respecting such duties towards another, as well as in other ways, one develops a friendship with another and by denying them one undermines or ends friendships.[13]

For my second example imagine that I own a Van Gogh painting. I therefore have the right to destroy it. I have an instrumental reason not to do so. I can sell it for a large sum. Furthermore many would derive great pleasure and enrichment if they could watch it. But no one has a right that I shall not destroy the painting. Nevertheless, while I owe no one a duty to preserve the painting, I am under such a duty. The reason is that to destroy it and deny the duty is to do violence to art, and to show oneself blind to one of the values that gives life a meaning. The duty exists regardless of whether I profess to be a lover of art. If I do so profess, then to deny the duty is to compromise my integrity.[14] But everyone has a duty of respect towards the values that give meaning to human life, even to those on which one's life does not depend for its meaning. The moral conception I am relying on here is similar to the one underlying the previous example. One's respect for values does to a degree consist in action expressing it. Where such action is particularly apt and urgent, there may be a duty that is then an intrinsic duty.

One common objection to such a line of argument is that although it is true that one ought to compensate one's friends and to preserve works of art, there is no duty to do so. One ought to do so because of one's concern for one's friends and one's respect for art and not out of duty. But the objection that if one has a duty one should comply with it because it is a duty is based on the wrong presupposition. One may well have a duty to do something because of one's concern for a friend or one's respect for art.

5. Rights and Narrow Morality

The examples I used to argue for the existence of intrinsic duties are unlikely to convince anyone who does not at least half wish to be persuaded anyway. They presuppose not only controversial views that I did nothing to defend but also a way of analyzing them that is not without rivals. Even if my examples do not convince, I hope they make the view that there are intrinsic duties more plausible, and less absurd or irrational. Sometimes a moral theory gains conviction because it seems to be the only one that is coherently statable. Whichever view we accept we always gain by being able to see them as just one of several alternative moral outlooks of various degrees of acceptability.

One objection that might be raised against the general way in which the argument about right-based theories was conducted is that it misinterprets the general nature of morality, or at least that it overlooks the fact that rights are supposed by their proponents to be the foundation of morality in the narrow sense.[15]

Morality in the narrow sense is meant to include only all those principles that restrict the individual's pursuit of his personal goals and his advancement of his self-interest. It is not 'the art of life', that is, the precepts instructing people as to how to live and what makes for a successful, meaningful, and worthwhile life. It is clear that right-based moralities can only be moralities in the narrow sense. An individual's rights do not provide him with reasons for action (though if he can expect his rights to be respected, they inform him of some of his opportunities). It is implausible to assume that an individual can conduct his whole life on the basis of the sole motivation of respecting other people's rights. Nor is there any reason to commend such a mode of existence. It would be a life of total servitude to others. On the other hand, morality in the narrow sense may be right-based. Rights do exactly what narrow morality is supposed to do. They set limits to the individual's pursuit of his own goals and interests. On the plausible assumption that the only valid grounds on which the free pursuit by people of their own lives can be restricted are the needs, interests, and preferences of other people, it becomes plausible to regard (narrow) morality as right-based.

We have reached here one of the fundamental divides between the right-based views and the outlook that informs all the preceding objections to the thought that morality is right-based. There is a fundamental objection to the very notion of morality in the narrow sense. Of course one may for convenience of exposition or other superficial purposes hive off any aspect of morality and discuss some of its problems separately. There can be no objection to that. The objection is to the notion that there is such a division at a fundamental level, that one can divide one's principles of action into those concerned with one's own personal goals and those concerned with others, in such a way that the principles are independent of each other. The mistake is to think that one can identify, say, the rights of others, while being completely ignorant of what values make a life meaningful and satisfying, and what personal goals one has in life. Conversely, it is also a mistake to think that one can understand the values that can give a meaning to life, and can have personal goals and ideals, while remaining ignorant of one's duties to others. There is no doubt a mutual independence at the superficial level. I need not decide whether to become a middle-distance runner or a professional chess player before I understand my obligation to others. But by the time that is the main remaining problem about the kind of life I would like to have, all the fundamental problems have already been settled.

It may be best to approach my objection to the conception of a narrow morality from the examples discussed earlier in this article. My duty not to destroy the Van Gogh is appropriate for inclusion in narrow morality, for it is not based on my interests nor does it depend on the preservation of the painting being part of my personal goals. It can be seen as a potential limitation on my freedom to pursue self-interest or personal desires. And yet I have suggested earlier that the duty is not exclusively based on the interests of others. Those would establish a reason not to destroy the painting, but not an obligation not to do so. There is no way of analyzing the respect due to art into two components, one representing a person's obligations to others concerning art, the other expressing the importance art has for his own personal tastes and interests. Consider a person who has no interest in the arts. Even he should respect them. Some will say that that requirement of respect is derived from the requirement to respect other persons, some of whom have an interest in art. But this is a partial and limited view. The general requirement of respecting art is one that people should regard not as a restriction on the pursuit of their personal goals, but as part of their general outlook on life. It is no mere internalization of a requirement based on the interests of others. It is part of the necessary process through which a person learns of the worthwhile options in life and through which he develops his own tastes and goals. It is also part of the process through which he relates to other people. It is crucial for the development of normal personal relations that each person understands his own tastes and goals in ways that relate them to other people's goals and tastes. He must regard his own goals and tastes as valuable because they exemplify universal values or values that form part of a mosaic which in its entirety makes for valuable social life. He must, if he is to be capable of personal relations, find room for other people's values within that scheme. If I recognize an obligation to preserve the Van Gogh, this is because I express thereby my recognition of the value of art and through doing so I have come to recognize some of the worthwhile options on which, even though I did not pursue them, my autonomy depends. By recognizing that very same value I also create the possibility of creating personal relations with other people, for those depend at the deepest level, on a sharing of values.

Personal relations, on which we have just touched, are another area in which the boundary between morality in the narrow and wide senses is invisible. Personal friendships, marital relations, one's loyalty and sense of pride in one's workplace or one's country are among the most valuable and rewarding aspects of many people's lives. Such relations are culturally determined forms of human interaction, and it is through learning their value that one acquires a sense both of the possibilities of one's own life and of one's obligations to others. The two are aspects of one and the same conception of value. Consider one's sense of belonging to a certain country as a factor determining one's sense of identity and consider one's sense of belonging to a country as requiring sacrifices in the interests of others. I do not deny that at times the two elements are separate. At times the obligation to one's country clearly conflicts with one's interests. In normal circumstances, however, one's relations to one's country help to shape one's interests, tastes, and goals. At all times one's obligations to one's country come from the same source. Whether they are perceived as restrictions on one's freedom or as determining one's identity and interests, they defy the division of morality into wide and narrow components.

We have come full circle to a consideration of the intrinsic value of some collective goods. If collective goods such as membership in a society are intrinsically valuable, then it is to be expected that they provide the source both of personal goals and of obligations to others. The confrontational view of morality that pitches a person's own interests and goals as not only occasionally in conflict with his obligations to others, but as deriving from independent and fundamentally different sources is essentially an individualistic conception. My objections to the view that morality is right-based derive from a sense of the inadequacy of the conception of morality in the narrow sense, which itself is a reflection of the rejection of moral individualism.

NOTES

1. R. M. Dworkin, *Taking Rights Seriously* (London: Duckworth, 1977), p. 171.

2. J. L. Mackie, "Can There be a Right-Based Moral Theory?" *Midwest Studies in Philosophy* 3 (1978): 350.

3. See "The Nature of Rights," *Mind* 93 (1984):194.

4. This argument is developed in greater detail in my "Promises and Obligations," in *Law, Morality and Society*, ed. P. M. S. Hacker and J. Raz (Oxford: Oxford University Press, 1977).

5. Action beyond the call of duty is naturally not just any action one ought to do but has no duty to.

6. I leave it open whether or not one has a duty to do that which is both necessary and sufficient to comply with a duty. My claim is merely that one has no duty to do something because it is sufficient to comply with a duty. I have reason to do that which is sufficient to follow a reason.

7. For a survey of different notions of individualism, see S. Lukes, *Individualism* (Oxford: Blackwell, 1973).

8. I am grateful to L. Green for drawing my attention to this distinction.

9. J. L. Mackie, "Moral Theory," p. 355.

10. D. A. J. Richards, "Human Rights and Human Ideals," *Social Theory and Practice* 5 (1979):461; "Autonomy and Rights," *Ethics* 92 (1981):3.

11. I have said a little more on the nature of personal autonomy in "Liberalism, Autonomy and the Politics of Neutral Concern," *Midwest Studies in Philosophy* 7 (1982).

12. There are intrinsic duties that do not presuppose any instrumental reason for the duty act. These are ceremonial or symbolic duties. But I shall not consider those here.

13. On the noninstrumental relation between friendship and its normative constituents, see further my comments in *The Authority of Law* (Oxford: Clarendon Press, 1979), pp. 253–58.

14. See on integrity Gabriele Taylor, "Integrity," *Aristotelian Society*, supp., 55 (1981):143.

15. On morality in the narrow sense see, for example, G. J. Warnock, *The Object of Morality* (London: Methuen, 1971), and J. L. Mackie, *Ethics* (London: Penguin, 1977), pp. 106f.

3

Act-Utilitarianism, Consequentialism, and Moral Rights

R. G. Frey

Claims to moral rights abound. In the United States today, one interest group after another has discovered that what it seeks is its of right. Thus, women's rights, children's rights, welfare rights, gay rights, animal rights, environmental rights, and much else have appeared on the scene. Declarations of human rights have become common, and such things as a minimum income, a job, and housing are now widely ceded us as of right. Such declarations often now are used to assist certain groups: homosexuals now appeal to some human right to freedom of sexual expression in order to object to certain pieces of legislation; political conservatives now appeal to some human right, for example, to religious freedom in order to make a case for the reintroduction of prayer into the public schools; political liberals now regularly castigate governments for their violations of their citizens' human rights; and those who would like to see more done for the people of the Third World often now appeal to those people's moral or human right to subsistence, which, it is maintained, is held against us, our incomes, and food supplies.

Even the most ardent rights-theorist must be somewhat dismayed as various interest groups race each other to convert their wants into rights, in order then to be able to demand their due and to place opponents on the defensive. To rights-skeptics, of course, this widespread indulgence of rights-claims will simply reinforce their doubts about moral rights, about how we are to distinguish between genuine and bogus rights-claims, and, as a result, about the fruitfulness of trying to discuss moral and social issues in terms of rights.

Not surprisingly, the present enchantment with moral rights has led to (further) disenchantment with act-utilitarianism. Because of its purported failure to cope with such rights, as their number has increased

61

prodigiously and as they have come to occupy a prominent place in much recent moral, legal, and social theorizing, act-utilitarianism has fallen (further) into disfavor.

In a sense, of course, this is a familiar terrain. Even in the very recent past, first duties, then rules, then absolute prohibitions have been seen as the instrument of the act-utilitarian's demise, and moral rights appear to be the latest, currently most fashionable candidate for this role. There is, it would seem, a perpetual need to kill off act-utilitarianism; all that varies, from period to period, is the precise instrument of death.

In the face of this widespread reliance upon alleged moral rights, act-utilitarians have not been unanimous in their response on how to deal with those rights; and it is this variation in response, and the movement towards a split-level ethical theory, that I want to discuss here.[1]

I

In its most general form, the argument for the rejection of act-utilitarianism on the basis of moral rights is this: (1) there are fundamental, individual moral rights that are essential for the protection of persons; (2) act-utilitarianism cannot accommodate these rights; (3) therefore, act-utilitarianism is either an inadequate normative ethical theory or, more weakly, less adequate than one that can accommodate such rights. The argument is made specific, obviously, by formulating (1) and (2) around some (alleged) specific right, such as a right to life or to autonomy or to equal concern and respect.

We can distinguish between two general sorts of act-utilitarian replies to this argument, depending upon whether it is (2) or (1) that draws the fire of the act-utilitarian. The former I shall call a reply in the spirit of Mill; the latter, a reply in the spirit of Bentham.

The Spirit of Mill

This is essentially a spirit of amenability and accommodation, and in the present context this spirit takes the form of trying to ground some scheme of individual moral rights in utility and so of purveying a utilitarian theory of moral rights. The above argument turns out not to work, then, because (2) turns out not to be true; it is not true that act-utilitarians cannot accommodate individual moral rights within their theories.

The Spirit of Bentham

This is a spirit of hostility and skepticism towards moral rights, in part the legacy of Bentham's treatment of natural rights and of the absence in his work of anything approaching chapter 5 of Mill's *Utilitarianism*.[2] In this context, hostility and skepticism can take different forms. For example, one form they have taken in my own work[3] is an attack on the claim that there is this or that moral right.

I do not deny that there are, for example, legal or, more generally, institutional rights; and if one wants to maintain that the law and social institutions generally can be and, perhaps typically, are regarded in a moral light, the I am perfectly happy to speak of these institutional rights as moral rights. But this is not what rights-theorists today typically have in mind when they write of fundamental, individual moral rights. The point is not that, say, a right to life or to autonomy or to equal concern and respect is not typically regarded by them as an institutional right. It is that the fundamental rights of the rights-theorist do not come into and go out of existence with this or that institution; rather, they antedate such institutions and serve as constraints on which institutions we should have. In the broad sense, in the sense of holding that there are preinstitutional moral rights, such theorists are natural-rights theorists. They are not all, however, natural-rights theorists in the narrow sense, since they do not all offer an account of the ground(s) of the rights they purvey in terms of (nature or) human nature. For instance, in *Taking Rights Seriously*, it is a tenet of Ronald Dworkin's position that our absolutely fundamental right to equal concern and respect is not brought into existence by community decision, social practice, or public legislation and survives contrary decisions, practices, legislation, and adjudication. Indeed, it constrains our decisions, practices, and legislation. But he does not ground this right in (nature or) human nature; rather, he simply affirms that it is 'fundamental and axiomatic'.[4] From it, from its positing, other dependent rights are derived. In short, this fundamental right, or this fundamental sense of a right, is a stipulated one. Whereas stipulation may enable it to evade the charge that it is nothing more than an alleged natural right in the narrow sense, stipulation is not something that will endear this or any right to skeptics.

Actually, my position on moral rights has been two-pronged. On the one hand, I am skeptical whether there really are any specifically moral rights, and I have tried to argue for this thesis by probing and exposing the way such rights are typically put into existence. To me, the rampant use of stipulation, recommendation, intuition, self-evidence, obviousness, and appeals to natural law in order to ground rights is open to attack. On the other hand, and no less importantly, even supposing there are moral rights, I think they are superfluous, to and distracting from argument about substantive moral issues. I have tried to argue for three theses in these regards. First, rights do not have a fundamental role to play in ethics; they are superfluous, in the face of a fully developed theory of right and wrong, which is all we need in order to decide how we will act. Second, we gain nothing in clarity, precision, and understanding by trying to discuss moral issues in terms of rights, among other reasons, because we lack a method of arguing about them, certainly, with any degree of finality. Third, rights actually get in the way of the issues: our attention is diverted from the important business of working out principles of rightness and justification of treatment in cases of the sort at hand, to the wholly speculative tasks of making something of (competing) rights-claims, of their (often many) alleged grounds, and of the vast number of competing criteria for rights-possession currently on offer.

In short, if we take theses of these sorts as illustrative of one possible Benthamite approach to moral rights, then the above anti-act-utilitarian argument turns out not to work, because (1) turns out to be objectionable; (claims to) moral rights are themselves suspect, and, accordingly, we have no reason to reject act-utilitarianism on their basis.

For different reasons, then, the Millian and Benthamite approaches to rights both reject the argument from moral rights. But whereas one camp seeks to carve out space in its theories for some scheme of individual moral rights, the other seems bent upon minimizing rights-talk in or eliminating rights-talk from ethics. In a word, natural allies are in conflict.

Whatever my particular view of the merits of the Benthamite approach to moral rights, I shall not argue it here, at least directly. Rather, I want to point to a problem at the center of the Millian approach, to the pressure this problem creates for the act-utilitarian seriously to complicate his theory, and to the particular form this complication seems likely to take, namely, a bifurcation in our moral thinking between theory and practice, with act-utilitarianism confined to the level of theory.

II

There is a problem at the very center of the Millian approach to rights: if Millians keep their rights away from their consequentialism, they will fail to be act-utilitarians; if they bring them into contact with their consequentialism, then the rights they incorporate into their theory are going to be pale shadows of full-blooded rights.

By consequentialism, I understand the view that acts are right or wrong solely in virtue of their (actual) consequences. That is, I regard consequentialism—if one wants to distinguish, then act-consequentialism—as a view about rightness, not about public choice; I take it to be an answer to the question 'What makes right acts right?' This view is the subject of many alleged (and some real) difficulties, among which some have wanted to include the charge that it betokens a corrupt mind; but I do not want to argue over this or other alleged difficulties here.

One may be a consequentialist without being an act-utilitarian, as is the case with ethical egoists; one may be a utilitarian without being a consequentialist, as is the case with the various types of rule-utilitarians; but one may not be an act-utilitarian without being a consequentialist. Consequentialism is not the whole of act-utilitarianism, but it is an integral part of it; and one cannot give up consequentialism without giving up act-utilitarianism.

The inclusion of consequentialism within his theory compels the act-utilitarian to treat moral rights, provided the case for there being some is made, in exactly the same way as he treats moral rules. The view that acts are right or wrong in virtue of their (actual) consequences is incompatible with any view of moral rules or rights that allows them even partially to determine the rightness of acts. At bottom, act-utilitarianism is a conjunction of (i) consequentialism, (ii) some standard of intrinsic goodness—welfarist in character—by which to evaluate consequences, and (iii) a range component, to the effect that it is the consequences as affecting everyone that count towards determining rightness; and there is simply no provision in the theory as a theory of rightness for moral rules or rights to play a role in opposition to consequentialism.

It does not follow, however, that an act-utilitarian cannot find some place in his theory for rules and rights. Indeed, in the case of rules, it is now usually agreed that he can argue for the inclusion in his theory of the very general rules of ordinary morality, on the ground that their utility, particularly in the face of general human weaknesses—such as succumbing to pressures, bias, and temptation—and of the possible lack of a clear view of acts' consequences, is far too high for them in practice to be easily set aside. Not *easily* set aside: when factors such as the above are absent or present only to a minimal degree, and when utilities so work out, the rules will be broken. Nevertheless, an act-utilitarian can concede these rules a role in moral thinking even if they play no role in his account of what makes right acts right.

It should be apparent, however, that the role an act-utilitarian concedes rules and rights is restricted. It is not just that they do not make right or wrong the acts falling under them or that they are not absolutely immune to utility; two further matters are at issue. First, rules and rights do not figure at the most basic level of act-utilitarianism. At *that* level is to be found utility, or, more accurately, consequentialism, a standard of intrinsic goodness for evaluating consequences, and the particular theory's principle of utility (in which 'utility' is interpreted in the light of the theory's standard of goodness). Unlike rule-theorists or rights-theorists, for whom rules or rights are basic at the level of theory, act-utilitarians can have rules and rights in their theories only at levels above the basic. Second, while rules and rights, at the level of practice, are not unimportant, their importance is a function of their utility, and their utility is a function of our human situation. That is, because of our human situation, rules and rights acquire an importance in act-utilitarianism they otherwise would not have, and, indeed, do not have, if our particular situation is not characterized by or improves with respect to the factors noted earlier.

Now the combination of these points makes of moral rights mere shadows of the rights of rights-theorists. To the rights-theorist, it is not finding a place in one's theory for individual moral rights but the place that is found for them that is crucial. On the other hand, to ground rights on the shifting sands of utility is to place them in jeopardy, since, under the right conditions, they would be set aside or violated. Possibly such conditions will obtain only infrequently; but that is a contingent affair, dependent upon how utilities fall out. And to rest the utility of rights on our human situation is obviously to make their utility subject to something that may well change.

But this way of putting the matter does not go deep enough. The real point is this: this combination of the above factors makes moral rules and rights *at best* mere appendages to a theory of right and wrong. If moral rules and rights are not basic in the theory and so do not form part of the theory's account of what makes right acts right, they are dispensable. All that prevents this happening are the practicalities of our human situation, which can and often do alter.

Rights that are theoretically nonbasic in a theory of rightness are what I shall call appendage rights, at least if we think, by way of contrast, in terms of the contemporary view of at least some moral/political rights as trumps. That is, I take the claim that some individual moral/political rights are trumps to be the claim that there are certain things that other individuals or groups may not do to one (e.g., in pursuit of the collective good), and what *makes it wrong* to behave in these ways is that such behavior infringes one or more of one's individual moral/political rights.

The situation, then, is this: consequentialism prevents the act-utilitarian from allowing moral rights a hand in deciding the rightness of acts, but anything less than this will mean that the rights an act-utilitarian incorporates into his theory will be theoretically nonbasic, appendage rights.

III

The most obvious way an act-utilitarian might move to take rights seriously is in fact not of use to the Millian. For not just any attempt to incorporate a scheme of individual rights into an act-utilitarianism is a move in the Millian direction; to incorporate rights but to retain them as subject to consequentialism is a case in point.

In *Essays on Bentham*, H. L. A. Hart ponders the question of why Bentham, the great apostle of utilitarianism, did not entertain a 'direct utilitarian theory of non-legal rights',[5] of why, that is, Bentham 'was not ready to accept a simple utilitarian theory of non-legal rights as something consistent with his adoption of an unqualified utilitarianism'.[6] What I want to stress, whatever the answer in Bentham's case, is that a directly consequentialist, utilitarian theory of nonlegal rights will still not make of such rights anything more than appendage rights.

Consider some scheme of individual moral rights of the scope that is fashionable today: if this scheme possesses the gravity and centrality for moral/political life that its supporters declare, then the act-utilitarian may argue that it has a high acceptance-utility, and, in view of the seriousness with which many people invest such rights as protectors of important human concerns, generally a high observance-utility. These high acceptance- and observance-utilities, including the utility to be gained in fostering among people a feeling of personal security through possessing these rights, are going to be offset only by a very substantial amount of increased utility through infringing a right in the particular case; and the number of cases in which this occurs is likely to be few. The argument, then, seeks to bar infringements of rights in particular cases for, it seems clear, merely marginal increases in utility.

The problem here, should the Millian act-utilitarian try to make use of this argument, is not the usually unsupported claim that cases in which rights can be infringed will be few (it is, after all, long, hard work to think through and calculate the utilities of a situation), but rather that the rights incorporated into the theory remain subject to consequentialism. All this argument does is make it more difficult for consequentialism, on a case-by-case basis, to override a right; it remains true that it is right to override rights if utility reaches the required magnitude and true as well that it is a purely contingent affair whether in a particular case utility reaches that magnitude.

In fact, then, the Millian act-utilitarian is not helped by this argument, and any act-utilitarian who does make use of it, because rights remain subject to consequentialism, can have at best only appendage rights in his or her theory. And this is true, I want to emphasize, even if the act-utilitarian were to accept one of the traditional ploys emphasized by G. E. Moore, such as that we will always give in to temptation or that we never command a clear view of acts' consequences, by which to argue that it would *never be right* to depart from rules or to infringe rights. For the truth is that even this Moorean position retains moral rules and rights as subject to consequentialism; all it does is to exploit some facet of our human situation in order to ground an empirical claim to the effect that we shall stand a better chance of maximizing utility *under these conditions* by adhering to the rules or rights. Even this move, then, even the move to exploit our human situation in order to have a scheme of rights that, because of that situation, never give way in the face of consequences is a move that does not solve the Millian's problem. For rights remain appendage rights: consequences make acts right or wrong, and it is only because we sometimes or often have difficulty calculating these or calculating them in a detached manner, that we do not use, or are reluctant to use, consequences to make right infringements of the rights.

IV

The traditional act-utilitarian ploy of finding additional sets of consequences by which to reduce the frequency of rule violations and right-infringements mislocates the problem. The problem is not what strength the rules or rights have—that is why use of the absolute/*prima facie* distinction can be misleading in these contexts—but what role they have in a theory of rightness. In a consequentialist normative ethic, they appear to play no role in the theory's account of rightness; they are appendages to that theory, and not even that, if our human situation clears up in certain specified respects. With this the case, a different strategy is required to deal with rights.

Of course, it may be suggested that I am exaggerating the differences between consequentialist-based ethics and rights-based ethics; in particular, it may be held that right-infringements can be included within consequentialist-based ethics by allowing such infringements to figure as part of an act's consequences.[7] This, too, however, mislocates the problem, though in a way different from the issue of strength. Merely being able to include the infringement of rights within one's consequentialism does not show that the rights in question count for anything in their own right in the theory. To show *this* what one needs to show is not something about infringements but rather something about the status of rights. Specifically, it must be shown how, even within a consequentialism, rights can acquire a status that enables them to count as factors for or against the rightness of some action, even though the act's consequences are plainly one way or the other. Nothing about the present suggestion shows that rights have this status.

In order to show that a right is not a mere appendage right, that is, a mere appendage to a consequentialist account of rightness, it must be shown how the right counts in and of itself in favor of or against some action, quite independently of *the consequences* of adhering to or infringing the right. Rights must count in their own right, to be worthy of the name and to be other than appendage rights; in a directly consequentialist theory, they do not count in their own right in favor of or against the rightness of some act. Only consequences count. Accordingly, even if the infringement of a right can figure among an act's consequences, because it does not follow that the right counts in and of itself in favor of or against the rightness of the act in question, rights are not obviously other than appendage rights. Here, too, then, a different strategy is required to deal with rights.

It seems perfectly clear what this strategy in the end will be: it will consist in the Millian finding a way of keeping his consequentialism and his scheme of rights apart, a way that, I stress, must be consistent with his consequentialism and with the nonbasic character of rights in his theory.

So far as I can see, there is only one way a Millian can move to achieve his ends under these constraints: he must radically complicate his theory by compartmentalizing our moral thinking, and assigning consequentialism and his scheme of individual rights to different compartments. I say this for two reasons. First, to urge the Millian to adopt, on act-utilitarian grounds, some scheme of rights that bars direct appeals to utility with respect to them will not, for the reason I have indicated, be of much use to him. Second, however, it also will not capture what the Millian actually wants. Such a move makes it appear as if what is at issue between the Benthamite and Millian is simply how many infringements of rights the act-utilitarian will justify, and this is to miss the point. It is not the number of infringements justfied but the fact that consequentialism can justify infringements at all that matters; for so long as it can justify infringements, act-utilitarianism will contain mere appendage rights. To avoid this, consequentialism and rights must be assigned different compartments so that they do not interact; it will then be true that consequentialism will not justify infringements of rights (except, if at all, at the limit of catastrophe), but this will have nothing to do with some worry about keeping the number of infringements small. Were *this* the central worry, then, as we have seen, an act-utilitarian such as Moore, who was prepared to have a scheme of rights in his theory, might resort to the device of appealing to additional sets of utilities by which to make it more difficult to infringe a right on a particular occasion.

Now the sort of complication of act-utilitarianism that will have to occur is at least clear in general outline; almost certainly, it will take the form of a distinction between theory and practice, with appeal to consequences occurring at the level of theory but not at the level of practice. But this *per se* is not enough; for, as we have seen, depending upon how the claim about practice and appeal to consequences is argued, a Moorean can have good reason for not appealing to consequences in the particular case, even though he remains a direct consequentialist. What must be added is that appeal to consequences is *not appropriate* at the level of practice, by which I mean that what it is right to do will not be determined by appeal to consequences in this case, even if there is nothing whatever to impede our assessment of them. And what will render appeal to consequences in the particular case inappropriate will almost certainly be the claim that utility will be maximized by foregoing case-by-case utilities. In this way, instead of a directly consequentialist act-utilitarianism, one will have generated an indirectly consequentialist one.

V

The best example of the sort of complication I have in mind—it is the best not only because of the detail with which it is worked out but also because of the originality, lucidity, and care with which it is developed—is to be found in R. M. Hare's *Moral Thinking*.[8] Hare distinguishes two levels of moral thinking, critical and intuitive, embraces act-utilitarianism at the critical level, and finds a place for substantive moral rights at the intuitive level.[9] For our purposes here, the crucial part of this split-level account of moral thinking is this: one uses act-utilitarianism at the critical level in order to select those guides at the intuitive level by which to conduct one's life; and the guides selected will be those whose general acceptance (Hare chooses between guides on the basis of their acceptance-utilities) will maximize utility. Thus, given that these guides have been selected with an eye to the situations we are likely to find ourselves in, action in accordance with them is likely to give us the best chance of doing the right, that is, optimific thing.

At one level, then, we have act-utilitarian critical thinking; at another, guides for living selected by that thinking. If the guides selected take the form of principles, then most of our moral thinking at the intuitive level will take the form of trying to decide what it would be right to do, on the basis of these principles. (Occasionally, to be sure, particularly when principles conflict, we are forced even in the practicalities of the situation to do some critical thinking in order to decide what it would be right to do.) In other words, given the principles selected by act-utilitarianism, what is right is what is in accordance with the principles; and if our principles at the intuitive level confer some rights upon us, then, unless we have a conflict of principles or are confronted with a situation our principles cannot readily deal with, an act is wrong if it infringes one of these rights. In this way, at the intuitive level, Hare's split-level account of moral thinking is only indirectly consequentialist.

Something like this Harean complication of act-utilitarianism can give the Millian what he wants over moral rights, namely, rights that are not appendage rights. On the split-level view, appeals to consequences and substantive moral rights occur at different levels; what is right at the intuitive level is determined by applying those principles selected by act-utilitarianism at the critical level as giving us the best chance of maximizing utility in the situations we are likely to encounter.

Some people have queried whether Hare's two levels of moral thinking can be kept entirely apart, that is, whether seepage will not occur between them; but I shall not bother with this issue here. Rather, I want to raise what for our purposes is a more pressing question: will consequentialists be attracted by the Harean complication to act-utilitarianism? There are a great many strengths to Hare's account of moral thinking; but will consequentialists avail themselves of these strengths? I want to suggest that they might not, and for four reasons.

VI

Calculations of Global Utility

Perhaps the strongest claim that Hare makes on behalf of the split-level thesis is that it deals effectively with the well-known clashes between common opinion and act-utilitarianism, of which so much has been made. It deals effectively with them, it seems, because Hare's theory is only indirectly consequentialist. That is, he appeals to consequences at the theoretical or critical level, but at the practical level, on grounds of utility, he bars any extensive use of such an appeal. Since the guides he gives examples of in his book as selected by utility are much of a piece with ordinary morality, and since action in accordance with these guides is nearly always right because appeals to consequences have been effectively barred at the practical level, clashes with common opinion effectively disappear.

In the past, consequentialism/act-utilitarianism was differentiated from other theories by its results. What Hare has done is to construct an argument for act-utilitarianism that, in terms of what the agent does, more or less removes the sharp, distinctive results with which the theory has usually been identified and puts in their place results that more or less are in agreement with those of rival theorists. Indeed, on Hare's position, there is no reason in theory—I do not imply that Hare would be at all attracted to the following possibility in practice—why one cannot be an act-utilitarian at the critical level and something approaching a Kantian at the intuitive level; all that is required is that the guides selected by utility at the critical level be of Kantian character and of Kantian ferocity with respect to the appeal to consequences. And it may not be difficult to meet these requirements, if one plays up our inclination to bias and temptation, our weakness in the face of pressure, our inability to be detached and clearheaded in thinking through moral problems, our lack of complete factual information about the various alternatives open to us, our lack of a clear view of acts' consequences, etc. If one bears in mind that the thinking of which the split-level thesis is an account is supposed to take place in a single agent, then one can see that Hare's account of moral psychology[10] is going to have to be sufficiently flexible to allow the agent to be comfortable with this bifurcation in his moral thinking and the act-utilitarian/Kantian dichotomy that may issue from it.

Now it seems to me that Hare's theory does not remove clashes with common opinion for the reason stated (viz., that the theory is indirectly consequentialist) and so for a reason *uniquely* to do with his split-level thesis; it removes clashes with common opinion, I think, because the guides he gives examples of as selected by act-utilitarian critical thinking, for example, about keeping our promises and telling the truth,[11] are of a piece with common morality. After all, nothing would have been gained by Hare's split-level theory, from the point of view of removing clashes with common opinion, if, though it barred consequentialist appeals at the intuitive level, the guides it selected at the critical level were of the order 'Always beggar your neighbor'. So, the central feature of Hare's accord with common opinion lies, I think, in his conviction that act-utilitarian critical thinking will throw up as guides at the intuitive level many, if not most, of those presently characteristic of common morality. Is this the case?

The utilitarian calculations needed to establish the point would be long and hard; calculating utility is time-consuming and difficult work, even at the best times. What I want to stress, however, is that the demands Hare's theory lays upon us make such calculations even more difficult to perform, so difficult, in fact, that I suspect we shall not have very much confidence in the claims made on the basis of those calculations and so in the claim that this or that guide is the one that maximizes utility.

Consider any case in which a reasonable amount of utility can be produced through the agent doing other than what his relevant guide directs him to do: on the split-level approach, in which the agent is using consequences or utility *not* as a means of deciding what it would be right to do, but rather as a means of selecting guides the application of which at the intuitive level determine what it would be right to do, the agent has to forego that particular dollop of utility. He does so in the name of overall utility; that is, when the agent uses consequences or utility as the means of selecting guides that, if accepted, will maximize utility overall, the agent has, in the name of overall utility, to forego the particular utility to be derived from doing other than the relevant guide directs. As cases mount in which a reasonable amount of utility can be gained through doing other than the guide directs, the agent has to continue to foresake particular utilities on behalf of overall utility. The problem is whether the act-utilitarian is really ever in a position to make this more global determination of utility.

At *some* point, of course, it may occur to the agent that by adopting slightly different guides, ones that increase the incidence of direct appeal to acts' consequences but that still serve the role his initial guides were designed to serve, he can capture more of these case-by-case utilities while preserving overall utility more or less as it was. To respond that such guides would not *in fact* maximize utility is simply not something that can be pronounced upon in advance of actually doing the calculations. And this is the point: there is not one but many principles to choose from, and what we must do on the split-level approach is to select that principle with at least as high an acceptance-utility as any other. But to determine this is by no means an easy task, even if we leave aside the uninviting prospect of our having to determine it for one after another candidate for greater acceptance-utility.

For example, does a principle of the form 'Keep promises' have a greater acceptance-utility than one of the form 'Keep important promises'? One can see how the issue is joined: if the determination of importance is left up to each of us, it is easy to see how disutility might ensue; if we are enjoined simply to keep promises, however, it is easy to see how disutility may ensue through overly rigorous observance of the principle. Disutility, then, *might* ensue on either principle. But will it? The question is asking us to estimate over the promise-keeping situations we are likely to meet with, the difference in acceptance-utility between the two principles. But think of how complicated making such an estimate will be and of the numerous factors that may affect it. I must ask myself the question of whether, for all the types of promise-keeping situations I am likely to find myself in, the one principle or the other has the greater acceptance-utility. Again, I must ask myself the question of whether, for all the types of speaking situations I am likely to find myself in, the principle 'Tell the truth' has more or less acceptance-utility than the principle 'Tell the truth in important matters'. The number of speaking situations I find myself in daily, however, are vastly numerous and widely varied and the factors that affect them multifarious. So what am I to do? Am I to think of only a few types of situations in judging acceptance-utility? Then, however, I will not be able to affirm that one principle has greater overall acceptance-utility, since I will not have examined all the types of speaking situations and all the types of contingencies that arise within them that I am likely to encounter. Or am I to think of *all* the types of speaking situations I am likely to be in, *all* the various principles that are on offer with respect to them, *all* the various factors that are likely to affect them, and so on? Then, however, there must be real doubt that I can do this, at least in a sense that does not put me in jeopardy of having my estimates of acceptance-utility amount to nothing more than guesses at acceptance-utility. And if estimating were to come down to guessing, it is by no means obvious that an act-utilitarian would pass up the particular utilities in the cases at hand.

Notice how, if our not infrequent lack of a clear view of acts' consequences is played up, it will feed our worry about guessing.

Notice, too, how the matter of confidence enters. It would seem far easier for me to estimate utilities in the particular case (I do not imply that this is itself an easy task) than it is for me to make the more global estimates of acceptance-utilities of different principles over cases of sorts I am likely to encounter. For this reason, I seem more likely to have greater confidence in my judgment in the particular case than in the broader, more global judgment. In other words, when I am told to forsake the particular utilities of breaking the principle in this case because the principle overall maximizes utility for cases of this type, I will not have all that much confidence that the principle does maximize utility overall, unless I am capable of performing feats of utilitarian calculation that I am not simply licensed in assuming I can perform. And if I lack confidence in this regard, including less confidence than in my judgment of utilities in this case, am I likely as an act-utilitarian to pass up these case-by-case utilities?

I must emphasize that the problem is not one of being able to say, on utilitarian grounds, that having some guide or other for cases of this sort is obviously more utile than having no guide at all; a Benthamite or Moorean act-utilitarian, with rules of thumb, can say this. The problem is to be able to say, and with confidence, that *this* guide maximizes utility overall for cases of this type. Whether we are reduced to guessing at acceptance-utilities, because of the pressure to take into account all the various contingencies, or reduced to not being able to determine greater overall acceptance-utility, because of pressure in the direction of taking into account no contingencies, we seem unlikely to have the requisite confidence.

Nor does this problem disappear, the more we flesh out the Harean complication to act-utilitarianism. To give but a single example, Hare subscribes to a desire or preference account of utility, and this means that, in deciding among guides at the critical level on the basis of acceptance-utility, we are looking for guides that maximize the satisfaction of desires or preferences. This refers to everyone's desires and preferences; that is, what we are seeking are guides whose general acceptance would enable us to maximize the satisfaction of the desires or preferences of those in and affected by the situation. To recall, we are not selecting guides for this case but for cases of this type, so feats of imagination—of contingencies, of people's desires and preferences, of all the desires and preferences of all those in and affected by situations of this sort—are once again required. It seems to me pressure will inevitably move us in one of two directions, to judge acceptance-utility on the basis of relatively full knowledge of the above factors or to make this judgment on the basis of relatively incomplete knowledge of these factors; and the problem set out above arises again. Put differently, utility-calculations on the Harean complication to act-utilitarianism either require us to know more than we are ever likely to know about factors that affect situations of that type, including different people's different desires and preferences, or judgments of overall acceptance-utility are going to have to be made under conditions in which the danger exists that such judgments will degenerate into guesses. Either way, the issue of confidence is a real one.

Finally, one might think to solve the problem by giving more narrow interpretations of the phrase 'situations of that type', that is, by breaking up types of acts into narrower types. If we start along this road, however, there are going to be vastly more principles for us to learn, master, and eventually deploy; and it is hard to believe either that a theory will be very usable in practice or that people will indeed maximize utility through trying to wield some great number of principles. The more types of acts broken up into narrower types, and the more narrow the types into which they are broken, the more acute these difficulties become. Nor must we overlook the possibility that rather frequent clashes with common opinion will begin to arise again, as many more principles, selected by act-utilitarian thinking, are deployed at the intuitive level, and over narrower and much narrower types of acts. Certainly, the assumption that all such principles, no matter how narrow the type of act in question, will be of a piece with common morality is a large one. In any event, Hare himself has shown in part one of his book the virtues for his theory of a small number of learnable, teachable principles; and the present suggestion, of breaking up types of acts into narrower types, seems likely to run afoul of his own position.

In short, it is not clear to me either that act-utilitarian critical thinking will throw up those guides that eliminate clashes with common morality or that, even if it does, we shall have very much confidence in them, enough in any case for us to forego the particular utilities in the case at hand.

VII

Human Shortcomings

There is a tension in Hare's split-level thesis between what we are capable of at the two levels, and this tension can lead to a particular result that may well affect whether the consequentialist will find the thesis attractive.

At the intuitive level, except in the sorts of cases I noted earlier, Hare thinks we are far more likely to do the right, that is, optimific thing by foregoing act-utilitarian thinking. As we have seen, however, the reason for this is not simply lack of time; the sorts of things Hare further has in mind are our inclination to bias and temptation, our weakness in the face of pressures, our frequent inability to be detached and clearheaded, our lack of factual information, our lack of a clear view of acts' consequences, our tendency to emphasize our self-interest and self-importance or to exaggerate the effect of acts upon us, and so on. These sorts of considerations—let us call them human shortcomings—are deployed at the intuitive level to contend against our setting aside a principle on consequentialist grounds; that is, they are used by Hare to cast doubt upon the reliability of our utility-calculations in particular cases.

There are, I think, three points (or three aspects of the same point) to be made in connection with this use of our human shortcomings. First, when we turn to more global utility-calculations at the critical level, either these same shortcomings are present or they are not. If they are, then these more global utility-calculations are as unreliable as those in the particular case; if they are not, then what has happened to them? More time and a certain remoteness from the actual situation will not in themselves dispel (all) such shortcomings; if a person is prone to special pleading, exaggerated self-importance, temptation, or bias, more time and remoteness *per se* hardly seem likely to make a new man of him. True, more time and distance from the actual situation may mean that one will feel the intensity of pressures less; but it does not follow either that, in a period of calm reflection, such pressures have no intensity at all or that, even if they have less intensity, they still do not have great intensity. What intensity they have is likely to vary from person to person and to depend in part upon the character of the pressures being exerted upon the agent. Moreover, we must not overlook what quite often happens outside the pressure of the moment and in a period of calm reflection: in the case of a person who exaggerates the effect of acts upon himself, for example, calm and reflection not infrequently make matters worse, through feeding the person's worries, anxieties, and dark forebodings about the future. In short, if human shortcomings infect utility-calculations at the one level, why not at the other?

Second, the assumption that all our human shortcomings have disappeared when we are doing our critical as opposed to intuitive thinking is simply implausible. If we do not assume this, however, our critical thinking is infected by our shortcomings, or, if this seems too strong, is at the very least rendered suspect or of doubtful reliability because of them. Either way, one of the central tasks Hare assigns critical thinking is in danger of slipping away from us. Critical thinking is supposed to assess our moral intuitions; it can do so, however, only if it is free of the effects of our human shortcomings, since, otherwise, it may, for example, be biased in favor of or against those intuitions.

Interestingly, Hare nowhere in *Moral Thinking* denies that our human shortcomings continue to plague us at the critical level. Though this means that he does not implausibly assume that they have disappeared, it also means that our critical thinking can be distorted by them. This, then, makes it appear as if the central difference between intuitive and critical thinking is simply the degree of distortion our human shortcomings inject into each kind of thinking. If this is so, then we seem to be in the situation of having to check one kind of distorted thinking by means of another and of hoping that the degree of distortion in the latter kind of thinking is less than in the former. Whether this hope is well founded will, as I say, depend (at the very least) upon the susceptibilities of the person in question and upon the nature of the pressures exerted upon him.

Third, our human shortcomings reappear at the critical level (we hope in muted form); they inject or can inject distortion into our critical thinking; and the degree of distortion so injected may be considerable in some of us. Are we all, nevertheless, to do our own critical thinking?[12]

If *each of us* is to do our own critical thinking, and if that thinking is suspect for the reason suggested, then we are effectively cut off from the rationale of our intuitions or principles at the intuitive or practical level. We are deprived of the theoretical or justificatory level at which our intuitions and principles are assessed and, in the appropriate sense, rationalized.

If *each of us is not* to do our own critical thinking, because not all of us can at the critical level achieve (relative) freedom from our human shortcomings, then those who have their critical thinking done for them—and it *may* be most of us—will be deprived of any rationale in themselves for the principles they wield and so for what they do at the intuitive level. They will be cut off from an understanding of the informed account of rightness and so from an understanding of the moral character of their own intuitions, principles, or conduct. They could be told what was right or wrong, but that is not the same thing. An elite among us would have been formed, as would a lesser class, and paternalism would be rife.

If *none of us* is to do our own critical thinking, because none of us in fact achieve (relative) freedom from our human shortcomings, then it is not clear what is achieved by the two-level thesis. For all of us should have to have our critical thinking done for us, and when Hare urges us to think through moral problems for ourselves, we should have to understand that to mean something other than what it says. Yet, the whole tone of Hare's discussion of specific moral problems is of us grappling with them; presumably, therefore, some of us must be able to do some critical thinking. (There would, in any event, be something very odd about insisting that we distinguish between our intuitive and critical thinking, between when we are employing our intuitive principles and when we are critically assessing them, and then denying that we can ever think critically or critically assess our intuitive principles.)

Overall, then, the problem is this: if one plays up our human shortcomings in order to impugn our utility-calculations at one level, and if our shortcomings reappear at the other level and with varying degrees of intensity, then can we really be confident that our more global utility-calculations at this other level are reliable? But even the slightest doubt on this score poses a danger for Hare; for it was the results of these more global utility-calculations that were supposed to deter the consequentialist from opting for the utilities in the particular case.

Finally, let me link this point to Hare's archangel.[13] There is a gulf be-tween archangel thinking, as Hare calls it, and our own critical thinking. If we confine ourselves only to our human shortcomings, then, while our critical thinking is distorted by them, more in some people, less in others, archangel thinking is entirely distortion-free with respect to them. What we as critical thinkers are supposed to do is to try in our own cases to come as close as we can, not, as it were, to the results of archangel thinking, but to archangel thinking itself. How close we ap-proximate to it, however, depends upon the amount of distortion in our critical thinking. If our critical thinking is very much distorted, then we seem hardly to approximate the model at all, in which case we are severed from the rationale of the principles revealed in our intuitive thinking. That is, we shall never in ourselves be capable of act-utilitarian thinking and so capable in ourselves of performing perhaps the most central task assigned critical thinking, namely, the selection and correc-tion of guides by which to conduct our lives. Accordingly, even if such thinking can be done, we cannot do it. If this seems too strong, then we may conclude that, even if such thinking can be done and that we can do it, we cannot do it well, with the result that doubts about the utility-calculations made by such thinking inevitably arise.

VII

Critical Thinking and Rights

Let us suppose that act-utilitarian critical thinking will select as guides for use at the intuitive level some principles that confer some rights upon us: two of the crucial differences between a directly conse-quentialist theory and an indirectly consequentialist one such as Hare's are supposed to be that, in the latter but not the former, (i) individual moral rights have a role to play in determining rightness and (ii) such rights are taken seriously. They have a role to play in determining rightness because, for Hare, what is right at the intuitive level is what is in accordance with the principles selected by act-utilitarian thinking at the critical level; rights are taken seriously because, given that they have this role to play in determining rightness, consequentialist appeals are effectively barred, with the exceptions I noted earlier, as grounds for infringing them. Conversely, in a directly consequentialist theory, rights have no role to play in determining rightness, and consequentialist ap-peals may always be cited as grounds for infringing them.

Now there is a problem here for Hare. He will secure no advantage over the direct consequentialist unless he builds into his theory some device that restricts the incidence of or occasions for critical thinking. The reason is clear: so far as rights are concerned, there seems an exact parallel between direct consequentialist appeals and Harean critical thinking. That is, just as the one view holds that alleged individual moral rights give way in the face of consequentialist appeals, so Harean theory holds that such rights are susceptible to infringement as the result of critical, that is, consequentialist/act-utilitarian thinking. If, in calm, reflective periods, therefore, I may always shift to the critical level and do some critical thinking, then the very dangers that have been thought to beset individual moral rights on a directly consequentialist theory will await them on Hare's indirectly consequentialist one. Indeed, what rights we have, if any, and what force they have to resist infringement will depend from moment to moment upon how utilities work out and upon what issues, with the utilities filled in, from my act-utilitarian thinking.

In short, if I may constantly shift from the intuitive to the critical level in my moral thinking, provided only that I have the time, then the security people allegedly feel through the possession of individual moral rights is in jeopardy; for my critical or act-utilitarian thinking could lead me to infringe them. If this is so, furthermore, then I seemingly fail to take rights seriously, since by constant shifts to the critical level I make them directly susceptible to consequentialist/act-utilitarian reasoning. Lastly, with such shifts, rights, as it were, are bypassed, in my determination of rightness; I use my critical thinking directly to think through what it would be right to do in cases of the particular type in question.

The problem for Hare, then, is that, unless some restriction is placed upon the incidence of or occasions for critical thinking, he would seem to find himself having to contend at the critical level with all the same complaints over rights with which directly consequentialist theories have to contend.

The restriction in question, moreover, cannot consist solely in the empirical claim that most of us do not have much time in which to do any careful, critical thinking; for such a claim hardly seems likely to underwrite a deep confidence in the security that individual moral rights allegedly afford us, a deep commitment to the seriousness and importance of such rights, and a significant role for them in the determination of rightness. All this would constantly be at the mercy of my finding time to do some critical thinking. The restriction seems bound up, not, or not solely with, empirical claims, but with claims about appropriateness. If two levels to our moral thinking are distinguished, then we need to know when we may appropriately shift from one level to the other. If our intuitive level thinking may, given time, constantly be subjected to and revised in the light of our critical thinking, and that is the picture *Moral Thinking* seems to purvey, then it is difficult to see how Hare's indirect consequentialism in the end gives a role and seriousness to rights at odds with the direct consequentialist's. If our intuitive-level thinking may not, even given time, constantly be subjected to and revised in the light of our critical thinking, then why not? Some further answer or complication in theory is needed, and I do not quite see now what that answer or complication is. (Nor do I quite see how the archangel model is to provide it: that model encourages us, *when* we do our critical thinking, to try to emulate archangel thinking as best we can; it does not tell us anything about how often we should strive to engage in critical thinking. But then surely we should need some reason for not striving to engage in it just as much as we possibly can, since, provided we are the sorts of persons who do any moral thinking at all, it is the paradigm of completely detached, fully informed, clearheaded moral thinking. Accordingly, it is not obvious why I am not licensed, during every calm, reflective period I enjoy, to engage directly in act-utilitarian thinking, and, therefore, licensed constantly to revise my intuitive thinking in the light of it. Thus, since substantive moral rights for Hare appear only at the intuitive level, they, too, are constantly subjected to direct act-utilitarian thinking, which is precisely where the direct consequentialist was supposed to go wrong.)

IX

Entrenchment

Hare quite rightly, I think, comes down hard against intuitionists, whom he sees as the main opponents of utilitarians, and his central criticism of them is that they ignore the critical level to moral thinking. To operate wholly on our moral intuitions, without the corrective device supplied by critical thinking, would, even if we were to ignore cases of *conflict* between our intuitions, leave us without any means of assessment of those intuitions; and that can hardly be a good thing.

Now intuitionists operate on principles or dispositions they have learned, and in this they are not *per se* doing anything wrong. For Hare himself favors, on act-utilitarian grounds, the inculcation of principles or dispositions, and one of the subjects on which he has laid stress, from *The Language of Morals* onwards, has been moral education. This consists, in his view, in building deep into our characters principles or dispositions of the sort that seem likely to foster utility. When I speak of building these 'deep' into our characters, I mean just that; for Hare wants us in the end, I think, in addition to our feeling great reluctance to depart from the way these principles and dispositions lead us to behave and so to feel remorse and guilt when we do depart from them, to have embedded them so deeply into our characters that they come in themselves to supply motives for us. Thus, if the appropriate principle or disposition has been embedded deeply enough, we come to want to keep our promises, not because of consequential considerations, but because promise-keeping has become a motive on our parts; this is, I think, Hare's rendition of what others would express by saying that, with a sufficiently deep internalization of the appropriate principle or disposition, we come to want to keep our promises for their own sake.

One can now see how this present discussion may possibly connect with that in the preceding section. For it might be argued that what prevents our constantly shifting from the intuitive to the critical level, considerations of time apart, is that we have so deeply embedded certain principles or dispositions (i.e., those selected by critical thinking) into our characters that we are greatly reluctant to depart from them and feel remorse and guilt when we do. In other words, the sheer depth of internalization of our intuitive principles may serve to prevent us from constantly shifting from them to critical thinking about them.

I think a consequentialist will worry about this kind of moral education and in a particular regard, which may only be a slight variation on Hare's view but nevertheless, as the consequentialist will see it, an important one. The worry has two aspects. First, if we so deeply embed into our characters a principle or disposition about promise-keeping that we come to want to keep our promises for their own sake, then even if we were to agree that act-utilitarian critical thinking would throw up such a guide for use at the intuitive level, we as consequentialists shall nevertheless want to be careful not to become insensitive to the consequences of particular cases. In other words, if we embed (at the intuitive level) consequence-disregarding principles so deeply into our characters that they come in themselves to supply motives for action, then how do we avoid freezing out particular consequences to such an extent that we cannot use them in the particular case to challenge the particular principle or disposition brought to bear on it? How, that is, do we keep deeply entrenched, consequence-disregarding principles alive to particular consequences? If the answer is that we constantly allow particular consequences to weigh against *this* application of the principle, then we are back with the discussion of the preceding section; if the answer is that we are not to keep such principles alive to particular consequences, then we seem to have a complete departure from any form of consequentialism, as well as an absence of any obvious way of challenging the principles; and if the answer is that the matter is simply another instance of something that must be settled by critical thinking, then we not merely have to envisage dramatic variations in what each of us as the result of our critical thinking may decide in the matter but also, and much more importantly, have to realize that we are being given nothing in the logic of Hare's position as an answer. What I mean is this: Hare can provide no guarantee *in theory* that our deeply embedded intuitive principles will be alive to particular consequences, since how deeply each of us in our critical thinking may think it wise to embed the principles such thinking throws up is more a psychological than a logical matter. It is not to the point to respond that all such principles are merely *prima facie* ones and so are of course alive to particular consequences; for the question is how, given deep internalization, even *prima facie* principles remain sensitive to particular consequences. If the answer comes down to some feature of a person's psychology, if, that is, the depth at which a person's intuitive principles are embedded in his character is a function of what, psychologically, he finds most amenable to the sort of person he takes himself to be, the consequentialist will be worried. For it will then be left up to each person's psychology whether his intuitive principles remain sensitive to consequentialist appeals, and people vary enormously in what they find amenable to the sorts of persons they take themselves to be.

Second, I think a rather important consequentialist point can be lost, if one considers the issue of entrenchment of principles in the context of intuitionist/act-utilitarian disputes. What worries a consequentialist is not the possible entrenchment of nonutilitarian principles or dispositions, as opposed to utilitarian ones, but entrenchment itself.[14] What Hare does is, on the one hand, to entrench certain principles or dispositions in us on the ground that they are likely overall to foster utility, and, on the other, to rely upon the empirical fact that we are not likely to meet with many occasions when it would be optimific to act in opposition to these principles or dispositions. The real problem with this procedure for the consequentialist is not Hare's empirical claim, but rather how the procedure is kept alive to the dangers of ossification. With respect to any deeply entrenched principle, the more difficult it is to bring yourself to violate it, the less you will do so, even when it has, so to speak, outlived its usefulness. Under these circumstances, Hare's empirical claim merely feeds your reluctance to violate the principle, with the result that you have become the victim of your own entrenchment of principles.

It is tempting, of course, to think that when, as I put it, a principle has outlived its usefulness, it will be discarded by act-utilitarian thinking, though if that thinking is infected with our human shortcomings or is curtailed in the way envisaged in the preceding section, then it is not obvious that the principle will be discarded; but this kind of response *can* miss the point. The point is not whether the particular principle in question does or does not foster overall utility, but rather how you prevent yourself on Hare's theory, no matter what the principle deeply entrenched, from simply being swept along by its deep entrenchment.

So, I am not sure consequentialists will want someone to come to want to keep promises for their own sake, unless they can be sure that the entrenchment of such a principle will not be so deep that the person has what has become, for all intents and purposes, an unthinking motive for action. Such a person would not be guilty of principle worship, but of allowing his principles to have become the sources of bias. This is what I mean by the 'dangers of ossification': the agent has become biased in favor of deeply entrenched principles because of (the depth of) their entrenchment.

The above explains why I do not think entrenchment can be the answer to the problem of constant shifts to the critical level raised in the last section. In order to prevent the entrenchment of principles exposing us to the dangers of ossification, Hare requires that these principles at the intuitive level continually be open to critical scrutiny; in order to prevent our constantly shifting to critical thinking and so perhaps evading these principles and the rights they impose, however, he requires that they not be continually open to critical scrutiny. (So far as I can see, therefore, the less deep we embed our intuitive principles the more open to direct consequentialist scrutiny they become, whereas the more deep we embed them the more likely they are to ossify and to become sources of bias.) This tension seems to me at the very heart of Hare's account of moral education; and though it may be held to be a further task of critical thinking to dissipate this tension, if what I have been suggesting earlier in this section, in connection with the point about entrenchment and psychology, is correct, the accomplishment of this task is more an article of faith than something guaranteed by the logic of the split-level distinction.

X

To conclude, compartmentalization of consequentialism and rights is only going to attract the Millian if the model of compartmentalization is attractive, and I think it possible that consequentialists/act-utilitarians may be somewhat reluctant to move in the direction of Hare's two-level theory. This, to recall, is what was supposed to give the Millian rights as more than mere appendages to a theory of rightness and so to enable him to distance himself from and to advantage himself over the Benthamite.

NOTES

1. This is a revised and expanded version of chapter 10 of my book *Rights, Killing, and Suffering* (Oxford: Basil Blackwell, 1983). I have benefited from discussions of it at Queen's University and the University of Toronto in Canada. I have also enjoyed the comments of a discussion group in Oxford, and the remarks in the group of R. M. Hare, Ronald Dworkin, John Finnis, and James Griffin have particularly influenced me. I am especially indebted to L. W. Sumner, for discussions in and around every aspect of the paper.

2. The contrast I am drawing here between Mill and Bentham I believe to be histori-cally accurate; but L. W. Sumner, through many conversations, and H. L. A, Hart, through his *Essays on Bentham* (Oxford: Clarendon Press, 1982), especially chapter 4 ("Natural Rights: Bentham and John Stuart Mill"), have shaken my confidence that the gulf between Mill and Bentham over rights is as wide as I make out. The reading of chapter 5 of Mill's *Utilitarianism* most in accordance with my view of that chapter is that of David Lyons, in his paper "Mill's Theory of Justice," in *Values and Morals*, ed. A. I. Goldman and J. Kim, (Dordrecht, Holland: D. Reidel, 1978), pp. 1–20. The point of Sumner and Hart, however, is that Bentham may not have been as hostile to moral (as opposed to natural) rights as I think.

3. See *Interests and Rights* (Oxford: Clarendon Press, 1980) and *Rights, Killing, and Suffering*.

4. R. Dworkin, *Taking Rights Seriously* (London: Duckworth, 1977), p. xii.

5. H. L. A. Hart, *Essays on Bentham*, p. 88.

6. *Ibid.*, p. 85.

7. Some such view seems likely to emerge from Amartya Sen's article "Rights and Agency," *Philosophy and Public Affairs* 11 (1981):3–39.

8. R. M. Hare, *Moral Thinking*, (Oxford: Oxford University Press, 1982).

9. I speak of 'substantive' rights here, since, for Hare, a right, say, to equal concern and respect is a purely formal right (*Moral Thinking*, ch. 9).

10. The moral psychology of a Harean agent is one of the features of Hare's split-level theory that I should on another occasion want to explore.

11. Hare, *Moral Thinking*, ch. 2.

12. The discussion that follows has been influenced by some unpublished remarks on act-utilitarian reasons for fostering non-act-utilitarian dispositions in ourselves and others by John Marshall.

13. The remarks that follow have been influenced by Peter Wenz's unpublished paper "Moral Intuitions in Hare's *Moral Thinking*."

14. I think C. L. Ten is making a similar point in his discussion of Hare's split-level theory and Mill's liberty principle, but I am far from clear that Ten's overall grip on Hare's position is a sure one; see Ten's *Mill On Liberty* (Oxford: Clarendon Press, 1980), pp. 37ff. See also John Gray, *Mill On Liberty: A Defence* (London: Routledge & Kegan Paul, 1983), pp. 36ff.

4

Rights, Utility, and Universalization

J. L. Mackie

Many different forms of utilitarianism have been put forward and discussed in some detail, and several very different right-based moral and political theories have been at least outlined.[1] But I shall be concerned mainly with the contrast between one form of utilitarianism, that advocated by R. M. Hare, and one right-based view, my own. Hare's theory has been fully stated, especially in his recent book *Moral Thinking;*[2] mine has not yet been adequately presented, but I shall indicate its main outlines, using comparisons with utilitarianism for this purpose.

The fundamental point of contrast, and conflict, between utilitarian and right-based views is that the former, at least in their basic theory, aggregate the interests or preferences of all the persons or parties who are being taken into account, whereas the latter insist, to the end, on the separateness of persons.[3] For the utilitarian, the ultimate determination and the ultimate justification of every moral requirement lies in its relation—perhaps a complex and indirect relation—to something that represents the pooling of all individual purposes. The rights-theorist takes it to be morally important to respect and protect—at all levels, not at some only—the separate interests of each individual in a way that goes beyond the mere counting of them, however fairly, as elements in the pool.

Of course this does not mean that a utilitarian must literally deny that persons are separate, or that any utilitarian has ever done so. What it means is that this separateness does no work in the utilitarian method of determining what is good or just, that in the utilitarian calculus the desires, or the satisfactions, of different individuals are all weighed together in the way in which a single thoroughly rational egoist would weigh together all his own desires or satisfactions: on a utilitarian view, transferring a satisfaction from one person to another, while preserving its magnitude, makes no morally significant difference.

A right-based moral theory attempts to develop and clarify the popular notion that everyone should have a fair go. This is something more than the utilitarian principle, enunciated by Bentham and echoed by Mill, that everybody is to count for one and nobody for more than one. It is also more than Hare, as we shall see, provides by saying that the moral point of view is that in which an agent imaginatively occupies in turn the positions of all those who would be affected by his action, and gives equal weight to all the preferences that he thus, in thought, acquires. One whose interests have been thus fairly taken into account may still, in the end, have much less than a fair go: the maximizing of utility may turn out to require that his well-being should be sacrificed, without limit, in order to promote that of others. It is this that a right-based theory is meant to bar.

The formal structure of such a theory will be something like this. Having started with the assignment to all persons alike of the rather vague right to a fair go, we first make this somewhat more explicit, in the light of ordinary human needs and purposes, by an assignment of some basic abstract *prima facie* rights. These, I suggest, will include the traditional rights to life, health, liberty, and the pursuit of happiness. We also need basic rights with regard to possessions. Here I suggest a right to the products of one's own labor, insofar as these can be distinguished, but also a right to share equally in or have equal access to all natural resources. I suggest also a similar right with respect to such products of the labor of previous generations as have reverted to the status of natural resources. This applies both when special claims are untraceable and when, though traceable, they are no longer in force. Such claims gradually fade out because the recipient of a bequest has a weaker right than the original producer, and this effect is cumulative. I suggest also a right to the fulfillment of reasonable expectations based on a fairly stable system of laws, institutions, and practices; and, finally, a right— which, unlike the others, can be not *prima facie* but absolute—to equal respect in the procedures that determine the compromises and adjustments between the other, *prima facie*, rights. Any specific moral or political theory or system can then be defended or criticized (or both) by considering to what extent its provisions and workings—including, no doubt, assignments of concrete, institutional rights, but also including rules, concepts of duty, the recognition and encouragement of certain dispositions as virtues, and the discouragement of others as vices—can be seen as applying, implementing, and realizing those basic abstract rights in view of the actual purposes, choices, negotiations, actions, and interactions of persons over the course of time.

Since the ultimate rationale of such a theory is the respecting and protecting of separate interests, it seems likely that any practical system that it would endorse and defend to any significant extent would center, as do most actual working moralities, on norms of reciprocation and conditional cooperation. Among other things, it will direct us to show gratitude, to help those who help us, to join in mutually beneficial enterprises and play our part in them, and to display the various sorts of honesty, fidelity, loyalty, and agreement-keeping that are in general likely to facilitate such conditional cooperation.

As this sketch shows, a right-based theory can and naturally will incorporate the distinction on which Hare insists between two levels of moral thinking. What I have called a specific moral or political theory or system belongs to what he calls the intuitive level, whereas the basic assignment of rights belongs to what he calls the critical level. The fact that most of the suggested rights are only *prima facie* ones, capable of being overridden in particular cases, does not mean that they are, like the rights that would be recognized in many utilitarian systems, merely derived principles whose rationale lies in their tendency to promote something else, say, the general happiness. The suggested rights are basic, though defeasible. They must be defeasible, since they can in particular circumstances conflict with one another. But the conflicts are to be resolved by balancing these *prima facie* rights themselves against one another, not by weighing their merits in terms of some different ultimate standard of value, such as utility.

This notion of balancing may seem obscure and may be thought to compel recourse to utilitarian methods at some point. This obscurity can be removed, and both the character of the proposed right-based theory and the contrast between it and utilitarianism can be made plainer, if we compare it also with the Marxist slogan, 'From each according to his ability, to each according to his needs'. My proposal incorporates Locke's two principles of property: that all natural resources belong, fundamentally, to all persons equally and in common, but that each individual has a private property in his own body, energy, talents, and labor, and therefore also in the traceable products of his labor. The Marxist slogan presupposes rather that not only natural resources but also each individual's labor, talents, energy, and perhaps his body too, belong to everyone in common: the needs of other persons constitute valid claims on whatever I can contribute. However, the second part of this slogan is ambiguous: just how are goods and services to be distributed in relation to needs? This might be read as proposing a utilitarianism of needs: utility might be equated with need-satisfaction (it being assumed that we can distinguish needs from mere wants or preferences), and the total of this utility or need-satisfaction maximized. But an alternative and more natural reading would give each person an equal *prima facie* right to have his needs satisfied, so that an ideally just arrangement would be one in which everyone's needs were satisfied to the same degree: the practical principle of redistribution would be 'Your need is greater than mine'. These two interpretations are not even extensionally equivalent. Equalizing marginal need may well not minimize total unsatisfied need or maximize the satisfaction of need: when A's and B's levels of need are equal, we may be able, by transferring resources from A to B, to increase B's need-satisfaction by an amount greater than that by which A's is reduced; B may be a more efficient converter of resources into need-satisfaction than A, even when their levels of need-satisfaction are initially equal. If we were choosing simply between these two readings of the Marxist slogan, the second would be not only the more natural but also the more attractive. There is a similar choice to be made between methods of adjusting conflicts between our more Lockean rights. The two principles of property quoted above are not absolute, either in my proposal or in Locke's own theory: initial property rights have to be weighed together with the rights to life, health, liberty, and the pursuit of happiness. Locke himself says 'so . . . when his own Preservation comes not in competition, ought he, as much as he can, *to preserve the rest of Mankind*'.[4] Conflicts between these *prima facie* rights might be handled by a utilitarianism of rights, so that what would count as the ideally just arrangement would be that in which total right-fulfillment was maximized, or total right-infringement minimized. Alternatively, they might be handled by assuming that, ideally, one person's rights should not be infringed more than another's. Again the two methods are not even extensionally equivalent, and again I suggest that the second is the more attractive. Such equality of sacrifice in compromises between our Lockean rights is, of course, not equivalent to the equal need-satisfaction in our second reading of the Marxist slogan, precisely because our rights include each individual's private property in his own body, energy, talents, and labor, and because each has a *prima facie* right to be free and to pursue happiness in whatever way he chooses, doubtless with very varying degrees of success. Does this mean that what I am advocating is equality of opportunity rather than final equality? Not if this means that justice would be secured if only each young adult started with equal resources and chances, no matter what happened thereafter. Rather we should include what we might call the prodigal son principle, that even someone who has squandered his initial opportunities has, later, some claim to be helped to make a fresh start. We want a continuing or at least a recurrent equality of opportunity, not merely an initial equality of opportunity, once and for all.

These contrasts have been drawn in terms of various ideal principles of justice. In practice each of the rival ideals could be realized only approximately and indirectly through some concrete system of institutions. Nevertheless, the ideal formulations are useful, both as guiding lights for the criticism or defenses of institutions and to bring out the contrasts between the different possible views. Our Lockean proposal is, not surpisingly, more individualist and less collectivist than the Marxist one. Yet even the latter, with the second, egalitarian, reading, is, paradoxically, *less* collectivist than any utilitarian principle. For a utilitarian principle also—as William Godwin in particular made clear— presupposes that everyone's labor, talents, energy, and body are in principle common property, to be used in whatever way maximizes overall utility. The utilitarian, no less than the Marxist, is committed to the clause, 'From each according to his ability'. And whereas 'to each according to his needs' can be read as prescribing *equal* need-satisfaction between individuals, a utilitarian is committed rather to *maximum* overall satisfaction—whether of needs or of preferences—that may well be at the cost of every sort of equality except equality of consideration, the right to be taken equally into account.

Hare's theory is based on features that, he believes, conceptual analysis shows to be characteristic of moral thinking: moral judgments are prescriptive, universalizable, and overriding. The kind of universalizability on which he relies is made very clear in his recent book: to endorse something as a moral judgment is seriously to prescribe it for a whole set of possible worlds each of which is exactly like the actual world in all its general features, but in which individuals change places in all possible ways. Essentially, this means that for me morally to choose some action is for me to prefer that action to any alternative with respect to an imaginary situation in which I not only occupy in turn the positions of all the persons affected in any way by this choice, but also take on all their preferences, detaching myself completely from my own actual preferences and values and ideals, except as those of one affected person among others. What is morally right, therefore, is what would be chosen from a point of view that thus combines or amalgamates all points of view. Hare infers that this will be equivalent to the output of a preference-utilitarianism, in which the 'utility' that is to be maximized is the balance of satisfactions over frustrations of all the preferences of all the persons concerned.[5] (The range covered by this phrase 'the persons concerned' is indeterminate: it presumably includes all actual human beings, present and future, but it is not clear whether it includes merely possible people, nonhuman animals, and perhaps all sentient beings whatever. But a right-based theory suffers initially from the same indeterminacy. This is a problem common to the two approaches and therefore irrelevant to the choice between them; so I shall leave it aside.)

The practical effect of this theory is very significantly affected by Hare's stress on the distinction between two levels of moral thinking. At the lower, practical, working level—the intuitive level, as Hare calls it—various rules, principles, and dispositions are in place; but thought at the higher, critical level has the task of deciding *what* rules, principles, and dispositions are to be adopted or cultivated for use at the lower level. This distinction provides two quick answers to anyone who complains—as so many recent writers have complained—that utilitarianism, including the proposed preference-utilitarianism, has counter-intuitive consequences. One answer is that the true consequences, for a practical working morality, of this preference-utilitarianism do not conflict but rather coincide with our ordinary intuitions. A prescriptively universalizing (and therefore utilitarian) critical thinker would encourage the adoption and development of firm principles and dispositions of the ordinary moral sort, rather than the direct use of utilitarian calculation as a practical working morality. There are at least six reasons why this is so. Shortage of time and energy will in general preclude such calculations. Even if time and energy are available, the relevant information commonly is not. An agent's judgment on particular issues is liable to be distorted by his own interests and special affections. Even if he were intellectually able to determine the right choice, weakness of will would be likely to impair his putting of it into effect. Even decisions that are right in themselves and actions based on them are liable to be misused as precedents, so that they will encourage and seem to legitimate wrong actions that are superficially similar to them. And, human nature being what it is, a practical working morality must not be too demanding: it is worse than useless to set standards so high that there is no real chance that actions will even approximate to them. Considerations of these sorts entail that a reasonable utilitarian critical thinker would recommend the adoption of fairly strict principles and the development of fairly firm dispositions in favor of honesty, veracity, agreement-keeping, justice, fairness, respect for various rights of individuals, gratitude to benefactors, special concern for some individuals connected in certain ways with the agent, and so on, as being more likely in general to produce behavior approximating to that which would be required by the utilitarian ideal than any other humanly viable working morality.

Since utilitarianism itself would thus generate an apparently non-utilitarian intuitive morality, it is idle to appeal against it to just such intuitions. Hare's second answer to the common complaint grants that there may be some very unusual situations, or some fantastic imagined situations, in which this reconciliation fails, in which utilitarianism, even after all the above-mentioned considerations have been allowed for, recommends choices that are at variance with our ordinary moral intuitions. But, it says, this shows only that these are situations with which our intuitions are not competent to cope. These intuitions have been developed in the real, normal world, and they are appropriate only for it: in fantastic situations they have no authority against the implications of universalizing critical thinking, if those implications are themselves clear.[6]

These answers are powerful enough to dispose of the majority of the stock objections to utilitarianism or to the kind of overridingly prescriptive universalization that, in Hare's opinion, generates it; it would, therefore, be both misguided and tedious to reiterate them. Instead, I shall raise three other objections.

One of these is internal to Hare's theory. Let us accept, provisionally, the thesis that first emerges from his kind of universalization, that what is morally right is, ultimately, what would be chosen from a point of view that combines or amalgamates all points of view. Is there, then, a uniquely correct way of amalgamating those points of view? Does it follow that what is right is what maximizes utility defined as the balance of the aggregate of the satisfactions of preferences over the aggregate of frustrations of preferences? Or might the appropriate amalgamation still be the one that took serious notice of the separateness of persons, perhaps in a way that would be expressed by the assigning of some basic abstract rights to each individual? If I am, for the purpose of ultimate moral decision, to be everyone, must I be everyone in such a way that all are blurred together into a mere aggregate of preferences, or can I be everyone with the boundaries between all these persons still visible and important? Can I not still want *each* of my multiple incarnations to have a fair go?[7] And, if I do, will I not assign to each of them *prima facie* rights that, when conflicts arise between one incarnation's rights and another's, are to be adjusted in the way indicated above, so that the ideally acceptable compromise will not infringe the rights of one more than those of another? In contrast with this, it is not enough that in the utilitarian method, or in Hare's utilitarian way of combining points of view, each individual is fully considered and his preferences counted, all preferences being given equal weight. The boundaries between persons are here being ignored, in that one person's satisfaction can simply replace another's and outweigh that other's miseries or frustrations.

An analogy between the different personae that one would assume through universalization and the different temporal phases of the life of an ordinary individual will throw some light on this issue. Suppose that as a young adult one could look forward to a fairly long life, and had some rough idea of the various satisfactions and frustrations likely to be experienced as a result of each of several alternative choices of a plan of life. Suppose that one could also allow for probable changes in one's preferences and ideals as one grew older, and was able to detach oneself from one's present youthful purposes and values and to look fairly at the alternative plans of life from the points of view of all one's future selves as well as the present one. Is it obvious that if a reasonable person were able to do all these things, he would opt for whatever plan of life promised the greatest aggregate utility? Or might he try to ensure that no substantial phase of his life was too miserable, even if very great satisfactions at other times were to compensate for this? I am not merely saying, as Hare might concede, that in general one would be most likely to maximize the aggregate of utility by providing for one's well-being at each successive phase. I am suggesting that looking after each substantial phase might be the sensible thing to opt for in its own right, not merely as a means to maximizing the aggregate. Yet the separateness of phases, in this case, just because they are only phases of the same person, would matter much less than the separateness of persons within the whole that is created and embraced by the adoption of the universalizing procedure. I might the more readily tolerate *my* misery over one five-year period if it were compensated by *my* great happiness over another five years simply because it is the same I that will be, or has been, happy. But if I adopt a way of thinking that commits me to being, as it were, both Smith and Jones, but separately, it is not so clear that I can tolerate unmitigated misery *as Smith* merely because that will enable me, *as Jones*, to be extravagantly happy. So if there is any force at all in the suggestion that the young adult might be reasonably concerned for the well-being of *each* of his temporal phases, it follows *a fortiori* that Harean universalization might generate a persisting concern for each separate individual.

I need not insist that what Hare's universalization leads to *is* a rights-theory rather than an aggregative utilitarianism even at the critical level: it is enough to point out that it does not give unequivocal support to the latter. There is no uniquely correct or rational way of amalgamating the indefinitely many points of view that are brought together by universalization, so there is no support to be derived from Hare's basic principles for utilitarianism as contrasted with a right-based theory.

My second objection is external to Hare's theory, in that it challenges even his basic approach through prescriptive universalizability. In earlier writings, Hare has placed great weight on conceptual analysis, maintaining that a correct understanding of ordinary moral concepts and moral language shows that overridingly prescriptive universalizability is built into them, and hence that to follow any other method would be tantamount to refusing to answer the moral questions we began by asking: while one can, without incoherence, simply opt out of the moral game altogether, this is the only consistent alternative. But this approach can be questioned on three grounds. First, even if analysis of established moral concepts shows that they involve some sort of universalizability, it is far from clear that they involve the precise sort that Hare is now using. His present method embraces all three of the stages of universalization that I have distinguished, but our ordinary concepts may well involve only the first, or perhaps the first and second, without the third.[8] Secondly, since there are these complications, opting out of the moral game and ceasing to ask recognizably moral questions is not the only alternative to using Hare's method. Thirdly, even if we accepted his conceptual analysis, we might well ask why that should matter, what power the analysis of existing concepts has to constrain our thinking, if there are other coherently possible ways of thinking about choices and patterns of behavior.

These points are important, since between them they destroy whatever force there might be in Hare's reliance on conceptual analysis and linguistic intuitions. Since there are coherent ways of thinking morally other than the one he describes, and moral language does not determinately involve his specific method of universalization, we have not only the choice whether or not to speak and think morally, but also, if we choose to do so, the further choice whether to speak and think morally in Hare's style or in some other. Since he vehemently advocates one specific kind of moral thinking, he is under pressure to find further ways of recommending it.

However, I need not labor these points here.[9] Hare himself now seems willing (at a pinch) to concede them. He says:

> If anybody either does not believe that I have given a true account of the moral concepts as we have them, or thinks that investigations of the logic of words in ordinary language are unhelpful, it is open to him to proceed in a different way. He could set out the logic of an artificial language, identical in its properties with the logic which I claim our ordinary words have; then he could show that anybody reasoning in such a language would have to think in the way in which *I* say our existing concepts constrain us to think;

and then he could, using the same arguments as I shall use, show that there would be an advantage in our adopting such a language. Though I should not like such a method as much as my own . . . I do not think that the difference between the results of the two methods would be very substantial.[10]

In short, he is now prepared to join with others in sawing off the branch on which he has been sitting all these years. But though the branch is sawn off, Hare does not fall with it: he has provided himself with alternative means of support, in the claim that 'there would be an advantage in our adopting such a language'. But what can this mean?

It might mean that adopting this as an artificial language (or retaining it if it is, after all, our ordinary moral language), and thinking in terms of it to determine a practical working morality, would do more than any alternative system of action-guiding thought to fulfill together all the preferences of all human (or perhaps all sentient) beings. Now, provided that it really is possible to think properly in terms of this language, this must be true, since what the use of the Harean moral language aims at is precisely the fulfillment of all these preferences—subject, of course, to the query in our first objection about whether there is a unique way of amalgamating them. Hare assigns his critical thinking to a class of 'archangels' presumed to be thoroughly rational and fully informed, and of course a system of thoroughly rational and fully informed thinking aimed at achieving X must be a better way of achieving X than any other sort of thinking. But precisely because this is so obvious, it is no real defense of, or support for, this kind of thinking.

Alternatively, this claim might mean that the adopting (or retaining) of such a language and way of thinking by *each* person is advantageous to *him*; in other words, that Hare is prepared to mount a prudential defense of moral thinking. And this is indeed what he does. He admits that to do what we ought to do is not always in our prudential interest and remarks that it is hard to see how anybody could have thought that it was always so in default of divine rewards and punishments. But he says that we can still 'achieve something more modest, which nevertheless is adequate for the defense of morality'. His argument is that if one were bringing up a child and had *only* the child's interests at heart, one would not inculcate in him a purely egoistic principle; rather, one would try to develop in him not only such virtues as courage but also 'moral *prima facie* principles of just the same sort as the act-utilitarian archangel would select'. The reason is that it is not easy to be a successful immoral egoist. 'Mankind has found it possible to make life a great deal more tolerable by bringing it about that on the whole morality pays'. Since 'by far the easiest way of seeming to be upright is to be upright . . .

perhaps the most effective way of bringing up our child to obey the principles would be to inculcate moral feelings'. And if this holds for the supposed case of educating a child in its own interests, it must hold also with regard to each agent on his own: it would be prudent for him, so far as he is able, to adopt or retain the moral way of thinking.[11]

What I have given here is a précis of quite a long discussion. Clearly it makes important empirical claims; but are they true? I agree that if one were bringing up this child with a view simply to its own interests one would not try to make it into a directly calculating egoist. One would try to provide it with such self-strengthening virtues as courage, perseverance, some sort of temperance, and so on. Also, one would try to provide it with the specifically moral dispositions of some sort of morality. But not, I think, exactly the same moral dispositions as would be selected by Hare's act-utilitarian archangels, even allowing for all the above-listed considerations that would make a reasonable Harean critical thinker settle for an apparently nonutilitarian practical working morality. Rather, one would develop in the child dispositions that would enable it to accept and take advantage of unequal social structures to a greater extent than would the product of an education directed by Harean critical thought. For example, if the child happened to be born into a slave-owning aristocracy, one would educate him so as to be a well-behaved member of that class, and no doubt so as to be disposed to treat his slaves reasonably well. But Hare's critical thinking might well say that we should develop even in so fortunately endowed a child principles that might lead him to support some tendency to reform this unequal social structure, rather than merely to accept it and flourish within it, if there were any real possibility of successful reform.

In short, Hare slides far too easily from the admitted point that to have some sort of morality is very likely to be to the advantage of any individual, to the conclusion that his specific sort of morality is so, and is maximally so. This thesis is, on the face of it, highly implausible; if Hare wants to make use of it, the onus is on him to defend it far more thoroughly than he has done. It is not enough simply to reiterate his belief that it holds.

However, let us suppose, merely in order to investigate a further step in the argument, that he is right in this empirical claim. Suppose, that is, that the practical morality that would be chosen with a view simply to the agent's interests coincides perfectly with that which would be chosen by a Harean critical thinker. Even so, this would not yield a prudential vindication of Hare's style of critical thinking or of its basic utilitarianism. The prudential support would go straight to the working morality, not by way of the utilitarian critical thinking. It would be at most a lucky accident that the two lines of thought led to the same practical results. Even if they did, what the prudential argument would vindicate would be something like our ordinary morality with its norms of reciprocation and cooperation, special duties of honesty and agreement-keeping, special obligations of loyalty to family and friends, gratitude to benefactors, the legitimacy of the pursuit, within limits, of one's own interests, and of resentment of injuries, and so on. It *may* be that, contrary to initial appearances, the universalizing critical thinking, interpreted in the aggregative utilitarian way, would recommend acceptance of just this same practical moral system. But this would not mean that we had thereby a prudential vindication of that sort of critical thinking; at most we would have an absence of any prudential case against such critical thinking, as a general program. In particular—and this is crucial—we should have no reason for regarding utilitarian calculation as the method on which we should fall back in really hard cases: these, like the basic method itself, would lie beyond the scope of the prudential vindication.

By 'hard cases' I mean ones in which appeal to the established principles of a practical working morality fails, either because those principles conflict with one another or because the situation is abnormal. Here, by Hare's own account, we shall have to suspend the normal operation of even the best 'intuitions', and since the assumed defense of the ordinary reliance on those 'intuitions' has been a prudential one, there is no case for saying that what we should fall back on here, to replace those 'intuitions' and principles, is the utilitarian style of critical thinking, merely because the output of this normally coincides with that of prudential critical thinking.

There is, then, no sound, nontrivial interpretation of the thesis that 'there would be an advantage' in adopting (or retaining) the moral language and the basic method of moral thinking that Hare favors. His alternative means of support gives way, and he does, after all, fall with the sawn-off branch of conceptual analysis.

But what else, he may ask, can we offer as a method of critical moral thinking? We surely need something on this level. We cannot be content simply to accept whatever morality is conventionally in force, or to respect all the threadbare 'intuitions' to which popular moralists appeal—particularly when we see how they conflict with one another and how some of them stem from religious traditions to which we have no good reason to ascribe any authority. We need some way of revising a community's working morality and of making adjustments when discrepant working moralities come into contact with one another. Certainly; but there are at least two possible rivals to utilitarianism as a guide to thinking at the critical level.

One of these, which Hare himself might on reflection find acceptable, results from my first objection, which is, as I said, internal to his theory. His thoroughgoing prescriptive universalization might amalgamate the points of view of all the individuals concerned in a way that took serious account of the separateness of persons, by assigning such basic abstract rights as I have suggested to each person. That is, we could have a right-based method of critical thinking, and it could be supported, with at least as much plausibility as the aggregative utilitarian one, by the approach through universalization.

But I would not myself support it in this way, because, as I have indicated, I do not find the argument from conceptual analysis for prescriptive universalization compelling as a method for choosing ultimate constraints on action. Rather, I would fall back on the thesis for which I have argued elsewhere, that right and wrong have to be invented, that morality is not to be discovered but to be made.[12] We have to start somewhere, simply adopting some basic practical principles, though no doubt not in an arbitrary or casual spirit, but with reflection on the range of alternative sets of principles, and on the entailments and likely consequences of each such set. I suggest that on reflection we might find an assignment of basic abstract rights to persons a more acceptable starting point for critical moral thinking than any other.

A second suggestion is harder to state succinctly. Let me approach it by way of a digression through a speculative account of the origins of morality. Hare has spoken as if our existing 'intuitive' moralities were the product of his style of critical thinking:

> It is no accident that the world and society are such that crime does not in general pay. . . . It is better for nearly all of us if social rewards and penalties are attached to socially beneficial and harmful acts; *and so it has come about that on the whole they are* (my italics).[13]

Similarly Hume, in the *Enquiry concerning Morals*, thinks that it is a sufficient explanation of moral rules and practices that they have utility:

> The rules of equity and justice owe their origin and existence to that utility, which results to the public from their strict and regular observance. . . . Common interest and utility beget infallibly a standard of right and wrong among the parties concerned.[14]

But this is emphatically not an adequate method of explanation. There is no sound general principle either of biological evolution or of sociohistorical development that tendencies or dispositions or practices will be fostered and encouraged simply because they are beneficial to the community as a whole in a utilitarian sense. The true explanation, of which this is a distortion, runs rather as follows.

Sociobiologists have outlined processes of natural selection by which genetically determined tendencies are developed in favor of 'kin altruism'—that is, helping offspring and other close relatives—and reciprocal altruism—that is, helping those who help you. Tendencies to cooperate in small groups, in which each agent's participation is conditional on that of most of the other members, can be fostered in similar ways, as can the resentment of injuries and hostile retribution. All these are what we might call spontaneous premoral tendencies: they can be found and understood in many nonhuman species as well as in humans. They are typically spontaneous, being genetically fostered, and give only an appearance of calculation: here, as elsewhere, natural selection mimics purposiveness. Further, social evolution is superimposed on biological evolution. Here the most important element is the development of conventions. These can be understood as arising out of and helping to resolve problems of several sorts: coordination problems and especially problems of partial conflict of interests, either of much the same form as the prisoners' dilemma or of nonsymmetrical variants of this form. Then the internalization of rules of behavior will turn conventions into norms. In this social evolution, as in biological evolution, mechanisms of interaction can generate spontaneous tendencies that mimic purpose and calculation, and the solutions of problems can be produced and maintained by the very forces that initially create the problems. Hume, in Book III of the *Treatise*, at least hints at this explanation of morality in terms of conventions, though in the *Enquiry* he substituted for this the simpler but less correct attempt to explain morality directly by its utility.[15]

If it is by such processes as these that first premoral and then specifically moral tendencies have actually developed, it is not surprising that actual moral systems have the features we usually find in them: norms of cooperation (including cooperation on terms that are differentially advantageous to parties of different sorts); norms of reciprocation; principles that secure various rights. In general, we find moralities that look like the product of many contractual or quasi-contractual relationships, although actual historical contracts have not as a rule contributed significantly to their development.

My second suggestion, which this digression has been designed to introduce, is that moral thinking at the critical level might resemble the processes by which practical working moralities really have developed, rather than the control by utility to which Hare, and Hume in the *Enquiry*, mistakenly ascribe their origin. That is, critical thinking might itself be a process of interaction, negotiation, and debate between diverse groups with different starting points, different traditions of thought. Rather than proceeding *de haut en bas*, being pursued by one or more detached thinkers who try to stand above the whole conflict of interests and ideals, it would work up from below, from those conflicting views and claims themselves. The details of this process would be contingent upon the input to it and are therefore not open to any precise description *a priori*. But it is reasonable to expect that any such process of interaction, negotiation, and debate would be roughly equivalent to some distribution of entitlements that are not merged into a pure collectivity—in other words, that this too would be, in effect, a right-based approach.

In criticizing an earlier draft of this essay, Hare has demanded that more should be said about the ground rules for such negotiation. This may, indeed, be a fruitful line of inquiry, but I cannot say much about it here. An attractive principle would be the above-mentioned one of equality of sacrifices in compromises between our Lockean rights, but realistic ground rules for negotiation would need to take some account of the strength of the bargaining positions of the parties. I would stress, however, that Hare's thoroughgoing universalization, which means that each party abandons his special interests, values, and point of view in taking on those of all parties alike, is not a ground rule for negotiation, but a move that would make negotiation unnecessary. Equally, Rawls's notion of a hypothetical contract made behind a veil of ignorance destroys what is characteristic of a contractual or negotiating method. In speaking of negotiation I mean real negotiation, conducted in the full light of day, while the parties retain their self-conscious individuality and divergent aims.[16]

This second suggestion is plainly different from the first, but it could be supported in the same sort of way, simply as a possibly acceptable starting point for critical moral thinking. There is, however, something else that might be said for it; and this brings me to my third main objection to Hare's theory, which, like the second, challenges his basic approach.

Hare's critically thinking archangels are supposed to be performing a task that Bishop Butler assigned more appropriately to God. (Hare has himself noted this in an earlier essay.)[17] Butler's God is presumed to have perfect knowledge and complete benevolence towards all his creatures; he therefore is in a position to choose the best practical working morality for human beings, with their limitations as he knows them, and to write it into their consciences in the form of moral intuitions. But this viewpoint that Butler plausibly ascribes to God is simply not accessible, either intellectually or emotionally, to anyone else.

It is obvious that it is not intellectually accessible. Critical thinking, it is to be remembered, is concerned primarily with the choice of sets of moral principles and dispositions, and this choice will affect indefinitely many present and future persons. No human thinker or small group of thinkers can possibly know what it is really like to be each of these people. Hare takes trouble to argue that one can really put oneself imaginatively in the place of *some* other people. This might be sufficient for universalization used as a test of the rightness of some particular choice of action; but it cannot be sufficient for the main task of critical thinking.

I would have supposed that the required viewpoint is also emotionally inaccessible, that no one can really *take on* the feelings of all persons, present and future, even if he could surmount the intellectual barriers to his discovery of them. However, Peter Singer, in a recent book, has tried to meet this challenge. His title, *The Expanding Circle*,[18] refers to the well-known thesis of Westermarck and others that the history of human moral thought has been, in part, the history of a progressive enlargement of the circle of persons towards whom altruism is morally prescribed and towards whom, to some extent, altruistic feelings and actions are really directed. Singer describes and accepts very much that same sociobiological account of the origins of morality in kin altruism, reciprocal altruism, and cooperation in small groups as has been sketched above. But he then argues that the expansion of the range of altruism is not due merely to wider practical opportunities for useful cooperation or to widening sympathies, but is rather to be ascribed to *reason* in something like a Kantian sense. This is not what Hume would have called reason: there is no strict deductive requirement to go on from altruism (or universalization) with respect to a small community, to altruism (or universalization) with respect to a large community or the human race or all sentient beings. But it is reason in a looser sense: it is the avoidance of an arbitrary cutoff. Singer appropriately compares this moral expansion with the gradual progress of arithmetic from the recognition of the integers from, say, 1 to 10, *via* the extension to an infinite sequence of integers, the introduction of negative numbers, fractions, irrationals, and so on, to the full modern development of mathematics. He connects both of these with biological theory. The growth of the ability to develop the higher mathematics could not be explained *in itself* as a product of natural selection: this ability could never itself have given its possessors a genetic advantage. But this ability may well be so closely linked with practically useful and genetically advantageous forms of intelligence that natural selection could not help introducing them together. We could not have the useful abilities to count sheep and to think conditionally without having also the useless ability and motivation that have led the mathematicians into Cantor's paradise. Similarly, Singer suggests, the kinds of moral thinking that are genetically advantageous, that would be and have been produced by the above-mentioned sociobiological mechanisms, together with the practically useful ability to generalize, tend automatically to produce the unrestricted prescriptive universalization of Hare's archangelic critical thinkers. And the latter, *unlike* the higher mathematics, may really be useful after all, although it could not have been selected genetically—or, I would add, culturally—for its usefulness.

If Singer were right, then, the archangelic viewpoint would in principle be emotionally accessible even to humans, not only to Butler's God, insofar as there would be a tendency in thinking, closely linked with reasoning powers that we already have, that would carry us from the already existing kind of morality (directly produced by biological and cultural evolution) to a Harean universalization.

However, this suggestion slides too easily over the contrast between a norm of reciprocation and conditional cooperation on the one hand and a norm of pure rational benevolence on the other. To go from the first to the second of these would be a qualitative change in moral thinking, different from a mere expansion of the circle within which altruism *of the same kind* operates. The 'reason' that avoids arbitrary cutoffs will not carry us over this gap. Also, the supposed evidence that there already is a significant amount of pure rational benevolence is weak. Singer makes much of the altruism of blood donors, but after all this is a comparatively inexpensive form of altruism. More spectacular forms of self-sacrifice typically come under the heading of the taking of risks within what is normally a cooperative enterprise, and are governed by norms of reciprocation. Despite Singer's argument, therefore, I still deny that the archangelic viewpoint is emotionally accessible to humans in any real sense, and I repeat that in any case it is not intellectually accessible.

There is, then, a good reason why critical moral thinking should take the form sketched in my second suggestion above, that of a process of interaction, negotiation, and debate rather than something closely analogous to the thinking of Butler's God, namely, that the former is humanly possible, while the latter is not.

This criticism may seem to tell not only against Hare's theory but also against my own first suggestion. But I think it is less damaging to the latter. We should need less close an approximation to divine omniscience and universal benevolence in order seriously to assign some basic abstract rights to all persons alike, and to criticize practical working moralities by reference to that assignment, than in order seriously to adopt an unqualified aggregative utilitarianism, even if we confined this to the critical level. There are two reasons why this is so. First, the right-based approach, since it keeps everyone covered to some extent, keeps *us* covered among others. And, secondly, since its aim is to keep everyone covered, it can proceed in a more piecemeal way. We can say roughly whether some local arrangement, over a finite geographical area and a modest time span, does or does not constitute a decent approximation to an application and realization of the basic rights of those directly involved, without necessitating sacrifices of the corresponding rights of persons outside this spatiotemporal region. We can say this more confidently than we can say that any scheme, however local its immediate bearing may be, is likely on the whole to come close to maximizing the aggregate satisfaction of preferences of the whole body of human (let alone sentient) beings, present and future. In effect, this means that while my first and second suggestions about possible methods of critical thinking—the first, universalization in the form of an assignment of basic abstract rights to all persons, the second, a process of interaction, negotiation, and debate—are in principle different from one another, they are still not very far apart: the second could be seen as a way of approximately realizing the first.

Let me sum up, then, the ways in which we might want to stress the role of rights in moral theory. First, it is clear that we shall want rights to be recognized and taken seriously as elements in our practical working morality. But this not a point at issue between Hare's view and mine: he would be emphatic about the importance of rights at this level, as was another utilitarian, J. S. Mill, when he wrote:

> Justice is the name for certain classes of moral rules, which concern the essentials of human well-being more nearly, and are therefore of more absolute obligation, than any other rules for the guidance of life; and the notion which we have found to be the essence of the idea of justice, that of a right residing in an individual, implies and testifies to this more binding obligation.[19]

The real dispute, then, concerns the choice between 'utility' and 'rights' as the central concepts in higher level, critical, moral thinking.

Secondly—and this is now a point at issue—I have questioned whether the analysis of moral concepts yields the precise kind of universalization that amounts to the identification of morally defensible choices with ones made from a point of view that amalgamates the points of view of all persons. But even if the analysis of existing moral concepts did have this as its output, why should this be seen as an important constraint on the kind of critical thinking whose function is to choose a practical working morality, that is, a body of rules, principles, and dispositions that would directly guide and control what people do? The authority of moral concepts is no more sacred than that of particular 'intuitions', and I have argued that Hare is not able to substitute for this authority a prudential vindication. The way, therefore, is at least open for a theory based on rights and the separateness of persons rather than on aggregative utility.

Thirdly, Hare's style of universalization assigns to his archangelic critical thinkers a point of view that belongs rather to Butler's God and is not accessible to human beings either intellectually or, despite Singer's ingenious argument, emotionally. Lacking this point of view, we could not really carry out the utilitarian critical thinking: rather, if we aimed at this, we should achieve only guesswork purporting to be an application of preference-utilitarianism. But two other methods are humanly possible. One of these accepts, as the moral point of view, one that amalgamates the points of view of all persons, but interprets this amalgamation in a way that still allows for the separateness of persons, and so issues initially in an assignment of basic abstract rights, in terms of which concrete moral and political systems and proposals can be defended or criticized. The other abandons the attempt to work down from any supreme principle or overarching point of view, and instead works up from below by a procedure of interaction, negotiation, and debate. Though different in principle, these two methods are not far removed from one another in practice. I suggest, therefore, that rights not only should be prominent in a practical working morality, but can also replace utility at the critical level.

NOTES

1. Right-based theories include those of Robert Nozick and Ronald Dworkin, and, if Dworkin is right, that of John Rawls. Another is sketched in my "Can There Be a Right-Based Moral Theory?" in *Midwest Studies in Philosophy* 3 (1978): 350–59.
2. R. M. Hare, *Moral Thinking* (Oxford: Oxford University Press, 1982).
3. Cf J. Rawls, *A Theory of Justice* (Oxford: Oxford University Press, 1972), pp. 23–27, 187.
4. J. Locke, *Second Treatise of Government*, sec. 7.
5. Hare, *Moral Thinking*, ch. 7.
6. *Ibid.*, ch. 6.
7. This point was made in discussion by Ronald Dworkin.
8. Cf J. L. Mackie, *Ethics: Inventing Right and Wrong* (Harmondsworth: Penguin Books, 1977), ch. 4.

9. Some of them are developed in the chapter referred to in note 8.

10. Hare, *Moral Thinking*, ch. 1, p. 20.

11. *Ibid.*, ch. 11.

12. Cf. chapter 1 of Mackie, *Ethics*.

13. Hare, *Moral Thinking*, ch. 11.

14. D. Hume, *Enquiries*, ed. L. A. Selby-Bigge, 2nd ed. (originally published 1902; reprint, Oxford: Oxford University Press, 1946, 1955), pp. 188, 211; see also pp. 202, 208, etc.

15. For a fuller explanation of these matters, see J. L. Mackie, *Hume's Moral Theory* (London: Routledge & Kegan Paul, 1980), chs. 6 and 9.

16. A proposal for basing a liberal theory of justice on 'constrained dialogue' has been put forward by Bruce A. Ackerman in *Social Justice in the Liberal State* (New Haven, Conn.: Yale University Press, 1980). I have criticized Ackerman's proposals in a review article, "Competitors in Conversation", in *The Times Literary Supplement*, April 17, 1981, p. 443.

17. R. M. Hare, "Principles", in *Proceedings of the Aristotelian Society* 73 (1972–73): 1–18.

18. P. Singer, *The Expanding Circle: Ethics and Sociobiology* (New York: Farrar, Straus & Giroux, 1980).

19. J. S. Mill, *Utilitarianism*, ch. 5.

5

Rights, Utility, and Universalization
Reply to J. L. Mackie

R. M. Hare

Mr Mackie starts with a contrast between utilitarianism and what he calls 'right-based' views or theories such as he has himself advocated.[1] I must therefore first ask some questions about this supposed distinction. My trouble is partly that some of the tenets which are said to distinguish right-based theories from utilitarianism are ones which I, a utilitarian, have no difficulty in assenting to; and partly that the basic distinction which is supposed to divide the two kinds of theory is one which entirely eludes me, although, to judge by the widespread use made of it, everybody else understands it perfectly well. Or can it be that what everybody else is doing is parroting a slogan with which John Rawls ends his otherwise more or less fair statement of his disagreements with utilitarianism? He says 'Utilitarianism does not take seriously the distinction between persons'.[2] This might suggest to a careless reader that utilitarians do not realize that there are distinct people in the world, with separate interests which have to be considered. But what utilitarian has ever denied this?

Mackie, at any rate, guards against this misinterpretation. But the question remains of what, if not this obvious truth, he is accusing the utilitarians of denying. What is it to 'insist, to the end, on the separateness of persons' (p. 86)? What the utilitarian is doing is not denying this, but trying to give meaning to the requirement, on which Mackie himself lays stress, 'that everyone should have a fair go'. It is hard to see what this could mean, except, in Bentham's words, to 'count everybody for one and nobody for more than one'.[3] But Mackie attacks the utilitarians for doing this. It is indeed rather mysterious that critics of utilitarianism, some of whom lay great weight on the 'right to equal concern and respect' which all people have, should object when utilitarians show this equal concern by giving equal weight to the equal interests of everybody, a precept which leads straight to Bentham's formula and to utilitarianism itself.

It should hardly be necessary to spell this out. To have concern for someone is to seek his good, or to seek to promote his interests; and to have equal concern for all people is to seek equally their good, or to give equal weight to their interests, which is exactly what utilitarianism requires. To do this is to treat others' interests in the same way as a prudent person treats his own interests, present and future. It is thus inevitable that having equal concern for everybody will lead us, as Mackie puts it, to weigh together the interests of different individuals 'in the way in which a single thoroughly rational egoist would weigh together all his own desires or satisfactions'. To do this is not to fail to 'insist on the separateness of persons'.

We can perhaps begin to understand why advocates of right-based theories get into the paradoxical position of advocating equal concern but dismissing the theory (utilitarianism) which secures precisely this, if we notice that certain rights, or the principles safeguarding them, initially demand *un*equal concern for people. Suppose that Tom (the lecher!) is consumed with a desire for the favors of Ann, but that she resists his advances because of a preference, though only a marginal one, not to indulge him just now. We say that she has a right to refuse, and indeed to be protected in her refusal by the law. But this is to show *more* concern for her than for him: we are frustrating a consuming desire of his in order to meet what may be a mere whim of hers to accommodate him later rather than now.

It is true that we should secure *formal* equality between them by adopting a universal principle forbidding rape by *anybody*. But the right-based theorist is very reasonably not likely to be satisfied by that. A principle universally *permitting* rape, or universally requiring females to yield to the advances of males, would pass this formal test just as well. Why then do we, in spite of our belief in the right to equal concern and respect, adopt, out of these principles, all of which are formally universal, one in particular—one which in this case requires inequality of concern?

Mackie has the answer, but does not explain how it is inconsistent with utilitarianism. He says (p. 87)

[A right-based theory's] formal structure will be something like this. Having started with the assignment to all persons alike of the rather vague right to a fair go, we first try to make this somewhat more explicit, in the light of ordinary human needs and purposes, by an assignment of some basic abstract *prima facie* rights. These, I suggest, will include the traditional rights to life, health, liberty, and the pursuit of happiness.

The right which stands in the lecher's way is presumably a particular case of the right to liberty: the liberty in question is the freedom not to have one's body interfered with contrary to one's wishes. As we have seen, the right demands *un*equal concern in this case.

These two stages in Mackie's account correspond closely to the two levels, critical and intuitive, in my own.[4] The explanation of how equal concern at the critical level can lead to unequal concern at the intuitive is that an impartial critical thinker equally concerned to give everybody 'the right to a fair go' would see that the right-assigning principles whose general acceptance would be most likely to achieve this aim would assign rights whose detailed observance in particular cases would sometimes require unequal concern. A two-level utilitarian theory makes this transition clear; whereas Mackie's phrase 'make more explicit, in the light of ordinary human needs and purposes' conceals the nature of the process of getting from 'the rather vague right to a fair go' to more substantial principles governing our actions in the concrete world among real people.

Is Mackie's 'formal structure' in fact different from my own utilitarian theory? The *content* of both theories might well be the same. Both, having set before themselves the aim of giving everybody a fair go, or having equal concern for all, find that the best way 'in the light of ordinary human needs and purposes' of achieving this aim is to devise a set of *prima facie* principles, some of them entrenching *prima facie* rights, for use in our moral thinking. My list of these could well be the same as Mackie's. But is the *structure* of the two theories different? I am inclined to think not.

I will not enquire what Mackie means by calling his rights 'abstract' (perhaps the point he is making is the same point as I commonly express by calling the principles used in intuitive thinking 'simple' and 'general'). But by calling them '*prima facie*' rights he seems at first sight to be accepting (as he does later accept) my division of moral thinking into two levels, and to be putting the moral judgements based on these rights into the intuitive level. This certainly seems to be their natural habitat; and that, as I have repeatedly stressed in my book, does not entail any diminution of the sanctity of the rights in question. I have given reasons why we should be extremely reluctant to let them be overridden, and even if we do, should feel bad about it.[5] Mackie himself sums up these reasons on p. 91 of his paper. But he also agrees with me that the rights have to be 'defeasible' (another word, we might almost say, for *'prima facie'*), because they can conflict in particular cases. This lays on the right-based theorist the task of giving a method for the resolution of these conflicts, as I try, in my book, to do in terms of my own theory. My account, though not entirely simple, does seem to me to yield a passably true-to-life model of the moral thinking that wise people actually do in such situations.

I am left somewhat in the dark as to the differences which he finds between a right-based theory and my own—or, which comes to the same thing, as to the sense in which his theory could be said to be 'based' on rights and mine not. For in so far as the rights are only *prima facie* and defeasible, it surely cannot be based on them; and the only right he produces which is more than *prima facie* is the right to equal concern and respect, which is preserved, at the highest level, and indeed really used as a basis, by my own theory.

This unclarity, it seems to me, infects the first of the new objections that Mackie makes against my theory. He puts it forward only after a very fair account of my suggested division of moral thought into two levels, which, he agrees, enables me to deal with the vulgar objections to utilitarianism based on counter-intuitiveness, examples of which are likely to be in evidence in this volume. He also recognizes the close relation between my version of even-handed utilitarianism and the quasi-Kantian universality of moral prescriptions on which I seek to base it. He goes on to attribute to me the view, in summary, that 'what is morally right is, ultimately, what would be chosen from a point of view that combines or amalgamates all points of view'.

We must notice that it is Mackie, and not I, who introduces the word 'amalgamate', with its suggestion, which he draws out, that 'all are blurred together into a mere aggregate of purposes', leaving the boundaries between persons no longer visible. What I actually say is rather different. In an article I published a long time ago I quoted the lines

> Momentous to himself as I to me
> Is every man that ever woman bore.[6]

My new book is full of the idea that we have in critical moral thought to think ourselves into the shoes of each of the persons affected, one by one—which is why, as we shall see when we come to Mackie's third objection, critical moral thought is so difficult for human beings. So far individual distinctions are preserved.

The question which then arises is how, when we think morally and therefore universally, we are to balance the preferences of these separate people against one another so as to be fair to them all. My answer is that we have to give equal weight to equal preferences, counting everybody for one. This is no more to *amalgamate*, let alone *blur*, the separate persons than it is when a judge, having heard what each of the parties to a suit has to say, tries to be fair to them all. As Mackie himself says, thinking this to be a point against me, 'Harean universalization might' (he implies that in my hands it does not) 'generate a persisting concern for each separate individual'. But in fact I do not in my critical thinking depart from this concern; I only seek a way in which concern for different individuals can be fairly balanced, and find it by treating their equal preferences as of equal weight.

As we have seen, this impartiality or equal concern at the critical level can yield principles which, in particular cases at the intuitive level, may require partiality or *un*equal concern, as when somebody's right has to be preserved at greater expense to somebody else. It is not clear how a right-based theory would justify this, since it purports to treat rights as 'basic'. I justify it on the ground that the general acceptance of such principles would on balance best serve the interests of all considered impartially. That is to say, there is no other set of principles which would do more for their interests in sum, when interests are counted equally in proportion to their strength.

It is the 'in sum' that Mackie is principally attacking. In the course of his attack he appeals to an analogy, which I also use, between adjudication of *inter*personal conflicts of interest and adjudication of *intra*personal but inter*temporal* conflicts. If I am now trying to decide between courses of action, of which one will in total maximally satisfy the preferences which I have at all times as to what should happen *at those times*, and the other distributes preference-satisfactions in some different way, I shall be forced into an adjudication between the interests of different phases of my own person which is analogous to that between the interests of different people. Mackie suggests that, contrary to the utilitarian solution of this prudential problem, someone in this position might 'try to ensure that no substantial phase of his life was too miserable, even if very great satisfactions at other times were to compensate for this'. How miserable is 'too miserable', and what 'compensates' for what? If we ask these questions, we see that even such a way of thinking requires us to place values on the preferences that we are going to have at the various times.

I say 'place values' and not 'assign strengths'. I shall not in this paper go into the problem of the 'interpersonal commensurability of utilities' which is discussed briefly in my book.[7] But, given that we can assess the strengths of the preferences, we still have to decide how much each of these preferences, present or future, our own or other people's, is to count for us, at the time when we are making the decision. My own answer is that, if we are prudent, they will count for us equally, strength for strength, irrespective of the times at which they are felt; and that, if we are thinking morally, other people's will count equally with each other and with our own.

The first of these theses holds because that is what we mean by 'prudent'. It has to be asked whether the person who follows the suggestion just quoted from Mackie is being prudent. On the face of it he is not; but it is perhaps possible to interpret what Mackie says in such a way that he is. All we have to say is that *by following the suggested policy*, he is showing that he places a greater negative value on the misery than the positive value he places on the sum of the spread-out satisfactions at other times that the misery makes possible. This involves taking 'compensate' in a Pickwickian sense. They do not really and fully compensate for the misery, in his present estimation, or he would not follow the policy. And he *is* being prudent in following it, if the actual values to him, at the times when they occur, of the various experiences will be the same as he now places on them (as manifested by his following the policy). If, however, they are not, he is being imprudent, most probably because he does not fully represent to himself now the values he will place upon them. Such imprudence is of course extremely common, but does not support Mackie's argument; on the other hand if, to support it, he were to allege that a *prudent* person could follow the policy in question, this, as I have just explained, will be because the satisfactions will *not* in fact compensate for the miseries; so the intrapersonal prudent calculation is, after all, analogous to the interpersonal utilitarian calculation, and the support for Mackie's argument collapses.

The second thesis, that, if we are thinking morally, other people's preferences will count equally with each other and with our own, holds because, when we make a moral judgement, we are prescribing universally for all situations of a given identical kind, irrespective of what individuals occupy the different roles in those situations (the preferences had by the individuals being part of the roles; they do not travel round with the individuals). But if we fully know what it is like to be a certain individual in a certain situation (and if we did *not* fully know, our moral thinking could be faulted for incompleteness of information) then we shall have the same preferences with regard to what should happen to us were we in that situation as the person who is actually in it and therefore actually has the preferences. For example, if I fully know what it is like to be burnt at the stake, I shall want not myself to be burnt at the stake just as much as does the person who is actually being burnt. Put these two premisses together, and it becomes inescapable that we prescribe, if we are prescribing morally, for all situations as if we were going to be in them forthwith, and therefore giving the same weight to the preferences of the people in them as *they* actually give to them. I have summarized the argument, and there is a lot more to be said about it; but it is not this part of my argument that Mackie challenges in his paper.

This, then, is my answer to Mackie's first, 'internal', objection: the objection that, even if my universal prescriptivist theory be accepted for the sake of argument, it does not lead inevitably to utilitarianism, but is consistent with his right-based theory. The answer is that, first of all, it does so lead, for the reason I have given; and that, secondly, if it is consistent with his right-based theory, then so is utilitarianism itself (as, indeed, I think it is, if 'based' is not taken too narrowly).

The first part of this answer, however, leads us directly to Mackie's second objective, which he calls 'external', because it takes issue with my underlying theory, universal prescriptivism. I myself base this theory on conceptual analysis or philosophical logic. The moral words do, as a matter of linguistic fact, have the logical properties of prescriptivity and universalizability on which my argument for utilitarianism is based. This is to be established by appeal to *linguistic* (not *moral*) intuitions: in our ordinary use of the words we do, as part of the meaning we give to them, assign to them these logical properties. We know that somebody who says 'He is in just the same situation as I am, including all his personal psychological characteristics, both occurrent and dispositional, and yet he ought to do it but I ought not' is offending against the logical rules which give 'ought' its meaning, in just the same sort of way as we know that somebody who says 'All the books in the shelf are blue, yet there is one which isn't' is offending against the logical rules which give 'all', 'not', 'is', etc., their meanings. It is open to anybody to adopt a different meaning for the word 'ought' (provided that he advertises the fact in order to avoid misunderstandings); but if he does so, when he asks 'Ought I?', he will, because he has changed the meaning and the logical properties which are linked with it, no longer be asking the same question as we were asking when we used the same words; it would therefore not be surprising if he were able to give a different answer. Compare the person who says 'All the books on the shelf are blue', but means what most of us would express by 'Some of the books on the shelf are blue', or by 'All but one (the one written by me) are blue'.

This position can be, and has been, attacked in two different ways. First of all, it might be alleged that we do *not* use the words consistently in that way; my linguistic intuitions are at fault. But secondly, it might be alleged that although what I say about ordinary language may be true, (or may be admitted for the sake of argument to be true), we do not want to be tied and bound, in our practical reasoning, by contingent facts about ordinary language. So somebody might say 'If the ordinary uses of words commit me, if I use them in my moral thinking, to being a utilitarian, to hell with the ordinary uses of the words!'

Mr. Blackburn, who was kind enough to comment on an earlier draft of my book, advised me, in view of these possible objections, to take a course whose availability I had, indeed, already seen; and I was respectful enough to add a paragraph pointing out the alternative course. Mackie quotes this passage as 'conceding' the basis of his second objection. Actually, it concedes at most one (the third) of the three premises that he needs (p. 94); and even concerning this one I make it clear in my book that this is not my preferred way of handling the matter. It is a long stop, in case anybody is so imperceptive as not to see the force of the arguments on which, in the main, I rely. The first and second of Mackie's three premises I would reject, because I appeal to only one kind of universalization (*MT*, p. 108), and that has a logical and linguistic basis which I have just reiterated. For this reason his first premiss, which requires there to be different kinds of universalization, misses the target, and so, therefore, does the second, which depends on it.

The 'alternative course' into which Blackburn wished to draw me was to say 'All right, let us admit for the sake of argument either that my linguistic intuitions about ordinary language are wrong, or that it simply does not matter what logical properties ordinary language assigns to the words. Let us rather tell ordinary language to go to hell, and devise an *artificial* language whose words do have, by stipulation, the required properties. Then any user of this artificial language will have to be a utilitarian in his moral thinking. It remains open to anybody, provided that he makes his use clear, to use those words in some different way from that laid down in the rules of this artificial language, just as he could escape in the same way from the rules of our natural language. He will then not be asking the same questions as we are. But he may not want to ask those questions. What we have to show him is that there is some reason why he should use that language and ask those questions, or, contrariwise, why we should not give up using our language and ask instead the questions that he is asking.'

At the end of my new book I address myself to the task of justifying the asking of moral questions (which is the same task, whether following Mr. Blackburn's advice I treat them as questions in an artificial language, or whether, following my own inclinations, I claim that our natural language already serves to ask them). After admitting the possibility of there being a character whom I call 'the consistent amoralist', who has abandoned the moral language and its rules (whether natural or artificial), I try to show what reasons there are for us not to become amoralists, and, still more importantly, what reasons there are for not bringing up our children to be amoralists, even if we have only their interests at heart. This part of my book amounts to a prudential defence of the institution of morality. As such it will raise eyebrows, but it is not my task in this paper to lower them.

———————

Let me make it clear, as Mackie does, that I am not merely giving a utilitarian justification of utilitarian morality; that would be trivial and easy. I am not, that is to say, only maintaining that an archangelic utilitarian thinker would come out with excellent moral reasons for inculcating the moral language with its rules. I am maintaining something much more substantial: that even a person who had nothing at heart but his own interest would do well to adopt this language and this way of thinking as a matter of ingrained habit. This, I maintain, holds for the world as it is and for people as they are; it does not hold for all logically possible worlds. The discussion, as Mackie says, is a long one, and my summary here will have to be even briefer than his. Note that I am not saying that the morally right *act* is always in the agent's interest; such a claim would be extravagant. I am maintaining that the interests of all ordinary humans (as opposed to impossibly clever devils) are likely to be furthered *in general* if they inculcate into themselves moral habits of thought—habits tenacious enough to make them actually suffer in mind if they transgress their morality, thereby giving them an added prudential reason for not doing so. The main reason, however, is that in the world as it is, and as we have helped, for reasons of self-interest, to make it, the easiest way of seeming to be upright is to be upright (an opinion which Xenophon attributed to Socrates).[8]

If anybody thinks that even this is an extravagant claim, I ask him to notice that the more thoughtful of us, when we have to think about the education of our children, and probably think much more about their good than about the good of the general public or about morality, in fact try, with varying degrees of success, to inculcate into them moral habits of thought. And it would go worse with the children if we did not.

There is, it goes without saying, room here for empirical differences of opinion as to whether this is so; for it is an empirical question what kind of education is most likely to lead to the maximal satisfaction of the children's preferences in the course of their lives. All I can say is that I believe that most thoughtful and experienced people, to judge by their practice, think it is so. The arguments which are brought against this position, like a lot of bad arguments against utilitarianism itself, rest largely on contrived examples, or too simple treatment of real ones. It is in this light that we should regard Mackie's example of the child brought up in a slave-owning aristocracy (p. 96). He suggests that critical moral thinking, such as I advocate, might lead such a fortunately endowed child 'to support some tendency to reform this unequal social structure, rather than merely to accept it and flourish within it, if there were any real possibility of successful reform'. But if there were any such real possibility, it could only be because there were factors at work, as there have been in many slave-societies before their reform, which made the foundations of the society shaky; and these same factors would very probably make it in the interest of its more fortunate members (especially if they they had regard to the interests of their posterity) to contemplate and work for a change to a more stable, because more equal, society. To substitute a more up-to-date example: does Mackie's argument commit him to saying that in present-day South Africa it is in the interest of a child to be brought up on diehard *verkrampte* rather than on more liberal *verligte* lines?

Although near the end of my book I do confront the question 'Why should I be moral?', I am not staking my reputation on the success of my answer to it. I should be content with something more modest: to have shown that the moral questions we are posing all the time are posed in terms whose meaning and logic generate a way of answering them which constrains us, once we ask the questions. If an amoralist refuses the questions themselves, that is another issue. However, I do believe that as a matter of fact there *is* a preestablished harmony between morality and prudence, to this limited extent, that if we were to bring up a child (or ourselves) to ask moral questions and answer them by means of the two-level structure of moral thinking which I say our language imposes on us, we should be acting in the child's (or in the second case our own) best interests.

———————

Mackie's paper contains an illuminating digression about recent sociobiological theories and Peter Singer's first-rate appraisal of them in his book *The Expanding Circle*.[9] I shall not go into the question in detail, as I have discussed Singer's book elsewhere.[10] I agree with his contention that the limited altruisms which 'the selfish gene' can produce (kin-altruism, group altruism and, more generally, reciprocal altruism) tend to escalate into a more universal kind of altruism, even though genetic factors might not by themselves *directly* produce this. The explanation he gives is that the power of reason evolves because it helps us to secure, by its more selfish applications, the survival of the genes which produce it; but that, once we have this power, we cannot stop ourselves using it in ways which lead us towards universal impartial benevolence. He compares morality with mathematics: counting and adding are good for our genes; but once we can do them we are on an escalator that carries us up to topology and other pursuits which, even if useful, could not have grown up because they helped our genes to reproduce themselves. In the same way, the kinds of thinking which, within a limited kin-group or small reciprocally helpful society, conduce to the reproduction of the genes responsible for them, may tend to escalate into a morality of universal equal concern for all sentient beings. And this, though not genetically produced, might in the end, in the present world-nexus of interlocking interests, prove to be genetically useful. To Singer's invocation of the escalation of reason, I would add a mention of the escalation of the moral *language* in which we reason; but the general lines of his suggestion seem to me promising.

But Mackie could agree, and still be left with his most powerful argument against me. It might be, he concedes, that the adoption of something like the standard system of *prima facie* moral principles for use in our ordinary thinking would be recommended both by a perfect moral thinker and by a similarly perfect prudential thinker. But if it were merely a contingent empirical fact about the world that this was in general the case, it would not, he thinks, support my prudential defence of morality. For although the *prima facie* principles would be the same, the route by which a prudential and a moral thinker would arrive at them would be different. And the consequence of this would be that in all difficult cases, especially those in which morality and prudence diverge, as I have admitted that they may, the critical prudential thinker may cease to agree. Though it may be prudent to cultivate a repugnance to lying, there are surely (Mackie could argue) cases in which, once the question has been raised whether I ought to tell a lie in my own interest although it would be morally wrong, the perfect prudential thinker will say that I ought, and the perfect moral thinker will say that I ought not.

As I have already suggested, the most promising way of answering this objection is by an appeal to contingent facts about human nature and about the world in which we actually live. First, I do not think it practically possible to bring people up so that they follow the *prima facie* moral principles with the consistency which even their own interest demands, without implanting in them quite strong feelings of aversion to breaking them. But if they have these feelings, it will become to that extent contrary to their interest to break them, because it makes them feel bad. So, when the perfect prudential critical thinker takes this additional factor into account, he too will recommend telling the truth. The original aversion therapy was in our own interest, and, once we have undergone it, it makes it in our interest to avoid the aversive events (e.g., lie-telling by us) even in those cases (which for my argument will have to be rare) in which it is otherwise in our interest that they should occur.

Secondly, even if the coincidence between morality and prudence in general were purely fortuitous (which it is not, though it is not logically necessary either), it would be sufficient for my argument (which is designed to show why we should not bring up our children and ourselves as amoralists) if there were this contingent correlation. For when we are bringing them up (at a stage when they certainly cannot *distinguish* clearly between morality and prudence) we shall cultivate in them the sound moral principles in their own interest. So there is prudential justification for the original aversion therapy. But what shall we, if we have their interests at heart, include in our education on the question of what to do when in difficult cases morality and prudence conflict? The time will come when they will be able to distinguish between moral and prudential critical thinking, even if, being humans, they cannot manage either at all well. My guess is that we shall warn them against supposing too easily that they can win the prudential game by abandoning the moral one. Critical thinking of any sort is extremely difficult, and, for my part, I think it both easier and wiser to do it in the moral way, by appealing to truly universal principles, than to attempt self-interested cost-benefit analyses. I know of so many people who have erred, even prudentially speaking, by supposing otherwise.

This leads me to a discussion of Mackie's third and last main objection, which will have to be brief. It relates to what he calls the inaccessibility of critical thinking to human beings. I do not find so much difference on this point between him and myself as he does. I stress repeatedly in my book that only a perfect being (God, or the character I call the archangel) could do it perfectly. Bishop Butler therefore, as Mackie says and as I have said in the past, leaves the whole thing to God, to find out the best *prima facie* principles and reveal them to our consciences. But, as Hobbes says, 'Though God Almighty can speak to a man, by Dreams, Visions, Voice, and Inspiration; yet he obliges no man to beleeve he hath so done to him that pretends it; who (being a man) may erre, and (which is more) may lie'.[11] If we either do not believe in God, or believe in him but also think that the line of communication between him and us is fallible, what are we to do? Intuitive thinking, as I hope to have shown in my book and as Mackie agrees, cannot be self-supporting, because we cannot without circularity appeal to intuitions to justify intuitions. So critical thinking has somehow or other to be done.

The question therefore turns into one about whether Mackie's or my suggestions about the best method of critical thinking are more promising. He first considers a method which, he says, could be put forward as an amendment to my own which on reflection I might accept. But no reflection is necessary, because the suggestion is entirely consistent with my views from the beginning and is no amendment. This is that my

> thoroughgoing prescriptive universalization might amalgamate the points of view of all the individuals concerned in a way that took serious account of the separateness of persons, by assigning such basic abstract rights as I have suggested to each person. That is, we could have a right-based method of critical thinking (p. 98).

As I have already said, this is how my own method proceeds: the abstract right in question is that to equal concern and respect (which is a mere rephrasing of universalizability). All the other rights which Mackie wants he calls *prima facie*, and therefore cannot think them to be the bases of critical thinking; and anything else he wants to put in as a basis of critical thinking could, I am pretty sure, be shown to be derivative from this right to equal concern.

But Mackie rejects this approach because he wants us not to base ourselves on conceptual analysis: 'Right and wrong have to be invented . . . morality is not to be discovered but to be made' (p. 98). This is surely not a bone of contention between us. For if he is here speaking about the concepts, of course I can agree that they had to be invented (or at least, to allow for a Chomskian innate grammar, that they had to develop somehow among men); and if he is speaking about the *content* of morality, it is in accord with my prescriptivist views, which have often been attacked on this very ground, to say that we have to come to our own moral principles and cannot look them up in any encyclopedia.

However, for whatever reason, Mackie rejects this approach, and suggests instead that

> critical thinking might itself be a process of interaction, negotiation, and debate between diverse groups with different starting points, different traditions of thought. Rather than proceeding *de haut en bas*, being pursued by one or more detached thinkers who try to stand above the whole conflict of interests and ideals, it would work up from below, from those conflicting views and claims themselves (p. 100).

This gets me quite wrong, if it was intended to suggest that on my view moral thinking can be done without discussing other people's interests, ideals, claims, views, etc., with them. Why should it be thought that I wish to dispense with such discussion and negotiation? But the question is, 'When we have finished stating our claims and views, what do we do then?' Some people, perhaps, are content to leave the issue thereafter to a power struggle. Mackie, with proper caution, says

> The details of this process would be contingent upon the input to it and are therefore not open to any precise description *a priori*. But it is reasonable to expect that any such process of interaction, negotiation, and debate would be roughly equivalent to some distribution of entitlements that are not merged into a pure collectivity – in other words, that this too would be, in effect, a right-based approach.

I find this suggestion somewhat obscure; but in so far as I can understand it, it seems not too different from my own. The main difference is that I, unlike any right-based theory so far produced, provide a clear basis for the negotiation: the prescriptions they come to in the end have to be such as they can all accept for universal application whatever individual role anybody plays. This is a method often in effect used in negotiations, and it works. The use of this rule in critical thinking will lead the negotiators to assign to each other at least one 'entitlement' at the critical level, namely the right to equal concern. It will also lead them to give each other a lot of *prima facie* 'abstract' (as Mackie calls them) entitlements for use at the intuitive level. In fact the whole thing will go just as I say it does, given this ground rule. If this is not to be the ground rule, what other way is there of disciplining the negotiations?

I will end with a suggestion. My own ideas were developed *pari passu* with fairly engaged and involved thought about a lot of practical moral issues such as often divide the negotiators in such disputes. I would be willing to let my method and a right-based method (when one has been fully worked out) be tried out on such issues, to see how well they serve to resolve them. I think it would turn out that the methods, in so far as they served, were not all that different.

NOTES

1. This and the paper to which it is a reply are the fruits of the last of several seminars which John Mackie and I held at Oxford before his tragic death. I must express the feeling of personal loss that I share with many others at being bereft of the delight and illumination of discussions with him.

2. *A Theory of Justice* (Cambridge, Mass.: Harvard University Press, 1971), p. 27.

3. Cited in J. S. Mill, *Utilitarianism*, ch. 5 end.

4. See my *Moral Thinking* (Oxford: Oxford University Press, 1981), chs. 2, 3.

5. *Moral Thinking*, esp. pp. 28ff.

6. 'Community and Communication' in *People and Cities*, ed. S. E. Verney (London: Fontana, 1969); reprinted in my *Applications of Moral Philosophy* (London: Macmillan, 1972), p. 115.

7. *Moral Thinking*, ch. 7.

8. Xenophon, *Memorabilia* I, 7; see *Moral Thinking*, p. 196.

9. *The Expanding Circle: Ethics and Sociobiology* (New York: Farrar, Straus & Giroux, 1980).

10. *New Republic*, February 1981.

11. *Leviathan*, ch. 32.

6

Respect for Human Moral Rights versus Maximizing Good

H. J. McCloskey

Utilitarianism and Natural Human Moral Rights

Jeremy Bentham saw clearly enough that utilitarianism can have no truck with theories of natural human rights. In *Anarchical Fallacies*, writing of the Declaration of Rights of the French National Assembly in 1791, Bentham made his celebrated statement:

> *Natural Rights* is simple nonsense: natural and imprescriptible rights, rhetorical nonsense, — nonsense upon stilts. But this rhetorical nonsense ends in the old strain of mischievous nonsense.[1]

In spite of this, Bentham's clear apprehension of utilitarianism's commitment to rejecting the view that there are certain basic natural human moral rights that hold of human beings as human beings, very many utilitarians today seek to reconcile their utilitarianism with theories of human moral rights, with theories of natural moral rights of persons of the kinds set out in the UN Declarations, according to which we are claimed to possess various basic, fundamental moral rights simply by virtue of being human beings, or human persons, and not by virtue of the utility of a belief in and action on the basis of respect for such rights. Utilitarianism denies, and is committed to denying, that there are natural moral rights that hold of persons as persons, of human beings *qua* human beings. If its ethic is to be expressed in the language of moral rights, it might be said to hold that it is the greatest good or the greatest pleasure that has a moral right to exist, that individual persons and animals have no moral right to a specific share in or of the greatest good, their roles being those of being instruments for achieving or vehicles for bringing into being and sustaining the greatest good, they having a moral right to contribute to the common good as vehicles or instruments thereof. Of course, strictly speaking, an abstraction such as the greatest good cannot in any literal sense of 'moral right,' possess moral rights, whilst the rights individuals may possess as vehicles or instruments of the greatest good would be a mixed bunch, including such rights as the rights to live or to be killed, to be free or to be constrained, to be helped or to be harmed or used—the rights varying from person to person, situation to situation, from time to time. Thus, if the greatest good could be realized by promoting the pleasure of only one or other of two distinct groups of one hundred persons, then, in terms of utilitarianism, it would morally be indifferent which group was chosen, and no member of either group would have a moral right to the pleasure. Similarly, if, in a war, the greatest good could be achieved only be sending a particular platoon on a suicide mission, the officer in charge would have the moral right to order the platoon to go on the mission, and the members of the platoon would have the moral right to be killed for the sake of the greatest good. This is a very different way of thinking about moral rights from that in terms of there being certain basic human moral rights.

Two considerations appear to have contributed to the belief that utilitarianism can accommodate within its framework the view that there are general human rights. The one is the mistaken belief that talk about rights in general, and about human rights in particular, is reducible without loss to talk about duties, this commonly being associated with another mistaken view, namely, that rights and duties are correlative. The other consideration is that utilitarianism has been thought by various utilitarians to imply that various general legal and social rights ought to be accorded to individuals, and this has been confused with the distinct view that individual persons possess general human rights *qua* being human persons.

It is not difficult to bring out that talk about rights is not reducible to talk about duties. We may have rights and there be no corresponding duties in the sense that whatever duties, if any, arise from the right, do not constitute the right. Thus we may have a moral right to appropriate the pearl we find in an oyster, money on a deserted road. We may have a right to follow the dictates of our conscience, yet others may have no duty to abstain from interference with us when we seek, on the basis of our conscientious beliefs, to violate the rights of others. There is the further consideration that with many rights—the right to life, the right to a fair trial, the right to education, the right to self-development—we determine what the duties of others are by reference to the right; and the duties that could follow from such rights may potentially be infinite in number and such as not to admit of being set out in a determinate list.

The view that rights and duties are correlative would, if true, lend support to the reducibility-of-rights-to-duties thesis. However, whilst duties and rights may be correlative—as when by a voluntary act a person enters into a promise, contract, becomes a parent—commonly rights, and more evidently, basic human moral rights, and duties are not correlative. This is so with the examples cited above. There may be no correlative duty to a right of conscience. With rights of recipience, rights to aids and facilities, the duties that arise from the right are not the determinate, fixed, finite duties, correlative duties are thought of as being. Equally, we may have important duties in respect of other persons, without those persons necessarily having rights against us. This is often so in respect of duties of benevolence towards determinate persons. The duty to maximize good, which dictates that we visit our lonely, ailing aunt in hospital, need give her no moral right to our visit.

It has been claimed that utilitarianism implies that various general legal and social rights, such as the rights to life, liberty, self-development, be accorded to persons. However this is distinct from ascribing a moral right to those persons. We may believe that there is no moral right to propagate immoral, false beliefs, nor to publish or read the obscene and pornographic. Yet we may rightly believe that there are good moral reasons for according the legal and social rights to do these things. Thus it was that St. Thomas Aquinas acknowledged that it may be permissible for a state to tolerate prostitution so as to avoid greater evils. It is relevant here that J. S. Mill is commonly interpreted as arguing in *Liberty* from ideal utilitarian premisses, that civilized, adult human beings have a moral right to liberty, a conditional right that holds only if certain conditions prevail. When these conditions prevail, it is a *prima facie* right, and an absolute right only if it is not overridden by other conflicting moral considerations. If Mill had indeed been arguing in this way, there would be a serious problem in reconciling his utilitarianism and his defense of the right to liberty. And Mill would have needed to show that his position was secure from Bentham's critique of natural moral rights theories. In fact, it would seem that Mill argued for liberty in the sense of freedom from interference by the law, by society through social pressure and public opinion, and by individuals as by organized boycotts—and this by reference to goods such as knowledge; rational, vital belief; self-development, including moral development; and pleasure. Where maximizing good dictated legal and/or social constraints as in many cases in which the individuals are either not the best judges or not the best guardians of their own interests, for example, the uncultivated in respect of education, as well as when others made it their business to prey on the weakness of others, Mill favored or entertained the possibility of legal and/or social constraints. So to argue, is to argue from ideal utilitarian premisses, not for the possession by individuals of various human moral rights, but for the according to certain individuals under certain conditions, the possession of various legal and social rights. The latter contention is consistent with utilitarianism.

A utilitarian might seek to accommodate talk about human moral rights within the utilitarian framework by arguing that there are good utilitarian reasons for attributing human rights to persons who do not possess moral rights, just as there may be good utilitarian reasons for ascribing responsibility to persons who are not morally responsible for their actions. This might be urged in terms of act-utilitarianism as a tactical move for maximizing good. Alternatively, it could be developed as an element of a rule-utilitarianism. Clearly it would be difficult to find plausible act-utilitarian reasons for propagating such a falsehood. On the other hand, whilst a rule-utilitarianism that incorporated such a human moral rights component would normatively be more attractive than many versions of rule-utilitarianism, it would remain exposed to the basic criticisms of rule-utilitarianism set out by J. J. C. Smart, myself, and others.[2]

The Concept of a Moral Right

In their discussions of the concept of a moral right, many philosophers have been influenced by their views about the nature of legal rights and have sought to assimilate moral rights to legal rights, explaining them as claims, legitimate claims, justified claims; as powers, powers we ought to be accorded or to possess or be permitted to exercise, or as moral powers; as liberties we possess or ought to possess; as expectations or as reasonable expectations; and also in terms of duties of others towards the possessor of the right such that to have a right against another is for that person to have a duty towards the holder of the right.

Against such accounts I have argued in various places that accounts of moral rights as claims, legitimate claims, justified claims, and the like, confuse what follows from the possession of a moral right, with the moral right itself.[3] We establish that a claim is morally legitimate, morally justified, often, if not always, by showing that it follows from a moral right. It is either unhelpful or inaccurate to seek to explain rights as powers of some sort. To explain them as moral powers is unhelpful as we need to explain what a moral power is, in terms of a moral right. On the other hand, explanation of rights in terms of powers we ought to possess, be accorded, or be permitted to exercise, does not fit the facts. A good deal of talk about rights has nothing to do with powers. Accounts of moral rights in terms of liberties give the wrong emphasis and note only one aspect of the possession of a right. To possess a moral right is to possess a moral liberty to do, enjoy, receive, demand, have demanded, that to which one has a right. However, with many moral rights, such as the right to life and to health care as an element thereof, the liberty aspect is the less important one, the provision of protection, aids, and facilities, the more important one. Much of the importance of claims about human moral rights lies in the fact that moral rights are quite distinct from expectations, more especially, reasonable expectations. Most of the many millions of disabled persons in the Third World today can have no expectation, reasonable or otherwise, that they will be aided in the way they have a moral right to be aided; yet it is true and important to acknowledge that they have a right to aid. The right is not simply a legitimate claim, nor merely a moral power, nor a mere moral liberty; it is *a moral entitlement* that gives rise to a moral authority to do what these individuals are entitled to have or to do, to be protected from interference, to receive aid, to demand or have aid demanded on their behalf. More generally, moral rights are moral entitlements that confer moral liberties on their possessors to do, demand, enjoy, have, etc., depending on the nature and basis of the right; and they are moral entitlements that typically but not always impose moral constraints on others to abstain from various actions and activities, or to do, assist, provide services and facilities, etc., again depending on the nature and basis of the right.

Basic Human Moral Rights as Grounded in Personhood

Whereas many special moral rights such as those of the creditor against the debtor, the promisee against the promiser, the child against its parent, are created by voluntary actions of one party, in the former cases, by virtue of the fact that the relevant party has a more general, more basic right to enter into the contract, to make the promise, the situation with basic human rights is very different. Their existence is not seen to depend on the occurrence of specific actions by others. How then are they grounded? How can it be shown that there are general, basic, human moral rights?

Historically, the main approaches to establishing the existence of human moral rights have been in terms of seeking to derive them from God, to ground them on human nature and what is necessary for human beings to attain their natural end through perfection of their nature, and in terms of contending that the basic, fundamental human rights are self-evident rights.

The first of these approaches, that of seeking to establish moral rights by deriving them from God, even though adopted by so famous an exponent of the existence and importance of natural rights as John Locke in the *Second Treatise Of Civil Government*, is rarely encountered today, partly because of the lessened importance attached to religion, partly because, if true, it would imply that really there are no natural, human moral rights, only rights possessed by God; and that if there were no God, there would be no moral rights. The second approach is that based on the Thomistic theory of natural law.[4] Space will not permit a detailed discussion of this approach here. However, it is to be noted that difficulties arise for such a theory in respect of its theses that there are ends or purposes inherent in human nature, that they are based on inbuilt 'inclinations' or 'appetites' that we have by virtue of our nature as substances, animals, rational beings, and that we have a self-evident right, by virtue of our right to be good as human beings, to align ourselves with these inherent natural ends to attain our natural end and be good as human beings.

The plausible approach, that upon which the major accounts of human rights of the late eighteenth century, the nineteenth century, and this century, and that which would appear to underlie the UN Declarations and their ready and widespread acceptance, is that the basic, fundamental, human moral rights are self-evidently so, that to become aware that persons possess such rights, we need simply reflect on the nature of human persons and on the concept of a moral right. (If J. S. Mill is to be interpreted as arguing for moral rights such as a moral right to liberty, as distinct from simply the according of legal and social rights, then his argument is to be construed as maintaining that there are moral rights to what is necessary as a means to or condition for attaining various intrinsic goods, where his premiss would need to be that there is a self-evident right to access to intrinsic goods).

Basic, self-evident rights of persons include: the rights to life, health, and to bodily integrity; to respect as persons, and hence to respect for one's moral autonomy and integrity, and as a possessor of feelings, creative imagination, and needs of many kinds; to self-development and to education as a condition and element thereof; to access to knowledge and truth. These are self-evidently rights and are to be defended as such. With certain minor qualifications, they are the same for all persons. The derivative rights that follow from these basic rights, which in UN Declarations are so often confused with basic rights, are not self-evident; and they vary from person to person, situation to situation. Hence it is that the very talented person, the person of only average capacities, and the disabled person may have very different derivative rights according to what is necessary for them to enjoy their basic moral rights as persons.

An adequate defense of the self-evidence of these rights would require very lengthy treatment of a kind that is not possible here. Instead of such a discussion, the features of persons that provide the bases of the claim that persons self-evidently possess such rights will simply be noted.

The right to life rests on the human person's nature as a morally autonomous being, and as a rational, emotional being with a capacity to control, create, and recreate his or her experiences. Respect for the existence and will of such a being is morally appropriate and confers the right to existence, that is to life, on those who possess such a nature. Thus the right rests on respect for and acknowledgment of the fact that possession of rational autonomy gives its possessor rights over his own existence—he has the capacity and hence the right to determine what he does or what is done to him; it involves respecting *his* will as it affects him. Usually he wills to live and not be killed. Given this, how can another have a right to override the will of a rationally autonomous being by killing him? Further, his nature as not simply a rationally autonomous being, but as a rational, emotional, imaginative, creative being has worth and value such as morally to require that it be protected, and neither harmed nor destroyed. The right to life that rests on these features of persons is a right not simply not be be killed but a right to be kept alive, a right to be saved if endangered. Such an account encounters obvious difficulties in respect of infants and fetuses. Infants evidently possess the right to life by virtue of their potentiality to be full persons. Although the fetus is usually—but by no means always—a potential person, the greater remoteness of its potentiality, combined with our awareness that a potential X is not an X and possesses very different attributes and value from an X, incline many not to ascribe the same right to life to the fetus, the more so as the fetus may be thought of in its early development as primarily a potential organism, although also a potential person.[5]

The right to health, like the right to bodily integrity, is related to but not wholly based on the right to life. Ill health and mutilation of the body need not threaten life. Deliberately to harm the health of persons is to violate their personhood, impairing capacities, causing needless suffering, overriding wills. So too with violation of bodily integrity, as with compulsory sterilization, barbarous forms of punishment such as chopping off hands, blinding, removing the tongue. In a real sense, although not in the sense suggested in Locke's labor argument for private property nor in the sense claimed by many feminists in their defense of abortion from a woman's right to control (and mutilate?) her body, our body is ours to care for and maintain as the vehicle of our personhood. Although it is true that we can lose an organ, a leg, an eye, and still be the same person, our body appertains to us as persons. The negative aspect of the case for the rights to health and bodily integrity is evidently strong. How can another have the right to injure, infect, disease a person? So to act is to violate a right. A very powerful moral justification would be necessary for such an act not to constitute a grave and illegitimate violation of a right.

The right to respect as a person and hence to respect as a morally autonomous being and as a rational, emotional, imaginative being, can only be grasped by reflection on the nature of a person as a person, and on what morally is the appropriate response to this nature. To deny respect to persons, not to respect a person's moral autonomy and integrity without good moral reason, is to treat the person as a thing. It is to deny his personhood. To force a person to act against his sincere, carefully thought-out moral beliefs, is to deny his autonomy in respect of the most important aspect of his life. Recognition of this right underlies the strongly and widely held conviction that conscientious objectors have a moral right, which should be recognized in law, to withhold their services in war, that those with moral objections to medical treatment should not be forced to undergo it even to save their lives, that attempts should be made to secure the rights of children whose parents object to medical treatment on moral grounds, without forcing the consciences of the parents.

The right of self-development and to education as a condition and element thereof relate to the nature and value of human self-development. The right is made manifest by bringing out the nature of self-development as a product of persons' exercise of their autonomy, and other valuable capacities and potentialities. The right to access to knowledge and truth is involved in the rights to self-development and to respect as a person, but it is also a right in its own right. Human beings have the capacity to acquire, grasp, use knowledge; and knowledge is of immense intrinsic and instrumental value. Recognition of such a right seems to be implicit in Mill's major argument for freedom of speech and discussion, however his conclusions are to be construed.

Basic Human Moral Rights as Intrinsic, Inalienable, but Not Always Absolute

The view that some or all of the basic human moral rights are absolute rights has a long history. Thomists have long argued to this effect, seeing such rights as the right to worship God, to live morally in accord with the natural law, and the right to life, as among the human rights that are always absolute. More recently, indeed, during the past quarter of a century, this kind of claim has been taken up by a very different philosophical school, that of the American libertarians and neolibertarians, of which M. Rothbard, J. Hospers, and R. Nozick are the best-known members, they arguing that the right to private property is always an absolute right.[6] It was because the theories and Declarations of Rights of their day were seen by them to embody this same kind of claim that certain human rights are always absolute, that both Bentham and Edmund Burke attacked theories of human rights as they did. Hence it was that Burke wrote:

> What is the use of discussing a man's abstract right to food or medicine? The question is upon the method of procuring and administering them. . . . Rights undergo so many refractions and reflections it is absurd to talk of them as if they continued in the simplicity of their original direction.[7]

Burke is clearly right in his rejection of theories that there are general absolute human rights. Major difficulties are encountered by theories that claim that any right, other than a purely negative right to freedom from interference of various kinds, are always absolute, the difficulties arising from the logical possibility of conflicts, and also from the fact of actual conflicts which are such that we cannot respect all the alledgedly absolute rights of all the persons who are claimed to possess them. Problems of a different kind are encountered by the claim that certain negative rights, for example, the right to life interpreted as a right not to be killed, are always absolute, namely, that such a claim leads to morally unacceptable conclusions. Different rights, for example, the rights to life and to moral autonomy and integrity, may conflict with one another, such that we have morally to determine which to respect and in what way; the one right, such as the right to life, may give rise to conflicts, such that we can protect, save one life, only by sacrificing or not saving another life. And rights may conflict with other values, such as pleasure or pain, in ways that morally oblige us to qualify our respect for the right, as in curtailing acts directed at a persons' self-development to prevent gross cruelty to animals. Thomists have offered partial, but only partial, replies to criticisms based on these difficulties in terms of theories such as the Doctrine of Double Effect, the theory of the Unjust Aggressor (who may be neither unjust nor morally responsible for what he does). However, these replies themselves encounter difficulties of many kinds, including those of involving their exponents in morally abhorrent conclusions not unlike those to which they object when such conclusions are shown to follow from rival theories. Thus the Doctrine of Double Effect permits the knowing, unintentional killing of thousands of innocent children for the sake of a proportional good; yet it commits its exponents to losing a just war if success can be achieved, and millions of innocent lives be saved, only by the intentional killing of one innocent person. Similarly objectionable conclusions follow about the permissibility of killing morally innocent 'unjust aggressors' to save one's life. At the same time, acceptance of these supporting theories amounts to an admission that human rights such as the right to life are not always absolute. How can it be so if we are said to have the moral right intentionally to kill the morally innocent unjust aggressor, and knowingly, albeit unintentionally, to kill innocent persons, when and if the intended good is proportionately good, and cannot be achieved without bringing about the unintended, foreseen good?

The problem of making rights-theory secure from Burke's criticisms is not to be solved along such lines. However, there is a much simpler, more plausible solution. Burke's objections are to be circumvented by acknowledging that the basic rights are intrinsic, inalienable rights, that they belong, are possessed by persons by virtue of their personhood, but that they are not always absolute rights. W. D. Ross, in *The Right and the Good*, applied the expression '*prima facie* duties' to duties that are always duties but not always absolute duties, Ross in his general account of obligation developing a theory very similar to that of Richard Price, Price being the object of much of Burke's vituperation in *Reflections on the French Revolution*.[8] A similar distinction needs to be drawn and a similar terminology is required in respect of basic human rights. They are always rights—inalienable, intrinsic rights—but they are simply *prima facie* rights; they are rights that are absolute rights only if they are not overridden by more stringent moral rights or other moral considerations.

The introduction of this distinction into human moral rights theory is both right and necessary. It does however greatly complicate the problem of determining what are the absolute, morally operative rights of a person in any concrete situation. Yet the acknowledgment of this feature of basic human rights is necessary for two reasons, the one because physical resources may be inadequate to allow all to enjoy their basic rights, and the other because, in specific situations, we may have to decide between the rights of different persons, and between respecting rights and securing other values.

To elaborate: some rights are such that it is in practice impossible partially or fully to respect them. This would be the case in respect to the right to life of persons on a sinking ship, when an inadequate number of lifeboats has been provided. Some must drown. Yet all, those chosen to be saved and those allowed to drown, possess the right to life as persons. Their rights impose duties on others to ensure that such a situation does not recur. This is not an unrealistic situation. Much the same situation prevails in the world at large in respect to the possibility of immediately respecting the rights to food, to medical and hospital care, and to education, especially higher education. Even if a redistribution of the resources of the world would permit all to enjoy their rights at a future date, the situation here and now is that many hundreds of millions of persons are now placed, in respect of the enjoyment of various basic rights, in a situation comparable with that of those who are left to drown for the want of adequate lifeboats.

There are many other situations in which the individual's right can fully be respected only at the expense of his or her life or that of someone else, or both their enjoyment of some other right or good, and this not because of scarcity of resources. Thus it may be the case that the only way effectively to safeguard the rights to health and life of many is to quarantine and treat those with infectious diseases such as typhoid, cholera, and the like, that is, to restrict their enjoyment of their rights to liberty and to self-development to a degree, for the sake of overriding rights of others. Conflicts of rights, similar to conflicts of duties arise; the parallel is not exact, but there are conflicts of real rights, not seeming rights; and the moral solution is to be arrived at by determining what are the overriding rights in the particular moral situation.

Even if rights are viewed negatively, as rights to freedom from interference and to protection from interference, conflicts may still be possible. We may have to choose whom to protect from being killed, constrained, interfered with. If the rights are rights of recipience, as the rights to life and health are so commonly seen to be today, many more conflicts that will need to be resolved will arise. To understand the nature of such conflicts, it is necessary to grasp that the status of the rights involved is that of being real rights, but *prima facie* rights.

There are also clashes between basic rights and other values — human rights and the preservation of the aesthetically excellent, the beautiful in nature, the maintenance of knowledge, the prevention of animal suffering. If, as seems to be the case, concern to lessen animal suffering may justify curtailing human rights, so too, concern for the preservation of the aesthetically excellent, the beautiful, or knowledge may do so too. Many, although perhaps not all, of the latter cases might be such as to admit of being interpreted as involving conflicts of human rights.

Prima Facie Rights-Theories as Distinct from Utilitarianism

Jonathan Glover argues that to accept a theory that rights are simply *prima facie* and not always absolute is to abandon the theory of moral rights for utilitarianism. His statement is a little more circumspect, or less reckless, than this, but substantially amounts to this contention. He states, for instance:

A doctrine of absolute rights goes further than this and excludes the possibility of ever justifying killing by its consequences. But the claim that we have only a *prima facie* right to life does not exclude this possibility. It is thus not clear that it significantly differs from the view argued for here.

The doctrine that we have an absolute right to live is a genuine alternative.[9]

Glover is very seriously mistaken here. His mistake arises from his uncritical assumption that the only moral considerations that may override *prima facie* rights are considerations in terms of good consequences, and further, that when good consequences justify overriding the right, it is as if there were nothing to override. In fact, it is not sufficient that an action that violates a basic human right, albeit a *prima facie* right, produce the best possible consequences, to be morally justified; it must produce the best possible consequences that are of such a nature as to justify the violation of the right. The best possible consequences by no means always provide such a justification. In any case, most commonly when a *prima facie* right is overridden, it is not overridden by good consequences, but by concern for other *prima facie* rights. A *prima facie* rights-calculus is essentially that. By contrast, various so-called absolute rights theories—that of Catholic moralists such as G. E. M. Anscombe—are heavily consequentialist and ideal utilitarian to a degree in the value and importance attached to the foreseen, intended consequences, such that they can justify knowingly infringing the right to life of innocent persons.[10] That such infringements of rights that derive their justification in these theories largely from the value of the intended good consequences (and partly from the fact that they are not 'intended') are not described as infringements, does not alter the facts of the matter. Glover may have come to misunderstand the nature of *prima facie* human rights theories because he interpreted them in the light of the consequentialism of such absolutist theories.

A theory of *prima facie* human rights could be to the effect that only rights, and never other values or consequences, can override rights. Such a *prima facie* rights-theory would have no affinities at all with utilitarianism other than having a maximizing calculus. However, it would be a calculus about maximizing satisfaction of rights and only that. Such a theory could be one in terms of a hierarchy of rights, such that, solely by reference to the rights involved and their place in the hierarchy, we could determine what rights were absolute. In fact, that is not the kind of *prima facie* rights-theory that is being developed here. However, it is both a logically possible kind of theory and one that deserves the attention of anyone who, like Glover, claims to be able, in a brief aside, to dispose of *prima facie* rights-theories on the grounds that they (must?) disintegrate, degenerate into utilitarianism.

The theory of *prima facie* human rights that is outlined here is one in terms of *prima facie* rights, many of which are rights of recipience, in which the rights create obligations and claims that collide with one another and with the moral demands created by other values. Many of these conflicts are to be resolved without reference, or with only negative reference, to consequences. When the consequences do enter seriously into the resolution of the conflicts, the solution arrived at is often very different from that which would be dictated by utilitarian considerations.

Resolving Conflicts Involving *Prima Facie* Rights

The points made in the preceding section may be illustrated by reference to conflicts of *prima facie* human rights such as the right to life, viewed as a right of recipience, the right to moral autonomy and integrity – and values such as pleasure and happiness, and the absence of pain and suffering. A consideration of the morally rightful resolution of such conflicts brings out the inadequacy of the utilitarian calculus as a basis for determining the morally right response to such situations and conflicts.

One kind of conflict situation involving the right to life is illustrated by the lifesaver who finds himself the only person available to seek to rescue twenty persons who have been swept out to sea by a rip, where all are at risk of drowning. Whom ought he to save? If, as the argument of this paper suggests, persons have equal rights to life, the lifesaver ought to acknowledge this in determining whom he seeks to save; he seeking to save, not the most useful, letting drown the least useful, but rather those in most dire need of saving. It would be immoral, and a grave violation of the right to life of those left to drown, for the lifesaver to seek to save only those whose survival would maximize utility. So too, in situations of urgent medical need, when there are limited medical resources such that only some can obtain the necessary aid. Equal *prima facie* rights dictate equal chances for all, that is, a fair decision procedure, for deciding between the competing claimants. By contrast, if we were to seek to resolve such conflicts by treating utilitarian considerations as decisive, we should select, or seek to select, those who are to be saved on a very different basis. Considerations such as life expectancy, health, likely future happiness and freedom from suffering, number of dependents, likely contribution to the general good, would then be seen to be relevant, even decisive, considerations, such that if the doctor could reliably know or estimate such considerations, it would follow that he ought to be guided by them in his decisions. In fact, those who take human rights seriously would and ought to regard such utilitarian considerations as of only marginal moral relevance. It may not be morally improper for a moral agent to resolve a specific difficult conflict on such a basis. However, to erect them into principles of general application for resolving conflicts involving rights to life would be to deny the basic importance of human rights. It would be tantamount to claiming that persons have, not equal, but unequal, human rights. This is because it would amount to the allowing of utilitarian considerations to override moral rights in conflict of rights situations, in a way that is seen to be morally intolerable when there is no conflict of rights, simply a conflict between a right and utility. Only the most weighty utilitarian considerations can justify overriding such a basic, important right as the right to life. This is true too in situations in which there are conflicts between equal rights to life. In fact, most such conflicts are morally to be resolved purely in terms of a rights-calculus. The rights of children, for example, may well determine that a parent, rather than a childless person, be saved.

Another conflict case involves the right to life and the right to moral autonomy and integrity, and the evil of preventable suffering. It is that in which a highly intelligent child suffering from spina bifida needs a blood transfusion if it is to live, when the parents morally object to the giving of such a transfusion. Respect for rights would entail that the child be given the transfusion and not be allowed to die, and that the parents not be forced to agree to nor to assist in bringing about the transfusion, but that they be prevented from frustrating attempts to give the transfusion. Utilitarianism, and even utilitarian considerations, might well suggest that such a child be allowed to die. Yet, weighing even *prima facie* rights and utility in such a situation, it is clear that the child's right to life must override all other considerations unless the child first gives its free, informed consent to its being let die. In the latter event, both rights-theory and utilitarian considerations might dictate the same course, that of letting the child die, although the rights-calculus would not be the simple, uncomplex one that the utilitarian calculus would be.

Respect for life and the right to life, and respect for persons as moral beings, may also conflict. Consider here the case of a very worthy member of society who morally rejects medical treatment and blood transfusions as immoral, who is involved in a car accident, is knocked unconscious, and comes urgently to need a blood transfusion, in which the attending doctor knows the patient and the nature of his or her moral beliefs. It is not at all clear what respect for rights would dictate here. Utilitarianism, on the other hand, would have a quick, ready, unequivocal answer, that the transfusion be given, if possible, before the person regained consciousness. Yet it is not at all clear that that would be the morally right course to adopt.

Another telling case involving the right to life relates to a person trapped in a burning car after an accident in a remote country area. His passenger, a doctor, has been thrown from the car unhurt. He sees that it is impossible to extricate the driver before he is burned alive. The driver is conscious. The doctor has a painless drug with which he can kill the driver instantly. He himself finds the whole situation unbearable to contemplate. On simple utilitarianism, and on the basis of Glover's interpretation of how utilitarian considerations override *prima facie* rights, it would be hard to resist the conclusion that the driver ought painlessly to be killed before he burn to death. Yet, if the driver apprehended the intentions of the doctor and if he believed that he had no moral right to take or to condone the taking of his life, and demanded that he be allowed to die from the fire, the doctor would have no moral right to take the driver's life. That it would be morally abominable for him to take the driver's life would in no way be affected by how nauseated the doctor was by the contemplation of the driver's death, nor by whether or not others discovered that he in fact did take the driver's life. That is because the rights to life and to moral autonomy are so basic and so stringent. To kill the driver in such a situation would be a total violation of a person.

Other cases can be alluded to only briefly, but they too illustrate the same general points. *Prima facie* rights-theory and utilitarian considerations and utilitarianism may well lead to very different, opposed conclusions in respect of rights of conscience of conscientious objectors to what is in fact a just, morally justified war. Punishment of conscientious criminals raises interesting problems for rights-theory and for utilitarianism. The problems facing one who accepts a *prima facie* rights-theory are very different from those facing a utilitarian. Consider the conscientious criminal who yields to his wife's pleas that he terminate her suffering by terminating her life, she suffering from terminal cancer. Consider the civil disobedient, who is civilly disobedient in order to change what is a gravely evil law. Consider the sincere but seriously misguided, successful terrorist who kills hundreds of persons. The rights-theorist is faced with the problem of resolving clashes of basic *prima facie* rights, the rights of the victims and the very stringent right of conscience of the terrorist. Utilitarians accept the need for, and the moral desirability of, reformative punishment. In all the above cases, reformative punishment, to be successful, would need to be directed at bringing about a moral conversion in the criminal. No one who respected rights, *prima facie* rights, could possibly countenance such punishment, although, out of respect for rights generally, he or she may favor punishment, even very severe punishment. It is hard to see that utilitarian considerations could ever override respect for rights in practical situations such that respect for *prima facie* rights was compatible with morally reformative punishment.

NOTES

1. *The Works of Jeremy Bentham*, ed. J. Bowring (Edinburgh, 1843), II: 523.

2. See J. J. C. Smart, "Extreme and Restricted Utilitarianism," *Philosophical Quarterly* 6 (1956), and my "An Examination of Restricted Utilitarianism," *Philosophical Review* 66, (1957).

3. See my "Rights," *Philosophical Quarterly* 15 (1965); 'Moral Rights and Animals," *Inquiry* 22 (1979); and "Handicapped Persons and the Rights They Possess," in *Problems of Handicap*, ed. R. Laura (Melbourne: Macmillan, 1980), ch. 10.

4. *Summa Theologiae*, I, II, 90–95; and J. Maritain, *Man and the State* (Chicago: Chicago University Press, 1951), ch. 4.

5. For a fuller discussion, see my "The Right to Life," *Mind* 84 (1975).

6. See M. Rothbard, *For A New Liberty* (New York: Macmillan, 1973); J. Hospers, *Libertarianism* (Los Angeles: Nash, 1971); and R. Nozick, *Anarchy, State, and Utopia* (Oxford: Blackwell, 1974).

7. *Reflections on the French Revolution* (London: Dent-Everyman, 1910), pp. 58–59.

8. *The Right and The Good* (Oxford: Clarendon, 1930), ch. 2, and R. Price, *A Review of the Principal Questions in Morals*, ed. D. D. Raphael (Oxford: Clarendon Press, 1948).

9. *Causing Death and Saving Lives* (Harmondsworth: Penguin, 1977), p. 83.

10. See, for example, "War and Murder," in *Nuclear Weapons: A Catholic Response*, ed. W. Stein (New York: Sheed and Ward, 1961), pp. 45–62.

7

Towards a Substantive Theory of Rights

James Griffin

1. The Need for a Substantive Theory

I want to take, as my point of departure, a dissatisfaction with the present state of philosophical discussion of rights that all of us, regardless of our views, feel. It is obviously unsatisfactory that the term 'rights', at least as it figures in the philosopher's lexicon, comes so close to being criterionless. It is still less satisfactory that the compound term 'human rights'—and it is on these rights that I want to concentrate—comes even closer. As a result, philosophers often give the impression of plucking human rights out of the thin air. For instance, in the middle of a justly well-known discussion of abortion, we find the author settling most problems by introducing a right to determine what happens in and to our bodies,[1] and if anyone should doubt, as many of us do, that there is exactly *that* right, we are unsure how to settle the matter. Also, we spend a lot of time these days arguing over the structural features of rights: whether they can be traded off against one another and against utility, whether they are, say, 'trumps'[2] or 'side constraints'.[3] Yet we all know that there is no hope of really settling these arguments until we can say what rights there are, what their extent is, and what makes them rights. We cannot, for instance, sketch out merely the rough outlines of a theory of rights—for example, rights as side constraints—and let the filling be added later. The filling is what settles whether one right can have different grounds on different occasions, whether a right can differ in importance from one occasion to another, and whether a right with one kind of ground may be traded off against other rights or against utility, while a right with another kind of ground may not be. In short, structural features and substantive features have to arrive in a theory together.

It would be perfectly safe to draw conclusions about the structure of rights in the absence of a developed substantive account if the answers to the substantive issues were obvious, but they are scarcely that.

But I think that virtually everyone agrees with these complaints, including those who make claims about rights that lack the foundations that the complaints desiderate. I doubt, therefore, that I have really to demonstrate a need for a substantive theory of rights, but no doubt I should explain further what I mean by such a theory. I think of a substantive theory in contrast to a formal theory—that is, one primarily concerned with the sort of structural features I have mentioned; and also in contrast to a conceptual theory—one primarily concerned to explore the relation of the concept of a 'right' to such concepts as 'duty' or 'permission' or 'entitlement';[4] and also in contrast to a taxonomic account—one concerned, as Hohfeld's was, with cataloging the different types of legal or moral relations that rights consist in.[5] A substantive theory overlaps these other theories, but it is unlike them in being mainly concerned with the content of the concept, with its criteria. And it does not just tell us, as some philosophers have usefully done,[6] the characteristics in virtue of which individuals are bearers of rights. It would also tell us why those characteristics justify the ascription of rights to them, and what else, if anything, does, and how, if at all, our present criteria might be improved.

2. First Ground: Personhood

If there are such things as human rights, then they are rights we have independently of laws, conventions, or special moral relations. Therefore, it is likely that their substantive theory will draw on, although also modify, elements from the natural rights tradition, and will go something like this.[7] Choosing one's own course through life, making something of value out of it by one's own lights, is what makes one's existence human. If we value our humanity, we will value what makes life human, over and above what makes it happy. Now, the freedom that makes life human is not a simple thing. The distinction between positive and negative freedom is by now familiar to us, but perhaps the systematic way to study all the complexities of freedom is to study the complexities of 'agency'. One component of agency is deciding for oneself. Even if I constantly made a mess of my life, even if you could convince me that if you managed my utility portfolio (on the usual understanding of 'utility') you would do a much better job than I am doing, I would not let you do it. Autonomy has a value of its own. But autonomy, on its own, is not enough. It is not enough to be able to choose one's path through life if one cannot move. One needs limbs and senses that work, or something to take their place. But that is not enough either; it is no good being able to choose and having the capacity to act, if one is so racked by pain or by the need to keep body and soul together that one cannot spare a thought for anything else. We surely also need some minimum health and leisure. Nor is this enough if others then stop us; we need liberty. We need other people not to interfere in those areas of our life that are the essential manifestations of our humanity— namely, our speech and associations and worship. Nor is this quite enough; it is not enough not to be fenced in, if we are unable to form any conception of where to go. We also need a mind capable of assessing things, which means that we need some minimum education and access to people worth hearing or reading.

This personhood consideration, to give it a not unfamiliar name, goes some way towards making the notion of a human right more determinate. It generates most of the conventional list of civil rights: a right to life, to bodily integrity, to some voice in political decision, to free speech, to assembly, to a free press, to worship. It also lends support to a form of positive freedom, namely, to a right to a minimum material provision.[8] And it says something about the extent of liberty: as far as the personhood ground goes, only a narrow liberty finds support; the right to liberty is not to do whatever fancy prompts (so that *any* restriction on satisfaction of desires is *some* restriction on liberty) but only, more narrowly, to do what is essential to living a human life.[9] It also provides a right not to be tortured, because torture aims at destroying one's capacity to decide and to stick to the decision.

We say that personhood concerns what is needed for human *status*, but it is tempting to be more generous and say that it concerns what is needed for human *flourishing*. Yet which should we say? What makes it so easy to shift between the two notions, *human* life and *good* human life, is the difficulty of knowing where to separate them. But it seems that the minimalist notion is the one that the philosophical tradition, with reason, supports. If we had rights to all that is necessary for the good life, rights would be too extensive. We should then have a right not just to a minimum material provision, but to any unsubstitutable component of a better life. If this were the way that the tradition regarded rights, then we should obscure the distinction, with no obvious compensation, between, on the one hand, what enhances well-being and, on the other, what rights demand.

However, the personhood ground, despite its importance, may easily lead us to underplay the dynamic side of life. For instance, we know that a person can be oppressed, can even be shipped off to the Gulag

Archipelago, and yet, because oppressors are not perfectly efficient, not only retain his autonomy and creativity but find them enhanced. But one who is oppressed can still ask of his oppressor, 'Who is *he* to have such control over me, whether it makes me or breaks me?' Rights, it would seem, must also secure the distribution of control over the central features of one's fate. Every responsible person must be granted control over certain matters affecting him. What is crucial is not just (human) status, but also control. The right to control the center is a strong form of negative liberty. Liberty is the absence of barriers to living out one's life plan. In its weak form, one is at liberty if, for whatever reason, one can live by one's life plan, as someone still can who has a form of life imposed upon him which, by luck, suits. But in its strong form, one is at liberty only if one could have lived by one's life plan, even if it had been different. The ground for the strong form of liberty is not obvious, but personhood must in any case be some of it. A person's values are not static; and fences that do not block now may block later. So personhood requires a strong enough form of liberty to guarantee the movement characteristic of human development. That still does not guarantee complete control of the center; it is not so strong a form of liberty as to stop a paternalist from arguing that his short-term violation of someone's control of his own life will make him freer in the long run. But the plausibility of a paternalist's claim has to be assessed. Given human limitations, how likely is it that a paternalist will deliver the goods? But now the justification for strong liberty is beginning to shift from personhood to practicalities, which probably deserve to be regarded as a ground on their own.

3. Second Ground: Practicalities

The personhood consideration leaves a lot unsettled. For one thing, it says that there is a right to *some* political voice. Yet how much? And what, too, is the *minimum* material provision? When life expectancy reaches 40? Or would it have to be 60? And what is *minimum* education? Literacy? Or would it have to be the ability to ponder the meaning of life? And we have, it says, *some* sort of right to bodily integrity, because without security of body we have no security of action. But, to raise Nozick's question, does this right bar a state's forcibly taking my kidney for transplant? Does it then bar a very accommodating state from demanding a pint of my rare blood that, it says, it will take in my own house while I sleep and leave me to wake the next morning as fit as ever?

Well, certainly it is no good expecting the personhood consideration to protect me against such an accommodating state, which threatens nothing essential to my human status. But there are practical considerations that are obviously relevant here. A line has to be drawn somewhere; the personhood consideration shows that much. And people and governments are not scrupulous, and are prone to domination and self-serving. Moreover, the line has to be clear and, for safety's sake, at some remove from the vitals. I can, it is true, still lead a human existence if the state takes one of my kidneys, but one might well fear that the chances of doing so in such an all-controlling and interventionist state would be slim. Whatever the result of this line of thought, there is no doubting the relevance of this *kind* of consideration. On any account of rights, I should think, practicalities play a large part in determining their final shape.

4. Third Ground: The Private Sphere

Personhood supplies only the weightiest sort of reason for rights, the survival of one's human status. However, Mill thought that whether something, weighty or light, falls within one's private sphere also counts. How I dress or part my hair is hardly central to my living a human existence. Still, it is *my* business: even if what I wear annoys and distresses you, surely I am within my rights dressing as I please.

Is the private sphere, then, a further ground for human rights? Personhood yields a right not to a general liberty but only to certain specific liberties. Mill, however, proposed that liberty should extend to whatever we wish to do, so long as it does not harm others. The harm test allowed him to define a self-regarding, or private, class of actions. But there are problems with Mill's broad conception of liberty. First, it lacks any clear value supporting it. Our status as persons is clearly valuable to us, but control over what is merely private is far less obviously so. Second, the justifications of the broad conception of liberty that carry weight, Mill's own for instance, seem really to be an elaboration of the old personhood ground rather than the provision of a new ground. Stopping me from wearing the clothes I want, as inessential as any particular set of clothes may seem to be to my human standing, certainly touches my self-respect. The idea of a person that we have already made appeal to is of a self-determiner. But to deny me freedom to express my own tastes does threaten my status as self-determiner. Exactly which clothes I choose may be trivial, but my status as an independent center of taste and choice is not.

In the interest of keeping the concept of a right as sharp as possible, one might want to keep the personhood ground as narrow as possible—

the absolutely minimum conditions for carrying out a life plan. If so, a right to dress as I please would not be supported by it. On the other hand, one might want to make it a bit more capacious—what is necessary for human dignity. One loses some sharpness with the extension, but one ought to keep in mind that, in any case, the narrow notion would not itself be especially sharp anyway. It turns on what is *central* to human status and what is *necessary* for carrying out a life plan, and what is central or necessary is essentially moot, and can itself be seen narrowly or broadly. So, in any case, there will have to be a lot of not very sharp-edged debate about these moot matters, largely in terms of practicalities, in order to fix the boundaries of rights. The loss, therefore, from adopting the slightly more capacious conception is not great. And the gain is a notion of liberty that is more in accord with the philosophical tradition, yet that still has a ground of some substance. This ground, although not as circumscribed as it might be, is not so extensive as to give us, as Mill thought we had, a right to general liberty. Mill focused on the private domain when it seems better to focus on one's status as a self-determiner. And some things that are 'self-regarding' are also too remote from one's being self-determining to be protected by this slightly more capacious conception.

5. Fourth Ground: Equal Regard

There is another consideration, very much to the fore lately,[10] that seems different from any of the preceding ones: namely, the moral significance of the separateness of persons. It takes a great deal of work to see what this consideration amounts to. It looks like a positive principle, but turns out not to be. It is explicit about what it does not like, but thoroughly vague on what it likes. The clearest thing about it is that it is anti-utilitarian. Utilitarian thought proceeds by the simple device of trading off goods and bads by their magnitude, paying no attention to whether the trade-off occurs within one life or between different lives. It is just this particular lack of attention that invites the rejoinders: one person may not be sacrificed, without limit, for the good of others; the well-being of one person cannot simply be replaced by that of another. Yet to say that it cannot *simply* be replaced implies that sometimes it can and sometimes it cannot. And to say that one person may not be sacrificed *without limit* implies that sacrifices are allowed but only up to a point. Each suggests a line but does not supply it. And it is not that we can expect rights to supply it, because this consideration is meant to be a more fundamental one from which rights are derived.

It might be hoped that the separateness consideration can be made more determinate through the idea of contracting. If persons have first to agree with one another, then each can exercise a veto in his own interest, and a veto seems the ideal instrument for expressing the separateness of persons. But we must give the contracting situation concrete shape, for instance, to decide upon what degree of ignorance to impose upon the contractors, in order to be sure that it will indeed express the separateness of persons. There are several different contracting situations. Which captures the right conception of separateness? It would help to have some rough independent idea of what that is.

I think that the way forward lies along these lines. One cannot sacrifice a person without limit because each of us has only one life, and each person's fate matters and matters equally. So we may take the separateness consideration as being, in effect, some form of a principle of equality, not a principle requiring equal treatment (say, meting out equal portions of resources), but that different and altogether deeper matter of treating people as equals, of showing them equal regard. Thus, the limit on trade-offs that the separateness consideration desiderates will be the limit imposed by equal regard. But what is that? Equal regard is a little less indeterminate than the separateness of persons, but is still notoriously indeterminate itself. Does equal regard require (i) merely equal weight ('everybody to count for one, nobody for more than one' in the way that utilitarians mean), or (ii) a minimum level of welfare, above which obligations cease, or (iii) an equal start with equal prospects, after which inequalities resulting from just transactions are themselves to be regarded as just, or (iv) equal goods, except when inequalities work to the advantage of the worst off, that is, Rawls' maximin, or (v) equal goods with equal prospects, or (vi) equal welfare, or (vii) equal opportunity? I know that many people believe that the use of notions such as 'the separateness of persons' and 'treating people as ends' is precisely to choose between those competing principles of equal regard. But this is to try to choose between these principles by appeal to notions so vague that they can be given content only by the choice between these principles. Nor can we remedy the vagueness by trying further to plumb the depths of our intuitions about either equality or separateness or respect for persons, because intuitions are superficial things. There will be no depths until we choose them and put them there. What we need is a well worked out theory of equality; such a theory would, at the same time, give content to all these notions.

However, if the indeterminateness is overcome in this way, and, as I suspect, one of the more demanding principles of equality emerges — say, for the sake of argument, maximin or equal welfare or equal resources — then equal regard constitutes a new ground for rights.

Personhood requires, among other things, minimum provision. Practicalities may lead us to define the minimum fairly generously. But equal regard requires something stronger than either: some qualified form or other of equal share.

The only reason to doubt that equal regard is a new ground for rights is that it may turn out to be reducible to the personhood ground, or *vice versa*. There is a long philosophical tradition which has it that, a few difficult marginal cases aside, we are all possessors of human standing and hence of human worth. Clearly we differ in the degree that we possess the various features that constitute human standing—for example, in our capacity for autonomy, rationality, evaluation, and action. But, according to this tradition, the notions of personhood and moral worth do not admit of degrees; anyone inside the boundary, no matter how far inside, is equally inside. If, in the end, it is this equal possession of human standing that is the ground of all rights, then it is not clear whether equal regard reduces to personhood, or personhood to equal regard, or each is only part of another, deeper ground that combines both. But the notion of equal regard is far too obscure to allow us to settle the matter now. So, until we have a theory of equality that makes the notion more determinate, it is best for the time being to treat it as a separate ground.

6. What Rights Does the Substantive Theory Yield?

These then seem to me the three elements of a substantive theory of human rights: personhood, practicalities, and equal regard. (The privacy ground, the fourth possible ground I considered, is best thought of as a development of the notion of personhood.)

Do these three grounds yield the human rights that moral theory needs? I have suggested that, in some form or other, they yield rights to life, to bodily integrity, not to be tortured, to autonomy, to the central civil liberties, to minimum provision, to a strong form of liberty (that is, to sovereignty at the center of one's life, so for instance, I think that it could be plausibly be argued, to sexual freedom and possibly, although less easily argued, to freedom to drink and take drugs), and finally to some form of equal share (that is, share in what makes a good life possible: although whether the equality is to be, for instance, only at some starting point or as far as possible continuously, and whether it is equality in opportunities or resources or need-satisfaction or desire-satisfaction, are all questions that the well worked out theory of equality will have to settle). And the equal share is not only a share in material goods but also in the powers and opportunities that matter just as much to a good life, and so it requires that advantages be open to all and that no advantages be denied without due process.

We have also seen, however, how much these three grounds leave indeterminate. Take, for example, the right to privacy. Is it a human right?[11] What are its boundaries? The personhood consideration would yield a right to whatever privacy is necessary to human standing: whatever privacy is needed for the thought and communication that go into forming one's life plan, whatever privacy is needed in developing the personal commitments central to one's life plan. But that, it must be admitted, is not a very extensive right. What, for instance, does it tell us about the invasions of privacy that worry us now: phone-tapping, electronic eavesdropping, access to one's medical or financial records? The only resources that the three grounds supply at this point are various tangled practical considerations. Why do governments want to tap phones? Which is now the greater danger—public intrusion in private life or private subversion of public life? What is at stake in debates about modern intrusions on privacy is a certain sort of power, and if nowadays the greater threat is from government power, and if the threat is great enough to undermine one's life plan, protection should go to individuals. But this sort of argument is not timelessly valid; it allows the possibility that at other times, in other circumstances, the powers should go elsewhere. In general, it would mean that, to the extent that practical considerations determine the boundaries of rights, they are subject to periodic redrawing. But I suspect that practical considerations are, at this point, all that we have to go on. And since practical considerations enter into the determination of virtually every human right, human rights have neither sharp nor fixed edges.[12]

Another important consequence of this account is that rights have more narrow boundaries than convention says. There is no general right to liberty, but only rights to specific liberties. There is no right to say or publish what one wants, not even a *prima facie* right subject to limitation by conflict with other rights, but merely a right to express what matters to the center of one's life. There is no broad right to determine what happens in and to one's body, only a limited right to the bodily integrity necessary to carry through one's central aims, where the boundary of the 'center' is essentially moot.

7. The Need for a Second Level to the Substantive Theory

Rights are linked to such values as autonomy, liberty, and equal regard. The substantive theory suggests that they are to be seen as protections of these values and so seen within a generally instrumental or teleological framework. That constitutes the first level in a substantive theory: showing in what rights are grounded. But, unfortunately, that does not yet get us very far towards understanding the structure of rights, for the teleological framework need not be utilitarian, nor even consequentialist. Autonomy and liberty are, on the face of it, not utilitarian values at all, and equal regard is less a consequence of respecting the corresponding right than a value the content of which is itself best expressed in terms of the right. And we need answers to many questions. Do rights conflict with one another? How can we settle conflicts? May rights be traded off against each other? Against utility? Do rights differ in relative importance? How is importance estimated? Are any rights absolute? Should we aim at maximizing the observance of rights? Can rights be forfeited, or diminished, by wrong-doing?

These questions raise parallel questions about the values to which the rights are linked. Do these values conflict? Can they be reduced to one value, or to one metric? Are they all the sort of values that we should seek to maximize? All of these questions, whether about rights or values, are unavoidable and require a second and deeper level of explanation. The first level in a substantive theory is concerned with how rights are grounded in values. But the second has to establish the character of the values themselves.[13]

8. Utility

So I turn now to the second level of a substantive theory, the investigation of the nature and structure of the values that rights protect. I want to consider just three of them: autonomy, liberty, and equal regard. I consider just these three not because I believe that all rights can be derived from them alone; on the contrary, there is much more to the personhood ground than just autonomy and liberty, and I omit the practicalities ground altogether. I take these three simply as examples for closer study. But to them one must add utility, with which I shall start.

Utility is best explained, I believe, not in terms of states of mind such as pleasure, but in terms of satisfaction of desire, where 'satisfaction' is meant without psychological overtones and implies merely that what is desired comes about. The desires that are relevant on this account are not only people's actual ones but also those they would have if they understood the nature of possible objects of desire; a person's own conception of what is in his interest, therefore, is not definitive. We should need, of course, some way of determining what a person's utility is, when his actual and these informed desires conflict, and that, though difficult, is possible. But the preference account of utility need not be wedded to any narrow Humean account of the opposition of reason and desire; it need not accept a Humean account of action or of the ground of moral obligation. It can agree with certain modern critics of utilitarianism that deliberation can be of ends as well as means. Nor should it be wedded to a simple-minded program of maximizing the number or the proportion of desires satisfied, as if all desires were on one level. Desires have a structure, a structure that comes from appreciating the nature and range of one's options. This appreciation yields not only local desires (say, for a drink) but also higher-order desires (to distance oneself from material desires) and global desires (to lead a certain kind of life). And any maximizing program would have to consider strength of desires, not 'strength' in the sense of felt intensity or motivational force, but in the sense of their place in an informed preference order, especially the order given them by global desires.

This interpretation has an important consequence. 'Utility' is not to be seen as the single overarching value, in fact, not as a substantive value at all, but instead as a formal analysis of what it is for something to be prudentially valuable. Therefore, utility will be related to substantive values, such as autonomy or liberty, not by being the dominant value that subsumes them, but by being an analysis of, and the related suggestion of a metric for, any prudential value. It should be seen as providing a way of understanding the notions '(prudentially) valuable' and hence 'more valuable' and 'less valuable'. Utility, therefore, is not what it is about objects that makes them desirable. What makes us desire the things we desire is something about them—their features or qualities. Making 'utility', in this way, a formal notion may seem to make it otiose. Why bother with informed desires when after all we can go directly to what it is about objects that shape the informed desires in the first place? But the notion of 'utility', although purely formal, is not otiose: it has clarity and scope that talk about particular substantive values, or desirability-characterizations, or reasons for action lacks.

That, anyway, is not an uncommon account of 'utility'; it seems to me the best account and the one that nowadays we have to come to terms with.[14]

9. Autonomy

The values that back rights—for example, the three values that I have singled out, autonomy, liberty, and equal regard—seem clearly to fall outside the ambit of utility. Now sometimes, at least, that is because the notion of utility in use is too narrow and would have seemed too narrow quite apart from this issue. Consider autonomy first. Would you, for greater serenity, surrender your autonomy? If you understand what is at stake, then unless the pain of autonomy is in your case very great, no doubt you will prefer autonomy. On the face of it, that preference can be brought within the ambit of utility. What reasons might one have for thinking that the value of autonomy is not the sort of value that utility represents? One thing that would show it is our deciding that autonomy is of absolute value, value greater than any utilitarian values. But few of us believe that; most of us think that there could come a point, say with a psychiatric patient, at which autonomy was so painful as to justify reducing it. Or, secondly, one might instead decide that the value of autonomy, while not absolute, is not given by its place in informed desires either, in other words, that reflectively wanting to be autonomous and recognizing its value to one can be at variance. But what then would one say is the difference between them? When, for instance, would trade-offs sanctioned by these different views of the value of autonomy diverge? It is hard to find examples, and that suggests that autonomy falls largely within the ambit of utility.

10. Liberty

Liberty, especially the strong sort of freedom to do not only what one in fact chooses but also what one might have chosen, seems a clear non-utilitarian value. It concerns distribution of power, not distribution of utility, even on the formal interpretation of utility, because what is distributed here is not what constitutes the value or significance of quality of life. It goes beyond quality of life to considerations of control: every responsible person must be granted control over matters that crucially affect him. This is the point that John Mackie makes in arguing that, if we understand goals properly, we see that they are less theoretically deep than rights:[15]

> A plausible goal, or good for man, would have to be something like Aristotle's *eudaimonia*: it would be in the category of activity. It could not be just an end, a possession, a termination of pursuit. . . . But Aristotle went wrong in thinking that moral philosophy could determine that a particular sort of activity constitutes the good for man in general. . . . People differ radically about the kinds of life that they choose to pursue. Even this way of putting it is misleading: in general people do not and cannot make an overall choice of a total plan of life. . . . I suggest that if we set out to formulate a goal-based moral theory, but in identifying the goal try to take adequate account of these three factors, namely that the 'goal' must belong to the category of activity, that

there is not one goal but indefinitely many diverse goals, and that they are the objects of progressive (not once-for-all or conclusive) choices, then our theory will change insensibly into a right-based one. We shall have to take as central the right of persons progressively to choose how they shall live.

All that Mackie says about goals seems to me true, but no stopping point. It is not likely that control would be valued for itself; it is valuable because of the value of what can be controlled. If others were to intrude but only at the very periphery of one's life, the power to repel the intrusions would not matter much. If the intrusion were at the center but were motivated, for instance as with some surgical intrusions, by an uncontentious and beneficial aim and carried out by sure techniques, again the power would not matter much. However, in the real world, intentions of intruders rarely are honorable, or values agreed, or techniques sure. So, in the real world, power at the center of one's life matters immensely. But its value derives from the value of the whole way of life at stake.

Mackie's argument is that since what is valuable in life is a kind of activity, a way of life, and since conceptions of the good life are diverse and developing, liberty must be 'central'. But liberty's being 'central' in this sense is compatible with its being derivative. Mackie's argument is meant also to establish that liberty is not part of a more fundamental teleological structure, but that is what it does not do. Certainly the fact that what is valuable in life falls under the category of activity would establish this only if an activity could never be a goal. But it can. It can even, on a proper conception, be something that has utility. 'Socrates dissatisfied' describes not a state at the end of activity, but a way of life. The fact that a person's conception of a valuable life changes and matures does not suggest that a right to liberty is in some important way more basic than goals. It suggests only that no *one* goal may be permanent or authoritative. But it is that we have goals, that we have the chance of making our life valuable, which gives value to the right to liberty. So, contrary to what Mackie suggests, it is not the right to liberty that is basic but the valuable life, *on some conception or other*. And the valuable life is basic in just the sense that Mackie tells us he has in mind: it captures what it is that gives point to the rest of the moral structure.

There is another reason that might lead one to think that liberty is a non-utilitarian value. Utilitarians, Mill for example, have claimed that we ought to respect liberty because, if we are at all wise to the ways of the world, we shall realize that paternalism is largely counter-productive and that in the long run general welfare is best served by strict noninterference.[16] All that is true, but many find it, with reason, a lame defense of liberty. Liberty, they would plausibly insist, is itself valuable, valuable apart from this link with utility. But when one spells this out sufficiently, one merely discovers a new link with utility. We value our status as persons and want to live recognizably human lives, and liberty is an indispensable condition for that. But then liberty, like autonomy, can be fitted into the scheme of our preferences, and its value explained by its place there. So there is more than one kind of link with utility. It is a mistake to move from liberty's being valuable in itself to the conclusion that utility does not encompass it. Using the formal notion of utility does not commit one to monism in values. One can value many different things, and value them not for any state of mind that they result in, but for themselves: leading a certain sort of life, having a certain sort of relation with people, being a certain kind of person.

Liberty seems, then, best understood as belonging to a teleological structure. Whether the ends of that structure, the valued ways of life, can be brought within the ambit of utility is contentious. But the contention is between conceptions of prudential value. Nothing that has so far entered the story about rights rules it out.

11. Equal Regard

Equality is a very different kind of value from the others. Unlike autonomy and liberty, which focus in a way on one life, equality focuses on the comparison of lives. It has to do with the weighing of different people's claims. It is not a prudential value at all; it is a moral value, in a way *the* moral value. So equality presents the best case for saying that rights are grounded in more than just prudential values.

Yet when we survey principles of equality, we are faced with an *embarras de choix*. I mentioned earlier seven perfectly familiar principles, and there are still more. So our first job is to make the notion of equal regard more determinate. Now when one reflects on these various principles of equality, one sees that some belong on different levels; they are not, after all, competitors but principles about different things. For instance, there is the most fundamental level, at which equality is to be seen as an interpretation of *impartiality*—that sort of impartiality that constitutes the moral point of view. We all agree that to look at things morally is look at them, in some sense or other, impartially, granting every person some sort of equal status. One well-known way of specifying this impartiality is by the device of an Ideal Observer: the moral point of view, on this conception, is a benevolent view from a god-like position above the fray, granting everyone equal weight. This can easily turn into the utilitarian conception of maximizing welfare, counting everybody for one. Rawls, of course, thinks that it merely turns into an undesirable impersonality and not the true impartiality of the moral point of view, which he sees as captured by a different device, the device of the Ideal Contractor: the moral point of view is the view of equal contractors from behind the Veil of Ignorance. And there are other competitors on this level. In any case, principles of *equality* can be principles of *impartiality* in this sense: they can express the spirit with which one will, if one is moral, consider the facts of the matter.

Then there is a second level, the level of substantive moral principles resulting from applying first-level principles to facts. For instance, Rawls derives, from his Original Position, his two principles of justice.[17] One should not overdo the sharpness of the distinction between these two levels. They have some distance from one another, simply because one can dispute, for instance, whether the Original Position yields maximin or average utilitarianism, and also whether the Ideal Observer's position does produce utilitarianism. But, still, these levels are not all that distinct. The principles on the first level are extremely vague, and the principles on the second level often provide necessary content for these rather empty conceptions of impartiality. There is a further wrinkle: even on this second level there are different *kinds* of principles generated that can reasonably claim to be principles of equality. There are, for instance, theories of rights that see people as possessors of equal basic protections and entitlements. There are also theories of distribution of resources that might, for instance, say that resources themselves should be equal, or that their welfare pay-off should be equal.

Then there is a third level of principles simplified for action on the social scale, where knowledge is short and justice rough. For example, a utilitarian might adopt a principle of equal resources, because on the level of social policy one cannot consult individual utility functions or hope effectively to control utility levels by manipulating shares of resources.

Hence, equality is a multi-level and, within a level, multi-dimensional notion. This is not surprising: equality is merely a formal notion (sameness of some feature), and sameness of different features matters in moral theory.

Now how do principles on these different levels support rights? Third-level principles, being rough rules of thumb, would support rights that were themselves only rough rules of thumb and so rights of a kind less strong than we are interested in now. First-level principles, on the other hand, principles that in effect express the moral point of view, would support perhaps too strong a kind of right. John Mackie and others think that they provide the one absolute human right, namely, a right to equal respect in the procedures that determine the compromises and adjustments between all the other, non-absolute rights.[18] But the doubt here is whether this is too much the whole of morality to be anything as specific as a right. It is absolute because it is moral standing itself, and morality can never recommend suspending the moral point of view. But whether or not it is best to regard this as a right, it is the principles of the second level that are the promising candidates for what we normally regard as human rights, and it is on them that I want to concentrate.

The competing principles on the second level provide rival ways of fixing the moral point of view. Some, as we have seen, seek to express the moral significance of the separateness of persons. Others give expression to the demands of everybody's counting for one in utility calculations. What they are all concerned with is what is permitted in the way of trade-offs between prudential values. They are all views about rights and distribution. The idea that certain of those principles are distributive while others are aggregative is an unfortunate contemporary muddle. No plausible principle of equal regard—think of Rawls' Difference Principle—could be purely distributive, without aggregative element, as if reducing everyone to the same level of misery could satisfy it. Every plausible principle of equality is based on the thought that everyone matters and matters equally, and to stress only formal features of distribution is to remember the *equally* but to forget the *matters*. Nor is the principle of utility aggregative, without distributive component; it represents another conception of the distribution that equal regard for persons requires. What we need are reasons for and against accepting it as, what it clearly is, a guide to distribution.

This also shows why we must pay attention to trade-offs. What is common to all conceptions of equal regard is the belief that *some* sacrifices of one person for another are permissible, but that a limit is imposed by everyone's equal status as moral persons. Well, what limit? To explain that is to explain our conception of moral status. And to explain it demands going beyond such edifying but empty formulas as 'no person may be sacrificed without limit' or 'respect for persons', which, like the characterizations of first-level principles (equal voice in an Ideal Contract, equal weight in the calculations of the Ideal Observer), leave so much undetermined that nothing can be got out of them until more is put into them. And the most promising way to do this is to use second-level principles as their further determination.

The way to fix the second level is to fix the principles restricting trade-offs.[19] One model is this: there is a line outside of which trade-offs are not allowed, a line that defines one's unbargainable personhood. Suppose one proposed the generous line supplied by maximin: the worst off to be as well off as possible. But if for the moment we allow ourselves to be guided by our intuitions, this is not a line we should long defend. Maximin, intuition tells us, has exceptions; rich societies in which the worst off are well off do, on the face of it quite reasonably, allocate resources—to art, for instance—in a way that further benefits the well off. Suppose then, to accommodate this, one redrew the line so that it prevented *sacrifices* of one person for another already better off, disastrous drops in welfare or, at least, drops to dismally low levels. But the French government knows that some people, through no fault of their own, die each year in automobile accidents because of the beautiful roadside avenues of trees, but it does not cut them down. So we do allow trade-offs between the common good and disastrous drops, even when the drop is as disastrous as death and the good is merely more aesthetic pleasure. Suppose, therefore, that one concluded that neither of these lines would do and that one looked for something weaker. Amartya Sen once formulated what he meant to be close to an absolutely minimum requirement, what he called the Weak Equity Axiom, which goes: if one person is a less good utility producer than another, say because he is handicapped, so that at any level of goods he is less well off, then he must be given *something* more than the other.[20] One might even make the requirement weaker still: the unfortunate one must not be given less, if he is below and the more fortunate one already above a minimum acceptable level of welfare. But these 'weak' requirements are still too strong. Surgeons, in choosing between patients for a kidney transplant, are often guided by a patient's prospects. If Jones has been chronically ill, below the minimum acceptable level for most of his life, with poor prospects of surviving long after an operation, and Smith, never as ill, has good prospects, Smith may be the one to be operated on.[21]

Intuitions, therefore, go against the model of an uncrossable line. Another model is this: there is no line that is the cut-off for trade-offs; there is instead a moral counterforce. In this model we fall back on the familiar structure of equipollent principles: say, a principle of welfare maximization sanctioning trade-offs and a principle of equal welfare restricting them, with sometimes the one and sometimes the other winning out in conflict. In the earlier case, the surgeons could help Smith, who is better off, a lot and Jones, the worse off, only negligibly; and it is obviously this great disparity that points toward their helping the one who is better off. So let us change the story: make the disparity less great. Smith, we shall say, is an otherwise healthy man of sixty who with a transplant will live another ten years; Jones is chronically ill man of thirty who with a transplant will live about another five years. Smith, we are strongly inclined to think, has had a fairly good go at life, and although his prognosis is better than Jones', the pull towards leveling the balance is obvious. The benefit to Jones is less but not negligible, and he has had, and will at the end of his life still have had, so much less than Smith has already had.

But if intuitions are to guide us, why should we stop there? Why not a policy of the more the better? We ought to exercise our intuitions on more cases with just the features that in the last case seemed decisive against a purely utilitarian trade-off. Suppose Jones were a six-year-old child with prospect of five more years, and Smith twelve years old with prospect of ten. Yet now intuition favors Smith. What if Jones were fifteen with five more years, and Smith thirty with ten? Now intuition is probably baffled. So, if intuitions are to guide us and, contrary to common practice, we consult a wide enough selection of them, they do not support this second model either.

Neither of these models is, on the testimony of intuitions, satisfactory. Nor, on the same testimony, is the utilitarian model. It is easy, altogether too easy, to announce attractive-sounding principles. But if one collected the trade-offs that fairly wide-spread intuitions support, and if one took the task seriously enough to collect a large number of them over a wide range of cases, this 'undisputed set of trade-offs', so to speak, would undermine every proposal that moral philosophy has yet produced of principles governing trade-offs. This is not fatal to them, but it certainly shows how far we are from having any satisfactory arguments on the subject.[22]

It shows too how far we are from having an adequate method of argument. The common method in normative ethics is piecemeal appeal to intuition. Recently, Richard Brandt[23] and Richard Hare[24] have argued, with deadly effect, that this method is not allowable, that intuitions on their own have no probative force. Intuitions are merely the attitudes, feelings, dispositions, inclinations that have been shaped largely, if not entirely, by social pressures, contingencies of personality development charted by depth psychology, and the like. Even if some intuitions have more respectable epistemological ancestry, inspection does not reveal which are the ones with respectable ancestors. Therefore, in the case of conflict between intuition and theory, there is no obvious sign of which should give way. Now, Brandt and Hare each draw a heroic conclusion from this: we must totally renounce appeal to intuition; and each offers his own very different proposals of an alternative method. The danger in the heroic stance is that many will find it untenable and therefore slip back into the old ways of piecemeal appeal to intuition, for lack of better. But there is better — for instance, some loose analog of Karl Popper's procedure in the natural sciences. Since we do not know by inspection whether a moral theory or a conflicting intuition is to be discarded, we must spread out theory as wide as possible and beyond the bounds just of morality, collect the potentially most embarrassing intuitions for any part of the theoretical structure, put intuitions under pressure by uncovering their origins, be innovative with theory, and modify sometimes intuition and sometimes theory until they are in balance. This is somewhat like Rawl's proposal for reaching reflective equilibrium,[25] but not exactly it, and not his practice in *A Theory of Justice*.

The most promising direction in which to look for the desiderated wide theory would seem to be this. We should look for a theory that allows trade-off between rights (and the values behind them) and between those rights and mere utilities, with no absolute rights except perhaps for an especially basic right to moral status. It would be a theory, therefore, that provided a technique for weighing these values, both within one life and between different lives, for both sorts of trade-offs are probably to be allowed. The principles governing these trade-offs are hard to see, but the common anti-utilitarianism of today — that, say, of Rawls, Nozick, Dworkin, and Sen — is based on assumptions that seem unpromising; at least; their attractiveness disappears once they are faced with 'the undisputed set of trade-offs'. And in view of this, some sort of very broadly utilitarian restriction on trade-offs seems again worth serious investigation.

The deeply troubling doubt about the utilitarian restriction is that it simply transfers the structure of intrapersonal trades to interpersonal ones. Does Mr. White's justified willingness to surrender some liberty now for his own greater liberty later also justify his losing the liberty for Mr. Black's greater liberty? And if it did, White might lose out not only in this trade to Black but, for similar reason, in another to Grey and another to Brown. Should we accept the cumulative effect of these trades even if, should things fall out awkwardly, they built up into something disastrous for White? But these doubts are ones we have already encountered. A typical non-utilitarian reaction to them is to propose a tougher standard of justification in trade-offs: namely, justification as compensation. White's later gain justifies *for him* his present loss. If the later gain goes to Black, then nothing justifies White's loss to White. Perhaps it is this conception of justification and this interpretation of the moral importance of the difference between intrapersonal and interpersonal trades that lies behind giving self-interest central place in the characterization of the moral point of view: for example, the way Rawls does with his Ideal Contractor, who, while not selfish, is rationally concerned to protect his own interests. But then to get an Ideal Contractor to contract at all, and at the same time to get the necessary degree of impartiality into the moral point of view, we have to build into it blindness to one's actual lot. But this characterization of the moral point of view can give us only a very limited number of answers. It may tell us about a few general arrangements for large-scale social groups — for example, that we should go for maximin. But with anything special or on slightly smaller scale — for example, the ill or risky social schemes, such as risks on roads or with health services, in which some will pay dearly — it would give distorted answers: if self-concern prompts the same extreme play-safe policy, very many trades that most of us think acceptable would be prohibited. Using self-concern as the theoretical device for introducing protection of individuals does seem a mistake. It seems, like Sen's Weak Equity Axiom, far too strong. It seems, therefore, that we should try to get protection of the individual into morality through a more flexible device.

Of course, as such anti-utilitarian restrictions on trades seem unpromisingly strong, the utilitarian restriction is bound to seem unpromisingly weak. We seem to need either to loosen the former or to tighten the latter. Here, too, I can offer only a speculation. There are restrictions in utilitarian value theory that, because of underdevelopment of the theory, have not begun to be appreciated. We have still to understand, and to work out, how radical the consequences are of the shift from a hedonist to a formal conception of utility. Since utility is not itself a substantive prudential value, it is the nature of those values that are that determines the structure of informed desires. Thus, there is nothing in the formal conception of utility that rules out one value's being incommensurable with another, in one sense of that highly equivocal expression — viz., that no amount of it could outweigh a certain amount of another.[26] There may be certain inflexibilities in prudential value theory that would therefore get transferred to a metric of utilities. If I had a friend prodigiously shrewd and overflowing with savoir faire who could save me a dozen minor false turns if he took over the management of my life, I should still value my autonomy so highly that I would not contemplate surrendering it. But what if he could save me, not a dozen, but a hundred minor false turns? But the trouble is this: minor false turns do not seem weighty enough, even in large aggregates, at least the aggregates that life presents us with, to balance the value of living life autonomously. Some things might indeed be weighty enough — great pain or anxiety, for instance, but minor false turns are not. Not even a thousand—someone might press—or ten thousand? But now the problem is to get one's mind around the question. If one's life contained a huge number of false turns—one right after the other—they would scarcely leave space for anything to go right; they would be a pretty good indication that something else, far more serious, was wrong. Or consider another case, liberty. Can the value of a person's being free to live what he regards as the only life of substance and significance open to him be equaled by the upset or distress that his doing so might cause others? Well, Mill has plausibly argued that upset and distress are simply not in the same league as a person's making something out of his life. The stakes are so different that, given the world as we know it, not even large aggregates of persons upset and distressed, hundreds of them or thousands, come into the same league. If it were a matter of some minor liberty, say one's liberty to bathe nude, one would expect upset and distress, if there were enough of it, to match the value of the liberty. But if it is one's most major liberty at stake—to live out one's life plan—why believe that life presents us with aggregates of upset and distress that will, judged simply on the values accounted for in a prudential theory of value, match it?

What all of this may indicate is that our moral notion of equality has fragmented. On the deepest level, on the level at which one does the ultimate and most authoritative weighing up of one person's fate against another's, trade-offs are allowed that these restrictive anti-utilitarian principles would block.

Yet perhaps these restrictive principles should really be given a different position in moral theory, on a less deep and authoritative level. Human rights mark the moral protections of our equal claims as persons. I wonder whether this second conception of equality, as protections due each individual, is at the base of several different weak (that is, overridable) principles of equality. First, it gives support to a principle of equal resources—for example, like Dworkin's;[27] it does not matter how admirable our individual conception of the good may be, what is to be protected is our living a human existence. And to protect that means protecting one person's capacity to live out his life plan just as much as another's. And this is a case for giving some place to a principle of equal resources.

There seems also to be a place, on the same level at which we admit a principle of equal resources, for a principle of equal welfare. Each person matters and matters equally, not just in the protection of his status as a person but also in how valuable his life actually turns out to be. It would be a waste to deny extra to someone who, through no fault of his own, had aspirations that were expensive in resources and who lived in a society in which most people thrived on relatively modest resources. It is not just one's capacity to live out a life plan that is valuable; the quality of the life that one manages then to live also matters.

There should probably also be some place on this level for an element of perfectionism, further qualifying these earlier principles of equality. Societies generally are not neutral between competing conceptions of the good, between poetry and pushpin. Arts councils attract government subsidies; pushpin clubs do not. And there seems to be good reason for this. For one thing, a society could not strike any balance between two values, say health and learning, unless it knew roughly how much it valued each. For another, if a society were completely neutral between competing conceptions of the good, it would pass up opportunities to educate people to forms of life that they themselves would be glad to lead. No doubt a little paternalism goes a long way; but there is a case for at least a little paternalism.

12. Utility and Rights

I started out by suggesting that the first level of a substantive theory will ground human rights in personhood, practicalities, and equal regard. Still, a substantive theory cannot stop there; it has to answer questions about the structure of rights, in order to do which it is forced on to a second level of theory about how these values and utility are related to each other. The most difficult case is equal regard. Although piecemeal appeal to intuition is the common way of arguing about it (and most moral matters), I think that we can bring almost all people to agree that it is not an acceptable method. Once we take a first step towards a more acceptable method, however, things begin to look different: prominent contemporary accounts of equal regard, motivated largely by anti-utilitarianism,[28] undeniably attractive at first glance, look unpromisingly strong or restrictive at second. Also, values such as autonomy and liberty can be brought within the ambit of a formal notion of 'utility'. It is on the second level, therefore, that utilitarian apparatus looks as if it might in some form usefully appear: to explain the structure of substantive prudential values and the moral significance of interpersonal trades.

To object to this substantive theory, contrary asseveration is not enough – for instance, to insist that it is of the essence of rights that they are 'side constraints' or that they are more potent 'trumps' than this theory makes them.[29] Those who object will have to come up with a better substantive theory, if they can.

NOTES

1. See J. J. Thomson, "A Defence of Abortion", *Philosophy and Public Affairs* 1 (1971).
2. Ronald Dworkin, *Taking Rights Seriously* (London: Duckworth, 1977), esp. Introduction, pp. xi–xv and chs. 6 and 7.
3. Robert Nozick, *Anarchy, State, and Utopia* (Oxford: Blackwell, 1974), pp. 28–33.
4. For useful discussions on the relation of 'rights' to 'duties', see for example C. Arnold, "Analyses of Right," in *Human Rights*, ed. E. Kamenka and A. Tay (London: Edward Arnold, 1978); on the relation of 'right' and 'permission', see Nozick, *Anarchy, State, and Utopia* p. 92; on the relation of 'rights' and 'entitlements', see H. J. McCloskey, "Rights," *Philosophy Quarterly* 15 (1965): 117.
5. W. N. Hohfeld, *Fundamental Legal Conceptions* (New Haven, Conn.: Yale University Press, 1923).
6. For example, A. I. Melden, *Rights and Persons* (Oxford: Blackwell, 1977), ch. 6; H. J. McCloskey, "The Right to Life," *Mind* 84 (1975): 413-14.
7. But also supported by Mill, and more recently hinted at by Isaiah Berlin, *Four Essays on Liberty* (Oxford: Oxford University Press, 1969), Introduction, p. lx; and appealed to, at least portions of it, by H. L. A. Hart, "Between Utility and Rights," in *The Idea of Freedom*, ed. A. Ryan (Oxford: Oxford University Press, 1979).
8. This positive freedom is suspect in many eyes. 'Poverty can be an evil', John Lucas writes, 'and great poverty is a great evil: but it is a different evil from lack of freedom'. See his *Principles of Politics* (Oxford: Clarendon Press, 1966), p. 147.
9. This is close to Dworkin's position, *Taking Rights Seriously*, p. 267.
10. See John Rawls, *A Theory of Justice* (Oxford: Clarendon Press, 1972), p. 27; Nozick, *Anarchy, State, and Utopia*, pp. 32–33.
11. It is, according to the United Nations Declaration of Human Rights. It is, according to the U.S. Supreme Court in its decision *Griswold v. Connecticut* (381 U.S. 479) and *Roe v. Wade* (410 U.S. 113); see discussion in Carl Wellman, "A New Conception of Human Rights," in Kamenka and Tay, eds., *Human Rights*.
12. Someone might hope that some of this indeterminateness could be dispelled by appeal to justice, that is, by appeal to the idea that rights are, roughly speaking, the claims that a just society would grant. But justice is no more basic than rights. The issues about rights before us now form a large portion of the stuff of a theory of justice, so there is no independent notion of justice to help us with these issues.
13. This is a good place for a brief further thought about what a substantive theory is. The theory grounds rights in, among other things, personhood. But to the skeptical eye this may look like no 'grounding' at all. It may seem merely a shift from one normative notion to another. After all, the content of the notion of a 'person', at least 'person' as it figures here in this substantive theory, is not a purely semantic matter; most of us would single out autonomy and living out one's individual life plan as central to being a person, but we well know that other people, especially in other ages, have not thought these features important. And if normative considerations enter in the choice of a concept of 'person', why not let them enter earlier with the choice of what is to be a human right? Why the indirection?

But this carries skepticism too far. True, not everyone uses this concept of personhood. In that sense, it is not totally outside the normative circle. But that does not mean that the notion of rights is not explained by it. Explanation in morals does not fail to be explanation unless it employs notions either that are not normative or that everyone employs. It is enough if it grounds a vague, troublesome, criterionless *explanandum* in an *explanans* that is more definite, clearer, and in the use of which we are more sure.

Also, think of the alternative. The skeptical spirit prompts us to make normative decisions at an earlier point, directly about human rights. Well, what would we then deem to be rights? What boundaries would they have? Are we to maximize their observance? If we are honest, we shall admit that we are baffled. We need help with all these questions, and the substantive theory is meant to give it.

14. I develop this account of utility more fully in "On Life's Being Valuable," *Dialectics and Humanism* 8 (1981), and "Modern Utilitarianism," *Revue Internationale de Philosophie* 36 (1982).

15. J. L. Mackie, "Can There Be a Right-Based Moral Theory?" *Midwest Studies in Philosophy* 3 (1978): 354–55.

16. See D. Lyons' useful discussion of Mill's view in "Human Rights and the General Welfare," *Philosophy and Public Affairs* 6 (1971).

17. *A Theory of Justice*, Sec. 11.

18. In his unpublished lectures, "Justice and Rights."

19. There well may be doubt about this approach: perhaps trade-offs, especially the sort that I shall presently consider, are not central to explaining moral status. John Rawls' approach, in contrast, is to suggest that we get straight the principles that apply to normal people, with normal capacities and health, and attend only later to the special demands of the abnormal. Otherwise, our intuitions, he fears, will be distorted by the special urgency of the ill and handicapped. (See his "A Kantian Conception of Equality," *Cambridge Review* 96 (1975): 96.) His approach would be possible if it were possible to work out a notion of equal regard without determining what morality requires in these hard cases. And hard cases would arise even in a society of normal people. They do not arise simply from illness and handicap, but also arise when a society makes hard choices about how to balance demands of saving life, on the one hand, and promoting the constituents of a good life such as art and education, on the other. But we do not have a determinate enough notion of equal regard to give us any answers, even in the relatively easy cases, independently of answers in the hard cases.

20. Amartya Sen, *On Economic Inequality* (Oxford: Clarendon Press, 1973), p. 18; for a still weaker version see his article, "Rawls versus Bentham: an Axiomatic Examination of the Pure Distribution Problem", in *Reading Rawls*, ed. N. Daniels (Oxford: Blackwell, 1975).

21. I argue this further in "Equality: On Sen's Weak Equity Axiom," *Mind* 90 (1981).

22. This argument, and the consideration of the two models leading up to it, is adapted from my paper "Modern Utilitarianism," *Revue Internationale de Philosophie* 36 (1982).

23. *A Theory of the Good and the Right* (Oxford: Clarendon Press, 1979), ch. 1.

24. *Moral Thinking* (Oxford: Clarendon Press, 1981), ch. 8.

25. *A Theory of Justice*, Secs. 9, 87.

26. I have discussed various interpretations of 'incommensurability' in "Are There Incommensurable Values?" *Philosophy and Public Affairs* 7 (1977).

27. Ronald Dworkin, "What is Equality?" pts. I and II, *Philosophy and Public Affairs* 10 (1981).

28. See H. L. A. Hart's excellent discussion, "Between Utility and Rights."

29. See nn. 2 and 3.

8

Contractarian Rights

Jan Narveson

1. Rights: What Are They?

There is a temptation to make a definitional connection between rights and contract, thus defining the contractarian view into truth. The temptation should be resisted, but it is of importance that the temptation is there, for there is something about rights that promotes it. Rights are (a) interpersonal, having to do with actions of some that affect others. Let us refer to the actors as the "agents" and those affected by a particular action as the "patients" in such transactions. Then (b) rights have the following important property: that although they can be had by either patients or agents, yet rights are essentially on the "patient" side of the centrally important transactions. Let us see how this is so and what it leads to.

To say that some party, A, has a right to do something, *x*, is to say that some other party or parties, B, have certain duties or obligations regarding A's doing of *x*. These will be either, minimally, the duty to refrain from interfering with or preventing A's doing of *x* or, more committally, to assist A in doing *x*, for example, by supplying certain necessary conditions of his or her doing so. To say that A has the right to have something, *y*, is to say about these other parties that they have the duty either, minimally, to refrain from damaging, destroying, or depriving A of *y* or, more committally, to supply A with *y* if A doesn't already have it.

It is possible that these definitions can be improved in elegance. They distinguish between rights to *do* and rights to *have*; but perhaps we can talk more generally of rights that certain predicates apply to A: A's right is the right *that* some F be true of A, 'F' being a variable. But what of the difference between the duty to (merely) refrain versus the duty to *do*? The distinction, applied to the above simplification, is now between the B parties' (merely) refraining from bringing it about that F *not* be true of A and their bringing it about that F be true of A, if A is not already F. (Note that the distinctions are different. The latter distinction, which is that between "negative" and "positive" rights, cuts across the distinction between doing and having. I may interfere with your doings, or I may damage your property; I may assist your efforts at doing something, and I may give you an ownable thing. And I can have duties to do any of these.) Is there any way of representing the duty to do and the duty to refrain as merely different values of the same variable? We can't say that both are "duties with regard to A's F-ing," for a duty to interfere would be a value of that variable, but such a "duty" cannot be generated by a right. Or more precisely, the duty to interfere with A's doing of x cannot be what is entailed by A's having a right to do x. However, the degree of elegance that would result from finding such a variable is not, I think, required for the present inquiry.

Now when A's rights are respected by party B, *B* is the agent so far as the "administration" of this rights-transaction is concerned. B could act (or refrain) in the way that A's right requires him to act (or refrain). A's right requires another party to do or refrain, and to do so in order to affect A in one way or another. Thus A is the "patient" in the transaction, even if the way in which he is affected is that he is left free to act in certain ways. This facet of rights will loom large in the following deliberations.

The plot thickens further when we ask who B might be. B is the party upon whom fall the obligations or duties generated by A's right. In many cases, B will be a particular individual or smallish group, as with typical contracts and promises. But if there are, say, human rights, then B is not a particular other person but rather, everyone in general. Those who hold that there is a natural right of all persons to F are holding that all of us must allow (or assist, as the case may be) all persons we can to F. But consider those narrower contracts between individuals. When we say that A, in promising B that he will do x, gives B the *right* that A do x, and thus that the promise imposes a *duty* on A to do x, are we making statements whose import for action is confined exclusively to A and B? I think not. We would, ordinarily at any rate, be saying that all of us come into it in minimal ways: for example, that *we* ought not to prevent A from carrying out this duty, *prima facie*; that we should recognize that the blame falls on A if he does not comply, possibly doing further things about him as well, by way of (at least mildly) reinforcing A's compliance-behavior. In short, there is a public aspect to private contractual activities. We may be called upon to intervene in some way, and the principles of contract are the guidelines for such interventions.

One further point about those "interventions": reinforcing behavior can range from the raising of an eyebrow to torture or execution. This is quite a gamut. Is it essential to the notion of a right that some degree of reinforcing activity is in order? It seems to me that it is. The distinction will be between the sort of reinforcement that is in order when we have a matter of rights and the sort that is in order when we do not. This has some plausibility, I think. Very roughly, rights can be *rein*forced by being *en*forced whereas other or lesser moral categories cannot. But the plausibility of the "institutional" view of rights, which would essentially embed them in arrangements we participate in, causes a difficulty for the enforcement view, since we can acquire trivial rights in institutional matters and why enforce them? However, we may perhaps resolve this by suggesting that rights are what *may* be enforced, but not necessarily what it is prudent, wise, or even morally desirable to enforce, all things considered. What would determine whether we may is the institutional arrangements; what decides whether we should is other morally relevant values.

Various other things have been said about rights: that they are "trumps," superior to considerations of (say) mere utility, that a charter of rights expresses the fundamental terms of human association, that to violate someone's rights is to do something destructive of his or her very person, for instance. And thus it is thought that rights are something buried deep in the soul, "inherent in the human personality." But most of what is true in these claims is, I think, due to enforceability. Externally imposed restrictions on one's sheer freedom of movement, damages, disabilities, and irritations to one's body, and the termination of one's very life, are impositions that one cannot ignore, and so to threaten such things by way of reinforcing certain kinds of behavior is obviously to attach great importance to those kinds of behavior; and if the behavior in question is identified by reference to certain statuses of others, then it is obviously to attach great importance to those statuses. On our analysis, rights are such statuses.

2. "Are There" Rights?

It is popular to talk as if rights "are," as if people "have" them in much the same sense as that in which they have pancreases or minds. But obviously such talk is at least misleading: if I maliciously slice you up, I violate your rights; but I don't slice *them* up. And those who don't believe that we have rights do not suffer from lack of vision if those who believe we do have them are in the right. But what *do* they lack? Things would be awkward if rights were the object of a special faculty for apprehending them. People who don't respect our rights are then readily excusable: they simply don't have one of those faculties; or if they do it's out of kilter. Surely it's better if such people have more nearly the sort of fault that those who don't see that $38 + 83 = 121$ have. We might then be able to fix things up by reanalyzing the arithmetic rather than just lamenting their lack of the right kind of moral miner's cap, or of its lamp being permanently on the fritz.

In legal contexts, or in more special ones, whether we "have" a certain right may be answered, hopefully, by going to The Law and looking things up; though it may prove to be very much less straightforward than that. What's on the books may not settle the matter readily. But in moral matters there are no books, so looking up the answers is not an available option. What then?

If we had a Creator who "endowed us with certain inalienable rights," how would he have done it? Where might he have put them? Accounts of that general stripe are useless, or likely worse because, again, misleading. What there "is" when there "are" rights, if indeed there are some, must be certain features or properties of those who "have" them such that we have *good reason to acknowledge* the obligation to refrain from interfering with, or possibly to sometimes help their bearers to do the things they are said to have the right to do, or have those things they are said to have a right to have. Their rights will be as real as those reasons are strong. Or rather, they will be as real as the features or properties mentioned above, given sufficient reason to accept the obligations in question.

Consider one of those unfortunate countries in which, we want to say, human rights are in a bad way. We oscillate between saying that the populations in those lamentable places have no rights, and saying that their rights are flouted, violated, ignored, trampled on, and in general not acknowledged. If they do not *have* the rights in question, though, how could they be ignored and trampled on? When we say that they don't "have" them, what we obviously must mean is that the relevant people—governments, usually—do not act in the way they ought, do not fulfill the obligations that would be theirs if their victims had the rights in question. But we do not mean that they ought *not* to act that way. In talking as we do, we clearly mean to be criticizing them, putting them in the wrong. On what basis do we level this criticism? It is redundant to say that the basis is failure to respect those victims' rights. The essence of the matter is that there is reason for obliging those governments or other agents to act otherwise, and that reason is identical with the reason for ascribing rights to those victims. There are not two separate problems, one of discerning the rights, the other of establishing the obligations. This one problem, of course, is a tough one. But at least there is but one.

On this account of the matter, then, everything depends on (a) the existence of those features or properties, F, such that (b) there is good reason to acknowledge the relevant obligations or duties toward F-persons on the part of those agents on whom they would fall. Obligations or duties are, on this view, assumed or acknowledged, or rejected or ignored. Are the obligations or duties still *there* even if not acknowledged? Clearly we must be able to say so. How can anyone ever usefully accuse anyone else of shirking his/her duty if the accused need only point out by way of defense that he or she doesn't acknowledge the duty in question? But we can make such accusations, for the obligations or duties in question are there if the reasons to acknowledge them are sufficient. In that case, those who nonetheless reject or ignore them are unreasonable and may be regarded in similar manner to those who have not done their homework; or, in some cases, to those who refuse to do it.

3. Agreement and Acknowledgment of Obligation

Clearly the present account puts a great deal of weight on "agreement" and "acknowledgment" of the obligations constituting rights. Such agreement or acknowledgment must be made by the agents who are in a position to interfere with the actions to which the right-holders have rights. Even more weight, of course, is put on the reasons *to* agree or acknowledge them, but we shall consider that below. Meanwhile, what we want to know is whether there might not also be, in addition to the case of those who have not done their homework, that of those who have done it and cheerfully agree that they have obligations of the kind in question, that is, that others have rights of the kind that entails those obligations, but who refuse to *do* what they admit they have obligation to do.

But I think there are not such. Or at any rate, those who *say*, at time t, 'I agree to do x at t_1" but who, at t_1, are nowhere to be found, can be said, in the absence of good excuse or justification for nonperformance, not in fact to have agreed. Such 'agreement' is a sham. In practical agreements, the type we have in mind, agreement is not acknowledgment of some abstract truth about differential equations, nor even of concrete facts—though either might well figure importantly in the background to practical agreements. But what we have in mind here is agreement *to act*. Such agreements are, in effect, settings of oneself in the direction indicated by the content of the agreement. Those who do that, yet at the time of performance say "what of it?" display the cheerfulness of the idiot to whom words have no meaning. One *cannot* agree, fail to perform, and be cheerful about it. Those who see that you have purported to agree and yet show no sign in action of having genuinely done so have a complaint, and if that complaint is not taken seriously by those against whom it is lodged, then the possibility of practical dealings with such persons is seriously undercut.

Here we must recollect the analysis proposed at the outset. Rights are statuses entailing not merely obligations, but enforceable obligations. To agree and acknowledge one of those is to agree to the propriety of such enforcement while one is at it. There are, therefore, two parts to such agreements: (a) agreement to do or refrain from the relevant acts, and (b) agreement to an enforcement procedure. But as Mill noted, rights in this regard are not unique. To agree to act at all is to agree that complaint is in order for nonperformance. Whether that is sufficient for talking of "rights" is perhaps a moot point. What is important is that often we shall need more substantial enforcement machinery than that. In such cases, we may say, the seriousness with which rights are acknowledged is measured in part by one's willingness to assist in establishing and administering that machinery. We establish and administer it in part on the verbal level, criticizing others in the light of the principles of right acknowledged; but in addition there might be subscription of taxes for formal machinery at the legal or even military level.

We can thus make a useful distinction. It might sometimes be rational to agree to do x, but not to expose oneself to a severe, or even a minor, punishment for nonperformance. But in other cases it might be rational both to agree to do x and to agree to the establishment of a penalty at some level, ranging up to the very severe, for nonperformance. The province of rights is the latter region. A rational schedule of rights will be a set of behaviorial constraints that is rational for all of the relevant parties to acknowledge, including enforcement as part of the bargain. And in the case of general human rights, the "relevant parties" are everyone (with a possible qualification to be noted).

Given all this, let us address ourselves to the question of why promises and agreements obligate. There is the temptation to say that this is a self-answering question: the point of agreements is to obligate, or to agree *is* simply to accept an obligation. It is a plausible view, and some appreciable portion of the truth about this must be in it. But we must be careful. Clearly the sheer utterance of the words "I hereby assume an obligation to do x" does not create an obligation to do x. The utterance of such words to another party, addressed to that party and, let us assume, accepted by that other party, normally does. But why?

The immediate effect, of course, is to make it *absurd* for the utterer to say, "But what does all that have to do with it?" The other party to such an utterance, if he presses his claim, is in a strong position, for he has a claim that the utterer of the promise cannot consistently deny. So far, so good. But there are *not* just two parties to an obligation. The principle that promises create obligations is a public principle. *Our* question is: should *we* take it that A, the utterer, is obligated to do *x*, which she has promised B she would do? Ordinarily, of course, our answer will be in the affirmative. ("Of course," but of course we need an argument; only this one will be pretty easy going.) But extraordinarily, maybe not. Perhaps both parties have overlooked side effects (*x* will produce pollution, for instance), or some background conditions have been unsatisfactory. Promises normally obligate, for the reasons that we all have to make it possible for individuals to incur obligations.

4. Hypothetical and Implicit Agreement

If A makes a contract with B, then A and B have obligations to each other. But if A only *should have* made a contract with B, what then? Certainly we would not normally put his case exactly on all fours with the case in which he in fact has made one. Indeed, we are more inclined to put it on all fours with the case in which nothing has happened at all. It would, let us suppose, have been most prudent had I bought B's car last week: prudent both for me, who needed one and would have had a very good one from B, and for B, who needed the money urgently. Still, neither of us *owed* the other a car or the money I would have paid. This case clearly creates a problem for aspiring contractarians. Obviously there has been no explicit contract between every person and every other person, even among those who are all alive simultaneously. And thus it has been suggested that the principles of justice are those that *would have* been agreed to by everyone, if _____. But whatever we might do about the blank, there is the obvious problem: why should this be thought to incur obligations? The situation is, of course, further aggravated if we fill in the blank by some such clause as " . . . if the party were behind a Veil of Ignorance," as in Rawl's now-famous theory.

Somewhere between explicit contracts, which standardly obligate, and purely hypothetical ones, which standardly do not, we have the idea of an "implicit" agreement. The idea *is* between the two, it is important to note: it is not off the board, or in some quite oblique direction from both. It is certainly appealed to in daily life. It is taken that one's actions can be such as to imply that one has accepted an obligation, with nearly the same force as if one actually had. In some of these cases, to plead "But I didn't *say* I would" is to put up a very weak case indeed; it would even, in some of those cases, be tantamount to lying. And that this should be so is not, on reflection, surprising. For after all, to make a promise explicitly is to convey a commitment by verbal means, which are the most precise and conventionally strongest means of so doing. But conventions are required for those verbal means to be possible in the first place. Why cannot similar conventions cause various other forms of behavior, in the right circumstances, to have much the same, or even precisely the same effect?

"Implicit promising" has most force between persons who are well acquainted with each other. But, for mankind in general, that is a condition that obviously does not obtain. And what is more, it is especially between strangers and persons who are at best indifferent to each other that the need for rights is strongest (as will be urged below). Does this weaken the case for the contractarian, then? Only, I think, if that case is seriously misunderstood. Let us reconsider.

The question of human rights and in general of moral rights, rights that are not enshrined anywhere in print, not formally built into any official administrative edifice, is the question of what *it is reasonable* to require of people, force them to do or to avoid. What else *could* it be? There are many with big chunks of theories of rights, or anyway with ample proclamations of rights, proceeding, one gathers, from the deep intuitions of their proclaimers: but these people *differ* among themselves. The question is, whose view, if anyone's is right? It is difficult to see what this latter question could mean other than, "Whose view has the (greatest) support of reason?" Of course, one can stick by one's guns no matter what, simply insisting that all others are in error—'guns' is likely not to be a metaphor in such cases. Or it might be that everyone shared the same intuitions anyway, though this is far from obvious at present. In either case, it would be hard to say, "Well, I admit that your view is *more reasonable*; mine, however, is right!"

Of course the reason in question is, in a sense, collective. This is not meant in a sense that would require us to suppose that there were collective entities with special reasons of their own. It is meant, instead, simply to remind us that since the problems stem from disagreements among individuals in the first place, they can hardly expect to get anywhere by simply insisting on what is reasonable "from their point of view"—each given his or her own point of view. The question is what it is reasonable for *us* to adopt in the way of restrictions on our several behaviors; and this can be done (if at all) only by discerning what there is in our interactions that can make it reasonable from *everyone's* point of view to adopt such restrictions. But if there is such a set of agreement-points among us, it is hard to see how we could do anything better, or what else could possibly do the job.

The claim that there is an "implicit agreement" among us, it seems to me, has two aspects to it. First, and most fundamentally, there is the question that is best answered by the idea of the hypothetical contract: What would it be reasonable for us all to agree on, were we to address ourselves seriously to the subject? Second, and of great practical importance, there is what, I believe, gives rise to the idea of "natural" rights: if the considerations supporting some or conceivably all of these hypothetical agreements are (a) obvious, requiring no enormous calculative facility or profundity of intellect to discern, and (b) practically pressing, so that human interaction on any considerable scale could scarcely proceed without some sort of mutual expectations of behavior complying with the principles that would be thus agreed on the part of those interacting, then those elements of the total set of proposed rights may well be said to be "natural" in the fairly straight-forward sense that it is reasonable to expect all to comply with them, reasonable to require all to comply, and reasonable to expect everyone to recognize those principles intuitively in practical situations.

Not all of the principles of justice, yielding the set of basic rights for persons, need have the foregoing status. On the contrary, we should expect that many cases will be very difficult indeed, involving subtleties and shades that require calculative ability and/or depth of insight of extraordinary kinds to resolve. And the principles on which such cases are found to turn, upon that kind of reflection, may well be difficult. What matters is that they are generated by the right kind of reasons, reasons that can be seen to be weighty from the point of view of everyone. Correct reasoning from such premisses must lead to what we want in the way of justice.

5. Why Contractarianism?

Contractarianism, I take it, is the view that the principles of justice are what would emerge from a general agreement (from—a vexed question—suitable baselines) of the above kind, in which each person reasons from his or her *own* point of view, in terms of his/her *own* values, interests, and/or desires, carefully considered. If we instead erect some supposedly basic value which, alas, many people do not recognize to be their own, reasoning out from that basic value what everyone ought to do, we are doomed to theoretical shipwreck. Or at least we are if the aim is to come up with principles that are compelling to *any* rational person. And that, I have suggested, must surely be the aim.

What we have said in the previous sections is that the principles of justice and rights are, roughly, those with which it is reasonable to expect everyone to comply, and to accept enforcement if need be. What was said just now is that those principles are the ones that would emerge from a general agreement—more precisely, from a properly conducted attempt to reach one—in which each reasons in terms of his or her own values, etc. Now some other theory might perhaps emerge were each to reason not from his/her own values, etc., but rather from some prescribed set that somehow had the imprimatur of Reason quite apart from the individual's own values and interests. A classic example here is provided by Henry Sidgwick, who, in the course of explaining the foundations of utilitarianism, appeals to the "self-evident principle that the good of any one individual is of no more importance, from the point of view (if I may say so) of the Universe, than the good of any other . . . ." Now, there is room to wonder just what it means to speak of the "point of view of the Universe" anyway; but supposing there is a coherent account of that, we must then ask why the individual should bother with that point of view. The point of view of the Universe would seem, on the face of it, to be an *alien* point of view. If the individual is to adopt it, it seems that we need an argument. And what, after all, could be the premises of an effective argument along that line? Would we not need to show that from the individual's own point of view, it would be rational to *adopt* the Universe's point of view? Sidgwick, notoriously, goes on to say that "It is evident to me that as a rational being I am bound to aim at good generally . . . not merely at a particular part of it."[1] But *is* that evident? One might be tempted to reply that perhaps that is evident, but that as, say, an *emotional* being I am going to aim quite decidedly at only a particular part of it. But that, though the positive part of it is surely plausible, is to concede too much. Why would not a quite rational being who was, let us say, in love with Tina, aim at Tina's good rather than Hortense's or, say, Albert's?

What Sidgwick's principle does, I think, is to conflate two very different sorts of impartiality. On the one hand, it rightly implies that the *principles* of justice and right must be impartial, and in that sense made, no doubt, from "an impartial point of view." But what it certainly appears also to imply is that those principles will require each of *us* to be impartial, impartial in our desires, interests, affections, and the like. And this, even if it is conceivable, is surely incredible.

Earlier contractarian theorists assumed that each individual is certain

to have at least one overwhelming and insurmountable partiality, namely, the partiality towards himself or herself. But it is unnecessary, as well
as false to fact, to assume that. Some will be found to be wildly partial
towards certain other individuals, some to certain groups of which they
are members, or even of which they merely aspire or wish to be
members. Moreover, these are partialities that may remain even after
the scrutiny of reflection in the light of long-run consequences, and so
forth, has been brought to bear by the person in question.

Many critics have insisted that the individual is not an "isolated
atom" whose values and interests are *sui generis*, even *ex nihilo*, and have
inferred from this that liberal contractarianism is a nonstarter. But to
argue thus is to miss the point. People get their values from many
places, and no doubt especially from their social settings. This, we may
agree, could hardly be otherwise. But how does this affect matters? It
would, for example, be ridiculous to infer that people do not really differ
on any important point of values. Members of the same societies,
however closely you narrow the bounds of the relevant "society," do in
fact differ on all kinds of matters. And of course different societies differ
very markedly indeed, as the history of the past couple of decades so
strongly brings home to us—even those of us who somehow managed
to miss the lesson of the preceding several millennia. Give what account
you will of human nature that is not ludicrously at variance with the
facts, and you are confronted with differences sufficient to generate the
problems that stimulate us to search for principles of justice. And that
is all we need.

The real question is, what does the reason of any individual tell him
or her to do? And it is to this that I am unable to see any other answer
than that it tells him to try to realize those things that he holds dear, at
least on due reflection. It is open to any theorist to try to show that due
reflection would homogenize all of those things he holds dear, making
each individual, carefully acquainted with all the facts, indistinguishable
from each other or indeed, from The Universe. A difficulty with that
idea is that it may take more time and breath than any theorist can find
in this mortal world to persuade many individuals that they should even
bother to try to acquaint themselves with *all* the facts! Nor is there really
reason to think that such an endeavor might be successful no matter
how ideal the circumstances. Perhaps we will remain different from
each other all the way down!

Meanwhile there certainly is no *workable* hypothesis other than the
one just advanced. What conceivable reason there may be for insisting
that each person *ought* to be reasoning from a standpoint other than his
own I do not know; but certainly to assume that he *is* doing any such

thing must be the height of absurdity. What solider edifice, then, could we hope to erect than one founded simply on the assumption that each person's reason will tell him to proceed from his own point of view? There is ample reason, starting from such premisses, to expect others to appreciate others' points of view, to allow for them, to take them into account; but that is not the same as literally *assuming* those other points of view. Aping Butler, perhaps we can characterize our starting point as the principle that "Every person is who she or he is, and not another person."

6. Contractarian Rights

We have rights against the other members of a group G, when it is mutually advantageous for all G's to assume enforceable obligations to us to refrain from interfering, or alternatively actually to assist, with our performance of what we are said to have a right to, and when there is recognition of this status. When G is mankind at large, however, we are faced with two major problems in proclaiming that there are rights. One is that the recognition factor is scant; the other is that it is not self-evident, at least, that there *are* any identifiable types of behavior such that it is mutually advantageous for all persons to assume the said enforceable obligations. Bear in mind here that "advantageous" is assessed via the values of the person concerned, not via the values of the theorist.

The recognition problem, I believe, is minor and is further assisted by the character of one of the rights that will, I think, be strongly supported by any reasonable analysis. The right in question is the right to be presumed to have peaceable, person-respecting intentions in the absence of good evidence to the contrary. Reflection quickly assures us that without such a right, we can get nowhere. For if your apparently innocent behavior is taken by me to be *prima facie* evidence of the extreme duplicity of which you are capable, calling for immediate violence from me, I now provide *you* with the justification for responding to my response in kind. That way lies the end of any possible civilized intercourse. But if this is so, then it follows that a sufficient sign of recognition of the right of personal security is nonviolent behavior. When we have no reason to suspect others, we are to refrain from aggression. This is weak, since bad intentions are compatible with very considerable amounts of good outward behavior, and the interpretation of "evidence" is plainly no easy matter in many cases. Nevertheless, it is very far from trivial. Apart from which, virtually universal recognition of the very minimal schedule of rights that could plausibly be advanced as human rights really does obtain, so long as we confine ourselves to the arena of individual-to-individual relations.

The other problem, however, is anything but minor. Bear in mind that our analysis requires that the "advantage" of the different parties is to be assessed via *their* values, rather than those of the theorist. And to begin with, it is very clear that at least *some* scrutiny of those values, some rational reflection (even reconstruction) may be necessary before the condition of mutual advantage can be shown to be met, at very least. For persons consumed by hatred, jealousy, or fanatical religious zeal (to name a few) may be related to certain other persons in such a way that the advantage of one is seen *ipso facto* as the disadvantage of the other. If we stop at that level, there is no possibility of arriving at a universally acceptable, rational schedule of human rights. Immensely compounding this problem is the factor of large-group solidarity, especially in the form of nation-state operation. This factor will delude people into supposing that they have a right to engage in behavior that would otherwise be transparently aggressive. Or it may make them suppose that they do not need to bother about human rights; for if their collective might is such as to enable them to force everyone else to do their bidding, then the condition of mutual advantage would at least appear not to be met.

In the face of these problems, a few maneuvers are available that will, I think, enable us to make some headway, as well as to disclose important problem areas. First, as against such phenomena as jealousy, hatred, and rivalry, the required strategy is one of containment. We must ask whether there are not underlying values—such as life itself— that do not, on reflection, have more weight than the defeat of one's rival; and whether it is reasonable to ask our fellow human beings to put up with behavior that, if generally practiced, would manifestly put an end to the possibility of cooperation and thus of all the blessings of society. Faced with such reflections, no rational person will persist in thinking that his or her behavior is right if it oversteps the bounds of peaceable and civilized life. A corollary, of course, is that justice cannot ask people to be nice to each other; it can at best insist that they refrain from being overtly nasty.

Second, we may face the issues raised by cohesive groups with two strategies. One is to remind every group that it consists of individuals, and ask those individuals whether the alleged gains of the group are in fact gains for them, especially when weighed against the benefits that may well be awaiting all those who are willing to deal on individual terms with persons of the supposedly opposing group. The other is to point out to any such group that it was able to attain such power as it has only by the previous forbearance of fellow groups and nations. Powerful nations that exercise their power in aggressive ways have certainly taken unfair advantage of their neighbors, who in the past could have prevented that growth of power had they so chosen. This is a consideration, of course, that tends to be advanced *too late*. Once in the driver's seat, it is difficult to accomplish very much by reminding the miscreant that he would not have been there but for the previous assistance of others. But our question, remember, is about the character and justification of rights; it is not part of the terms of reference of such a project to show that appeals to considerations of right must always be effective. Manifestly, they will often not be.

And finally, we should in part concede the objection. Conceivably some would not be parties to any general agreement on enforceable restrictions on behavior. Complete universality may not be attainable. But how much need this worry us? On the contractarian view, rights are due to agreement. Those who will not agree have no rights, and we have no duties toward them. It is, I think, not really possible that anyone would, on due reflection, prefer the condition he may expect if the rest of mankind are united against him with *no* restrictions on what they may do to him to what he may expect if he is willing to make at least the most minimal concessions. But if there are such persons, they are beyond the reach of a theory of rights, except in the very important sense that they afford no counterevidence to it. Their existence does not show that rights are impossible or pointless, given that they are of the character I have been proposing above.

Rights are relative to reasonable agreements. The grand general rights are two: the right to enter into agreements and have those respected, and the right to inviolacy of one's person in the absence of infractions of other rights. Neither is "absolute": considerations of long-term mutual advantage among all persons could justify bending in special cases. And because a multiplicity of considerations enter into the reckoning of advantage, not to mention standing difficulties in determining what agreements actually obtain, we should not expect to find easy and definite answers to the question of what our rights are in nonglobal cases. What has been maintained here is only that the contractarian analysis makes sense of rights and affords a definite line of approach for those difficult cases.[2]

NOTES

1. Henry Sidgwick, *The Methods of Ethics*, 7th ed. (New York: Macmillan, 1907) p. 382.
2. The general line of thought in this paper was stimulated by David Gauthier, though he should not be held responsible for details. See his "Reason and Maximization," *Canadian Journal of Philosophy* (March 1974). See also my "Human Rights: Which, If Any, There Are," in *NMOS* 23, ed. J. Ronald Pennock and John W. Chapman (New York: New York University Press, 1981).

9

Utility and Ownership

Alan Ryan

Any theory of rights ought to have something serious to say about rights of ownership. Property rights may not be the most important rights we have—supposing that we can draw a clear line between property rights and other rights. Nonetheless, one can hardly imagine a sociology that did not concern itself with the causes and consequences of the distribution of titles of ownership; and one can hardly imagine a normative jurisprudence that was unconcerned to lay down the proper duties and powers of owners. There are three ways of taking property rights seriously that I shall here have in mind: they do not exhaust the possible approaches to the subject, but they cover enough of them, I think, at any rate to show what is at issue in any account of the nature and purpose of ownership. The first of these is the doctrine that there are natural rights of ownership and that taking any sort of rights seriously must start from a conception of individuals as 'self-owning'. Thus, much of Robert Nozick's criticism of John Rawls's account of justice boils down to the objection that Rawls supposes that society originally owns all the talents of all its members, and this supposition is at odds with taking seriously the rights of individuals over themselves.[1] What it is for individuals to have rights over themselves is explained in terms of individuals owning themselves in something like the 'liberal conception of ownership' explicated by Professor Honoré[2] On this view, individual rights are either natural or else created by contract between individuals who are *essentially* proprietors.

The existence of natural rights of ownership is denied by both of the other two ways of thinking about property that are at issue here. Both of these positions see property rights as essentially artificial creations, essentially the creatures of the law, and dependent for their moral weight on instrumental considerations. The second of our three views,

175

then, accepts that individuals have *rights* that are in an important sense 'natural' or at any rate 'nonartificial' and certainly nonlegal; what property rights individuals may be granted by the law is constrained by the rights they have prior to the law, and what rights individuals ought to be granted by the law may—depending on the full development of the theory of rights in question—be more than merely constrained. If our theory of rights yields rights to welfare or even rights to employment, we may find that the best way to embody these rights in positive law is by giving people proprietary rights of some sort of other. More plausibly, however, we are likely to find that such considerations would simply limit the freedom of owners to do what they liked with their property—welfare or employment rights would plausibly constrain owners of capital in dismissing their employees or paying them whatever wages the market would allow them to pay, rather than yielding anything resembling 'job ownership'.

The third of our three views, and the one to which most of what follows is devoted, is the utilitarian account of property rights. This normative theory of property rights is distinctive in that it is not merely insistent that property is essentially the creature of the law, justified or not for instrumental reasons, but that those instrumental reasons do not themselves involve references to rights. The justification of property rights is, in general, a matter of showing how a system of legally defined and enforced rights and duties best promotes the general welfare; there will be all sorts of questions raised by an attempt to show which system is optimal from a utilitarian standpoint, but these will not be questions about the protection of people's natural rights. Now, in what follows I shall be concerned to argue that a utilitarian account of property rights is generally able to take property rights with all the seriousness they deserve; this is quite a different matter from saying that traditional utilitarianism can take *all* rights as seriously as they deserve, but I shall also argue in passing that property rights are not *basic rights* of the kind utilitarianism is commonly said to misrepresent. My view is that the utilitarian rejection of rights as a fundamental component in morality does create problems at the point at which a utilitarian's liberal intuitions come into conflict with the demands of the general welfare; but the rights that these intuitions seem to presuppose are not property rights.[3] As always in this area, J. S. Mill presents us with some difficulties, in that he did want to show that utilitarianism was deeply committed to the existence of *moral* rights; but here I confine myself to defending the consistency of his claim that all property is the creature of the law with his defense of individual liberty in *Liberty*.[4] I reach my conclusion slightly episodically by tackling four familiar issues in the theory of property—the problem of 'initial appropriation' of unowned things, the state's rights of taxation and compulsory purchase, the legitimacy of slavery, and whether we 'own' our bodies; but before tackling these issues, I begin by making five fairly obvious points about a utilitarian account of property rights in order to show that these episodes are episodes in one theoretical story.

I

Part of the importance of the utilitarian account of property rights, both in its historical impact and now, lies in its disconnection of the defense of property from appeals to liberty. There are, as we shall see, various ways in which this disconnection is effected. The first, which goes back to Hobbes at the latest, is the disconnection of the analysis of property rights from the defense of traditional republicanism and its account of the role of property rights in maintaining civic liberty.[5] Traditionally, the defense of republican government was the defense of civic liberty; this, for instance, is the whole point of Machiavelli's *Discorsi*, a work that takes it for granted that one thing a constitution maker must attend to is the regulation of property to preserve liberty.[6] This was not an archaic concern by the time Bentham discussed property rights in his *Civil Code*.[7] Rousseau acknowledged his debt to Machiavelli in the *Contrat social* and, perhaps even more clearly though inexplicitly, in the provisions of the *Economie politique*.[8] Jefferson, too, knew that his defense of the small proprietor belonged to a classical tradition, and the Scottish social theorists of the eighteenth century are interesting just because they live in two intellectual worlds, one of them thinking in terms of civic virtue and civic liberty, the other thinking in terms of progress and prosperity. But 'liberty' in this sense means nothing to the utilitarian theory of property. Or, to put it more moderately, it cannot be the central concern of the utilitarian theory, and even if it becomes an important concern of some utilitarians, it cannot become so in quite these terms. To Bentham, as much as to Hobbes, 'freedom' consisted in the silence of the laws, not in those laws that did exist being self-imposed under a republican constitution.[9] *If* you were concerned to recreate some of the characteristics of classical republican politics, there were, no doubt, various things you might well be advised to do about property; but none of them were best described as creating liberty. This conceptual point about what 'liberty' *is* was, however, made with the casualness it was partly because neither Hobbes nor Bentham had any time for the republican virtues anyway. It is noticeable that when J. S. Mill came to defend producer cooperatives as incorporating the best of private proprietorship and socialism, he revived the classical emphasis on self-government and broadened the concept of liberty to include virtue as part of freedom.[10] I will not labor the point further, since I have tried to spell it out at some length elsewhere.

II

The second aspect of the disconnection of property and liberty is better known, and is more to our present purposes. This is the insistence that there is no natural right to property and that in whatever ways the property laws of a state may be misconceived, or its taxation and welfare policies, too, it is not in violating a man's natural liberty to do what he chooses with his own. There is no such thing as natural ownership, and whatever natural relationship you may establish with things external to you does not amount to ownership until the law makes it such. Since all the property rights you *could* have would be created by the law, whatever rights you do have are simply what the law says they are. Whatever laws there are about property do not diminish your liberty by removing a former right of ownership.

Now, this claim must be understood quite carefully. It is not the claim that the law cannot abridge your liberty at all. For Bentham, as for Hobbes, the whole point of law is to abridge liberty for the sake of making more useful the liberty it leaves us with. The laws protect us in using the liberty they leave us by restraining others from interfering with us; that is, they remove the liberty to interfere with one another in various areas, in order to allow us to live more securely and more contentedly. In the state of nature there would be liberty to seize what you could, liberty to hang on to it, liberty to defend yourself against attack, but liberty to attack others, liberty to seize what they had got, and so endlessly on. It is this useless liberty that the law abridges. And what that useless liberty does *not* achieve is the creation of a property right in whatever you succeeded in seizing and holding.[11]

In Bentham's account of these issues, it sometimes seems that Bentham's attachment to legal positivism stems from the view that duties are logically prior to rights. That is, Bentham holds that rights exist only when there is some power capable of laying upon others the obligation to refrain from interfering with us. For my *de facto* possession to ripen into *de jure* ownership, I must be the beneficiary of a rule backed up by sanctions that essentially says to others that under such and such conditions, they must not interfere with my use and control of whatever it is. My rights in the thing are the shadows cast by your duty to allow me to exercise my abilities unimpeded.

But, of course, there are two distinct issues here: one, whether some rights defy such analysis; the other, whether duties imply positive laws. There is, I think, one kind of right that Bentham's account has great difficulty in dealing with. This is the right to decide one's future conduct that one can transfer to another by a promise made to him or her. Suppose I promise a friend to accompany her to the cinema; once I have made the promise to her, I have transferred to her the right to say whether I shall or shall not go. This seems to presuppose that in the absence of any such promise I had just such a right as I transferred; and this right seems not to be the shadow of anyone else's duties, but rather to be the basis on which their duties are to be understood. It is, on the face of it, a general right to liberty on the one hand and a power to bind ourselves by transferring that right on the other.[12] If promising only becomes intelligible in terms of our having this kind of underlying right, Bentham's program of eliminating rights from the foundations of morals runs into difficulty. This, however, does no great damage to the program of giving a utilitarian account of property rights since there is no reason to construe promises as if they are a transfer of *property*.

The point can be enforced by turning to the writer who talks of our having a property in our own persons, and in the process we can see the second point at issue, namely, that it can be perfectly plausible to argue that there are natural property rights, even if rights are the shadows of duties—or, less aggressively, even if rights are secondary to duties and duties are the creatures of law. Locke's talk of 'having a property' in ourselves is very far from implying that we are our own property; we are, he says, the property of the God who made us. Locke's account of our capacity to make promises to one another is an account of how men have a limited sovereignty over themselves, limited because it is granted by God for His reasons.[13] In relying on such a case Locke takes it for granted that duties are prior to rights. All the same, men have some elaborate property rights in the state of nature; the reason is clear enough. God requires us to go about His business; we must therefore have the powers that we require for the fulfillment of those duties His business lays on us. It is not just that many of our rights can be explained in terms of other people's duties—that my right to life, for instance, is to a large extent the shadow of your duty not to kill me except in self-defense; it is also that I have a duty to preserve myself, and therefore a right to do so. My quasi-legislative capacities to make something mine, and to make it yours by transfer, are not understood solely in terms of your duties of non-intervention; rather, they are powers I must have if I am to make the most of God's endowments. What rights I have in the state of nature become intelligible in the light of a rational understanding of God's purposes, which is why Locke thinks it is clear that the requirement that we must not let anything perish uselessly in our possession is a distinct requirement from that of leaving as much and as good for others. 'Spoiling' is a matter of God's purposes rather than human whim.[14]

In the same way, my right to positive aid from others as well as to noninterference stems from others' duties to God. They are obliged to preserve all mankind as much as may be, where their own preservation comes not into competition; this means that they have a duty to preserve me if I am likely to perish otherwise. I do not merely have a right that they do not impede me in looking for food elsewhere than among their goods, I have a right to some portion of those goods too.[15]

It is thus clear that in any simple fashion the view that duties are prior to rights does nothing to show that there could not be *natural* property rights; conversely, the view that rights are prior to duties and that there are moral rights as well as legal rights does nothing to show that there are natural *property* rights. But there does lurk here a view that Bentham ought to have found congenial, although so far as I know he does not embrace it. In essence, he could have argued that duties are prior to rights, that duties are imposed by law; Locke believed this, believing as he did that obligation depended upon the will of a superior. Locke, therefore, believed quite consistently that under natural law, with a divine lawgiver, men had rights in the state of nature. Once God was dead, natural law was dead, natural duties were dead, and natural rights were dead. A secular natural-law theory is simply incoherent, and a secular natural-rights theory is therefore incoherent too. Against a writer like Nozick, the argument still has some force.[16]

III

A third feature of the utilitarian account of property then becomes clearer; this is the view that the nonexistence of a system of property rights enforced in law is not an infringement of anyone's rights, not itself a restriction of their liberty, and not straightforwardly an injustice to them. Any positive system of property rights will, as we have seen, certainly restrict their liberty; on an instrumental but nonutilitarian view, a positive system of property rights may also infringe rights, though it will not infringe property rights—for example, the legal enforcement of slavery does not violate the slave's *ownership* of himself, since he has no such ownership by nature, but it does, on this view, violate something like his right to equal treatment as a moral personality among others.[17] To do this to him is to perpetrate an injustice against him. But the absence of a system of property rights seems on the face of it to leave everyone at liberty to manage as best they can; this does no injustice to anyone and violates no rights.

One thing that a more elaborate utilitarianism will, however, want to say about this is that the absence of a system of enforceable property rights is, at least, a missed opportunity to do a lot of good. The interesting question is, what is the best account of the good undone? Take a society in which there is no adequate patent law, say; any utilitarian view of ownership will agree that an inventor here lacks an incentive to develop an invention properly—no man will sow where another will reap. This will mean that society at large does not benefit as it might from his talents. Mill, I think, would have gone further than that; given his view of liberty as enlargement of choice as well as absence of coercion, it is plausible to say that we should increase the freedom of the inventor by creating property rights in the forms covered by patent law, so that one form of good left undone in their absence would be the creation of liberty. Again, it seems plausible that Mill might also have held that the primitive notion of justice ties individual deservings to individual doings; the absence of natural ownership rights is not the same thing as the absence of natural deserts, and even if patents are not the only way to secure natural deserts, they may be such an obvious way that it would be right to say that their absence constitutes an injustice, or certainly a failure to secure justice.[18]

Once there is a legal system of some sort in operation, the justice with which it distributes benefits and burdens among different classes of person will interest the utilitarian as much as anyone else.[19] In that sense, the nonexistence of some particular sort of property right against a background of the existence of many such rights will certainly raise questions of justice, because the burdens of abstaining from other people's property will be imposed on everyone, but only some people will get a reasonable *quid pro quo* for that abstention. The difficulties of giving a persuasive account of the place of these distributive questions occupied Mill a good deal and can perhaps be left to one side here, since they relate to the utilitarian treatment of rights and justice generally rather than to the utilitarian treatment of property rights in particular.[20]

Still, it is worth noticing what follows for the *extinction* of a given property right. Since the right is not a deliverance of natural liberty, it is a mistake to complain that the proprietor's liberty has been reduced. Rather, he has had a privilege or an immunity removed. Nonetheless, considerations of justice do enter into the case, though less as rock-bottom considerations than by way of the principle that expectations legitimately acquired ought not to be frustrated without good cause and on equitable terms.[21] This requirement is met readily enough if the proprietor gets some form of compensation for what he loses. Suppose a mine owner buys his mine in good faith, and some years later has to give it up upon nationalization. There is no injustice in this and no important direct loss of liberty—there may well be important issues about the concentration of power lurking in the background, but these have to be taken care of separately; what the coal-mine owner cannot fall back on is any cry equivalent to 'it's *my* coal mine'. What he can properly do is complain if the terms on which his ownership is abolished impose undue burdens on him.

IV

A fourth feature of utilitarian accounts of property is that they face a characteristic problem, that of reconciling security and equality. The most famous discussion of this is Bentham's own, but in one guise or another, it runs through the literature ever since.[22] Because the utilitarian is not moved by claims such as Robert Nozick's, to the effect that there can be no place for redistributive action in a world in which everything comes into existence already attached to an owner,[23] the forward-looking nature of utilitarian justifications of any distributive arrangement means that the utilitarian is always wondering whether existing rules for the distribution of the society's stock of resources could be improved.

On the face of it, an equal distribution of goods is likely to best serve utility. If goods generally possess diminishing marginal utility, and people have much the same tastes and psychology, then as a rule of thumb, equal shares maximize total utility. But the essence of ownership is surely security. The point of having a property right in something is that I can control what happens to it, whether or not it gives me much, or indeed any, utility at that point. The benefit to society of having rules that secure people in their control of things is obvious enough. A man will not sow where another may reap, and the social cooperation needed for anything more elaborate than small-scale sowing and reaping is unimaginable unless there are rules allowing people to plan ahead and to rely on others performing in due season. The world would simply not be used efficiently in the absence of such rules.[24] It does not follow that those rules have to exactly like those of full private ownership in our sense—communal ownership and longer or shorter leases would be sensible enough, or family ownership plus trustee discretion—but they do have to provide certainty and security.

The conflict between security and equality then develops inexorably. Productivity demands security, that is, laws that do not change quickly, rights that can be relied on no matter what. But the process of production will steadily create increasing inequality as the clever and fortunate do well and the rest less well. At any given moment, there would be an increase in welfare if we were to divide up everything equally; but to do it would set at risk the environment of security and predictability that we rely on to create the wealth to redistribute in the first place. To put it simply, the utilitarian has to discover what distribution of the golden goose's eggs deters the goose from laying.

The dilemma itself compels no particular resolution. Moreover, as all discussions of the disincentive effects of taxation reveal, the argument is clouded with special pleading, as well as bedeviled by the obvious problem that what deters people and what doesn't depends a lot upon what moral, political, and other beliefs about the world they hold. Bentham and James Mill argued in a way that has recently been popularized by von Hayek and that rates security very highly indeed.[25] Over the long run the only way the state can maximize overall welfare is by creating private property rights, and then policing a *laissez-faire* economic order. This, moreover, appeals even to the more egalitarian sort of utilitarian; it might be true that at any given moment the worst-off person *now* would benefit from an equal division of the social stock, but over any long run the worst-off person in the *laissez-faire* order will be better off than the worst-off person in any other system. Bentham in practice did not stick to quite such a rigorously 'hands-off' position. Since there is nothing in the utilitarian calculus to forbid the sacrifice of one sort of gain for another, Bentham is not tempted to suppose that we should never tamper with expectations at all. The crucial point is to avoid frustrating the sort of expectations we ought to arouse. If my father cannot pass on his property to me now, I, having come to expect to get it, will feel frustrated; had he been told when he acquired it that *I* would not be able to pass it on, there would have been no frustration—he could have satisfied his expectations, I would satisfy mine, and my unborn children would have no expectations in the case.[26] The general position adopted by Bentham seems to be that the government may properly encumber property with taxes and restrictions from a future date in order that persons in future take possession knowing what they are getting, and people presently do not stand a loss at once. Compared with a theory that is wholly committed to the *rights* of owners, this is casual about the loss of the ability to decide exactly what shall happen to one's property; a utilitarian sufficiently impressed with people's attachment to the distant future might be more tender to the desire to tie up one's property, but this would be a matter of political psychology rather than direct moral theory. The crucial point is simple. As against the theory which holds that all redistribution is illicit because what it is proposed to distribute already has *owners*, the utilitarian holds that the artificial device, which is what a legal system is, can be constructed in whatever way we choose; but the importance of creating and satisfying stable expectations means that it is almost certainly wrong to attempt anything more than slowly operating methods of redistribution.

V

In all this, there is one point we have skirted but not confronted. This is the claim that for society to establish rules regulating property rights, society must claim something like initial ownership of the property thereafter confided to private hands.[27] The fifth and final point that needs to be made about the utilitarian theory of ownership is that its conception of rights is quite at odds with this view. There is a sort of natural affinity between the utilitarian justification of property rights – in general and in particular – and the legal positivist view that what property rights exist at any time and place is a factual matter to be settled by inspection of the local legal system. The conceptual question of what property *is* is divorced from the question of what property rights there ought to be; and an implication of this is that the utilitarian simply denies that the state must claim ownership to create ownership. Once there is a legal system, it is, of course, true that *individuals* do have to own things before they can transfer them. It does not follow that the relationship between the state and the individual is in positive law the same, and it does not follow that the relationship between society and the individual is in morality a shadow of the legal relationship between individuals. When the state claims the power to tax, to take by compulsory purchase and all the rest of it, this need no more rest on claims of ownership than I have to claim *ownership* of my neighbors' houses to have the right to pull them down in the event of their threatening to set my house on fire.[28]

What this means is that the utilitarian theory of ownership is in the last resort not very bothered about *ownership* at all. Ownership is to be analyzed as a bundle of rights, and the bundle can be unpicked in various ways and reassembled as we choose. To wonder who *really* owns a vast corporation like ICI, seeing that rights to income, rights to control the day-to-day operations of the company, and all the rest of it are scattered among so many different people – and seeing that the shareholders who own the company do not in any simple way own the company's property – is not an anxiety that comes naturally to utilitarians.[29] To suppose that things *must* have owners is habitual with Kant and Hegel but alien to the utilitarian tradition. On the utilitarian view, ownership is a convenient device, but one whose functions could largely be replaced by other sorts of rights, and it would be no lacuna in a legal system if many things were simply unowned and were dealt with in quite different ways.[30]

To insist that the state has no right to alter ownership rights save by the grant of such a right from the owners is, in effect, to start from the prejudice that only rights can generate rights and that rights are essentially proprietary in nature. This, however, is an odd view to take; its oddity comes out in interesting and curious ways in Nozick's *Anarchy, State and Utopia*, where the distinction between offenses against the person and offenses against property is simply collapsed—all are illicit boundary crossings.[31] Anyone tempted in that direction, as was Kant, who wished to grant the state the same range of economic powers that most utilitarians would wish to, then has the awkward task of justifying the introduction of a fictional communal ownership of the earth as a starting point and a fictional contract empowering the state to regulate subsequent private ownership in appropriate ways.[32] The awkwardness is so extreme that it makes the utilitarian view of the conventionality of property rights and their dependence on the activities of the state all the more attractive in comparison.

VI

These considerations can be fleshed out a little more by taking four issues in which the arguments alluded to so far have been put to work. The first of these is the proper way to treat 'original acquisition'—the question of what rights persons can plausibly claim over unowned things. The second is the question of the legitimacy of slavery. The third is whether the state's right to tax is equivalent to a right to impose forced labor upon its subjects. The last is whether we own our own bodies. The point of taking up these issues is that they show up neatly the differences between utilitarian and natural-rights theories, and show in addition that even when utilitarianism perhaps cannot deal with everything a natural-rights theory can deal with, we need not resort to natural rights of ownership. At two points at least these are issues that embarrass utilitarians whose liberal instincts and utilitarian arguments pull in different directions. Mill is often accused of incoherence in arguing that people ought not to be allowed to sell themselves into slavery; it seems to be a breach of his own prohibition of paternalistic legislation; he seems to depart from strict utilitarianism in just assuming that there is nothing to be said for slavery; and he cannot give a coherent account of the individual's rights over himself or herself—if the individual is sovereign over himself in what harms nobody else, how can he not have the right to sell himself into slavery?[33] Again, when utilitarians are accused of being willing to sacrifice one person for the welfare of another, an example often employed against them is what one might call 'compulsory transplanting'. What is the objection to killing an innocent person in order to distribute his or her bodily organs among sick patients who would otherwise die for lack of them?[34] As we shall see, the utilitarian is not without resources to answer this question, but the natural-rights theorist is, at first glance, perfectly equipped—he simply says that our bodies are *ours*, not part of a publicly available stock of medical resources.

The rights a person can claim over unowned things are the subject matter of Locke's theory of property most famously, but they must occupy any theorist's attention. In Locke's account, the crucial and contested claim is that a man who acquires something by catching it, picking it, drinking it, or whatever, mixes his labor with it, and in the process makes it *his*.[35] The question is whether a utilitarian like Mill who is sympathetic to the thought that individuals have moral rights as well as legal ones is forced to concede that people's moral rights amount to ownership. The answer seems to be no. On the doctrines of *Liberty*, what a person may do with an unowned object depends on just the same considerations as govern a person's rights generally; that is, he may do what he likes so long as he doesn't threaten harm to others. Does this mean that when he picks an apple from a tree, he comes to own it? The answer cannot be straightforward, depending as it does upon prior assumptions about what the central elements of ownership are. But suppose we agree that since picking the apple harmed no one he was permitted to do it; we can then go on to agree that once he had picked it, it would then be an unwarranted interference with his liberty to stop him eating it. The more interesting question is what happens if he tries to pass it on to someone else. If his taking and eating harmed nobody, it is likely that giving it to someone else will harm nobody, and that he ought not to be prevented from doing it.

Is this, however, a transfer of property rights? I think it is not. That is, the new possessor's right to noninterference comes from the fact of his *de facto* possession and the general rule that whatever he does ought to be tolerated unless it does harm to others. Similarly, if the previous possessor imposes restrictions on what can be done with the apple—suppose he insists that the new possessor eat the apple himself rather than pass it on in turn—these restrictions are intelligible as the result of a promise made to the former possessor rather than as features of the property in question. One could envisage many of the incidents that attach to property and run with it as restrictive covenants being mimicked by a string of promises, and promises to exact further promises, but these would still be matters of personal rights not real rights. The obligation to exact a promise from whomever we pass the apple to is an obligation holding us to the particular person to whom we made the promise only.[36]

The temptation to say that a person who takes an unowned thing must become its owner seems to stem from two things. The first is that because we identify actions by their doers we cannot but agree that it is 'his' or 'her' taking that alters the status of the thing taken; it was *his* taking that moved it from a state where nobody had it to a state where he had it. The temptation then is to think that he has mixed what was his with what was nobody's and thereby made it his too. It should not be a strong temptation, though, since the sense in which our actions are *ours* is not much like the sense in which a car is ours.[37] The second temptation lies in the idea that a person who takes an unowned object does so with the *intention* of becoming its owner, rather as the King of Spain took possession of the New World from his study in Madrid with the intention of thereafter controlling its destiny. This is fundamentally the way Kant and Hegel tackle the issue.[38]

The objection to tackling the issue in this way is that it simply begs the question by presupposing what it tries to explain. It more or less ends by asserting that a person who takes an unowned thing asserts a sovereignty in it that has to be acknowledged as a corollary of the principle of respect for persons. There are two things a utilitarian might wish to say in response. The first is that utilitarianism can give a perfectly sensible account of why first occupancy ought generally to be treated as a step towards legal ownership; asking what conventions would maximize utility, we are likely to end by thinking that *ceteris paribus*, we should confirm the title of those in possession, those who have mixed their labor, and so on.[39] The second is that no utilitarian would accept respect for persons as a fundamental principle; it is altogether too like the doctrines of 'abstract right' that Mill deplored. The idea that people establish themselves in the world as owners of external things would have struck him as an implausible derivation from an implausible principle. It might be argued that someone who held an instrumental theory of *property* rights, but who held that individuals had some rights— perhaps a right to equal concern and respect among them—which were not conventions established for instrumental reasons, might be more inclined to think that the rights one might have over unowned things did amount to ownership. Even so, there is no great pressure in this direction.

VII

I turn now to the question of slavery. Rights-theorists have had various views about the institution. One extreme view, associated with Grotius, and perhaps with Nozick,[40] is that since we begin by being the outright owners of ourselves, we can give that ownership to anyone we choose; once the transfer has taken place, we no longer own ourselves, of course—we are owned by whomever we have transferred ourselves to. His or her ownership of us, like anyone's ownership of anything, is a matter of tracing how he came by the title; since we once held it and transferred it to him, he has a good title. The other extreme view is that slavery is incoherent; it presupposes that the slave is both mere thing and fully fledged person, and he or she cannot be *that*. The rights essential to personality cannot be transferred, either because, as in Locke, we do not hold them in the absolute way we hold rights over things or because, as in Hegel, there is felt to be some incoherence in basing the right to extinguish our personality on the fact of that personality.[41] Neither view looks to the utilitarian advantages of slavery versus other economic arrangements; both look to one question only, which is whether slavery necessarily violates the slave's rights in such a way that even a voluntary act of the would-be slave cannot make him a slave.

The utilitarian cannot go along with those who think that slavery is conceptually illicit. On the positivist account to which utilitarians subscribe, slaves exist if some legal system or other provides for their existence. The only question is whether it ought to be possible to own another human being, and whether a person who tries to sell herself or himself into slavery can be held to the terms of any such agreement. It is for all that, true that before Bentham turns to discuss the issue at any length, his first step is to condemn the defenders of slavery by inquiring if they would be happy to change places with slaves—no doubt a good question but dubiously utilitarian in spirit.[42] The more interesting response is offered by Mill in his discussion of perpetual contracts, in which, he perhaps a bit contentiously, links slavery and marriage. The difficulty Mill is in is obvious enough; if people are to be allowed to do whatever they wish so long as they do not damage the interests of others, we seem to be committed to letting them sell themselves into slavery—or marriage. But Mill denies that society ought to enforce any perpetual contracts of this kind. The way he presents the case, moreover, suggests that he, too, may have thought it an awkward one—a paternalistic interference with free choice but justified in terms of the enlargement of freedom rather than in the usual paternalistic terms of the interference being 'good' for the person interfered with in terms which he or she might no appreciate.[43]

A more accurate view dispels the air of paradox. The defense of leaving people to do as they choose is not based on the thought that they 'own' themselves and can do as they choose with all their various pieces of property, themselves included. There is no natural ownership, whether of ourselves or of others. What a person who wishes to be a 'slave' can do is promise to do whatever he or she is asked to do by the person he nominates as the 'owner'. He cannot be a real slave in the absence of a legal system that recognizes servitude as a legally enforced condition; he cannot do more than set out to behave slavishly. With that, we ought not to interfere—save by engaging in those activities that Mill groups under the general heading of exhorting and entreating; more crucially, we ought not to side with his 'owner' if he changes his mind about the whole business and decides to stop behaving like a slave. This seems to meet the case—it is not that we stop people doing what they naturally can, but that we decline to provide institutional sanctions to make them go on doing it. It may be compared with the case of suicide; we ought not to prevent someone's committing suicide— under appropriate restrictions about making sure that he or she knows what sort of choice he or she is making. It does not follow that we are obliged to *assist* anyone to do away with himself. To do the latter is to limit our own freedom of action; perhaps we are so convinced that a given person's life is a misery that we do feel we ought, say, to lend him our gun to make a quick job of it, but this will be a matter of particular cases, not a matter of a general obligation to help someone to realize his choices no matter what. If I think him or her mistaken, I am under no obligation to help.[44]

One possible argument to show that Mill is still in trouble would be to claim that the obligation on the rest of us to enforce a perpetual contract stems from the fact that it is a promise like any other. If in general we think we ought to enforce the rights people get from others in virtue of being the beneficiaries of promises, why ought we not to enforce this promise—what grounds are there for saying that the 'owner' gets no rights, no matter what promises the 'slave' makes? It plainly is not like the case in which what I promise is something I have no right to do, such as the case in which I promise you that I will murder someone else. I have the right to act slavishly, and I promise to do just that. The reply, I take it, is that for a writer such as Mill, the way in which promises are to be understood is as a social device; promising is a device for enlarging the scope of choice. Promising belongs in an institutional framework that society offers to its members for the better conduct of their affairs. The rationale for it is in part libertarian, that is, it is partly out of a concern that people should be able to make arrangements facilitating future but as yet unknown projects that we mind so much about promising. But this rationale is at odds with enforcing self-enslavement.[45]

This, of course, is to stick within the framework offered by rights-theorists who raise the question whether we have the right to enslave ourselves. On the rather wider issue of how to respond to arguments about 'respect for persons' that rule slavery out of court as a morally tolerable institution, Mill's position is impeccably utilitarian. That is, he thinks that slavery was once justified as the only way of allowing enough economic advance to promote human progress generally. Once civilization advances, it is clearly intolerable. But, in the nineteenth-century context, he still argues that although slavery is quite wrong and ought to be abolished, the owners of slaves should get proper compensation; there is no suggestion that their complicity in an illicit institution rules out a claim to compensation.[46]

VIII

Armed with the utilitarian view that property rights are entirely conventional, we can give a straightforward account of the state's right to tax, expropriate, or otherwise dispose of the property of individuals. The utilitarian's commitments to both individualism and collectivism balance out quite elegantly here. In a manner of speaking, the ultimate beneficiary of our efforts and the world's resources ought to be the community at large or 'all sentient creatures';[47] yet, the community only exists as discrete individuals, the only satisfactions there are are satisfactions of particular individuals. We must be tender to individuals for the sake of the whole collection of individuals. Therefore, in principle governments may create and extinguish titles of all sorts, and tax at any rate they choose.[48] But three sorts of consideration ought to animate them in making up their minds about what property rights to recognize and what taxation policies to adopt. The first is the need to keep up incentives, to avoid depressing initiative, and the like. This, we have seen already, may lead to a cautious policy about trying to redistribute resources; but it may leave plenty of room for maneuver about what we tax—we may go gently on earned income but have a large accessions tax, on the grounds that this would increase the incentive to *earn* an income and does not much reduce incentive in general by making it less easy to give wealth to the already wealthy.[49] This is the place in utilitarian theory in which an answer comes to the recently popular question whether taxation isn't the same thing as forced labor. The reply is that on this view it is not. Certainly, taxation is a forced contribution to social costs—even if we approve of all the measures the government takes, we have no choice whether to pay our contribution to its expenses. But not all forced contributions are forced labor, and the utilitarian knows why *corvées* cause social unrest in a fashion income taxes usually do not. An income levy is much the least painful way of extracting taxes—tithes are worse and labor duties worse yet. Moreover, viewed in the utilitarian framework, there is no particular anxiety about the status of taxation generally; it is not that we have a property right in our incomes and then reluctantly hand over some portion to government. *Morally*, as opposed to *legally*, there is no reason to think that we do have that sort of right to our pretax incomes; rather, we are entitled to some share in the net proceeds of social collaboration, even if the simplest way of organizing the business is a way that gives more comfort than it ought to the nonutilitarian.

The second consideration is the need to do justice to different classes of person. Here, once more, we have to take it on trust that utilitarianism possesses an adequate account of justice; if it does, we must recognize that in addition to the considerations of incentive and the like just mentioned, we must take care that fairness is not neglected, either in the allocation of tax burdens or in compensating those whose property rights are extinguished. But all this is bread and butter to social theorists like Mill, who took considerable pains with his evidence to parliamentary committees on just such topics.[50] The last consideration is perhaps the most interesting. If the utilitarian justification of property rights is to enlarge choice and create security, it may be that we ought to break up the property rights characteristic of a capitalist economy based on individual private property and the joint stock company for much the same reasons that animated the putting together of those bundles of rights in the first place. For instance, we may want to divorce the ownership of capital assets from the right to appoint managers; we may want to divorce the right to receive an income from a shareholding from the right to receive a share of capital gains; and we shall certainly want to insist on separating the state's right to insist, say, that any firm above a certain size is run as a workers' cooperative from any suggestion that the state should try to monopolize the right to decide prices and output in the manner of a command economy.[51] But what is above all to be noticed about what all this implies for the utilitarian theory of ownership is that when a rights-theorist might begin by asserting that people just *are* originators of value, creators of moral worth in the world, and the begetters of their own projects—all of which requires expression in the appropriate ownership institutions—the utilitarian is content to say that although people are not essentially anything of the sort, this is what with luck and good social design they may become—and a rational justification of property rights justifies those rights which that progress requires.[52]

IX

I turn, lastly, to the suggestion that if we do not start with a doctrine of self-ownership, the utilitarian is driven to treat as serious moral proposals ways of treating people which we all know to be simply wrong. The thought experiment of the argument for compulsory transplant surgery is a good example. We suppose a ward in which two men are dying, one for lack of a suitable kidney, one for lack of a suitable heart, say; to the news that no spare parts are available, they reply that they are—all the doctors need do is kill some unsuspecting donor and save two lives for the price of one.[53] It is, I think, clear that no sensible utilitarian would give the suggestion houseroom for reasons familiar to all insurance companies—it creates a moral hazard in that it gives people an incentive to ruin their own organs, seeing that they stand to benefit from transplants if they are ill, and they stand not to be used for spare parts if they aren't fit to be so used.[54] But some writers appear to think that this misses the point. The difficulty is to decide what that point is. One suggestion is that because the donor's organs are *his* organs, it violates his rights to take them. Even if all we did was take a pint of his blood and leave him to recover quietly after we had done so, it would still violate his rights, just because it was *his* blood and not ours.

It seems to me that there is not much to be said for trying to explain the illicitness of treating people as resources in terms of property rights—save perhaps negatively in recalling that we are not one another's property. But it is not because we are each our own property that we are not one another's property. We draw a sharp line between theft and assault, and a theory of rights that blurs the distinction is unattractive. It was precisely because we cannot be injured except in our own bodies that Kant had to go to such lengths to explain the nature of property in terms of our being 'injured at a distance' by mischiefs done to it.[55] It seems peculiarly unattractive to make the case the other way round—to explain injury as a sort of theft close to. Another consideration in the same vein is that whatever one thinks about rights in general, property rights are at least often through and through artificial; but rights over our own bodies come as close as anything can to being natural rights. Even to walk down the street presupposes that I have the right to move my legs in the appropriate fashion. It's hard to see what rights would be like at all if they did not include rights over one's body—but it is not hard to see how there could be such rights and no property rights.

In short, if there is something distasteful about such a suggestion as the compulsory transplant surgery, it seems to be for two reasons. The first is moral. The idea treats people as mere means to an end, treats them as resources. I do not think that utilitarianism can do very much to accommodate the idea that this is intolerable; this is one reason why many writers have thought that an instrumental theory of property rights was correct, but resisted the thought that the best instrumental theory is utilitarian. All the same, utilitarianism can do a good deal to embrace the same conclusions as the theorist of a right to respect as a person would reach. If people just do passionately mind about not being treated as an object, even for benevolent purposes, that launches the utilitarian case for treating people's own wishes with extreme tenderness.[56]

The second reason that may underlie this desire for being the controller of our own fates is more nearly metaphysical. It is the consequence of our human embodiment that for each of us *this* body is special; we and it are so closely bound up with one another that we cannot coherently see ourselves as both selves and mere collections of parts. It is quite unclear to me how far one can press this point, and equally unclear to me how much metaphysical baggage utilitarianism has to carry or jettison. Happily this does not matter, since the only point I have to make in conclusion is that these considerations do not affect the analysis of property rights. If an inability to give an account of the categorical imperative in its various guises is a defect in utilitarianism as a complete system of ethics, it makes no difference to utilitarianism's capacity to give a persuasive account of property rights. As we have just seen, there may be some rights—the right not to be sacrificed, say—for which utilitarianism cannot offer a very compelling rationale. But such rights are not property rights. Of those rights that are genuinely property rights, utilitarianism gives the plainest and most compelling account we have.

NOTES

1. R. Nozick, *Anarchy, State and Utopia* (Oxford: Blackwell, 1974), p. 228.
2. A. M. Honore, "Ownership," in *Oxford Essays in Jurisprudence*, ed. A. G. Guest (Oxford: the Clarendon Press, 1961), pp. 107ff.

3. G. W. F. Hegel, *The Philosophy of Right* (Oxford: the Clarendon Press, 1941), pp. 54, 57.

4. J. S. Mill, *The Principles of Political Economy*, in *Collected Works* (Toronto and London: University of Toronto Press and Routledge Kegan Paul, 1965) II–III, p. 201ff.

5. T. Hobbes, *Leviathan* (London: Dent, 1914), p. 113.

6. N. Machiavelli, *The Discourses* (Harmondsworth, Penguin Books, 1970), pp. 42-43.

7. J. Bentham, *Theory of Legislation* (London: Trubner French, 1887), pp. 93-198.

8. J-J. Rousseau, *Social Contract and Discourses* (London: Dent, 1973), pp. 117-53.

9. *Leviathan*, pp. 110-11.

10. J. S. Mill, *A System of Logic*, in *Collected Works* (1973), VII–VIII, p. 841.

11. *Theory of Legislation*, pp. 112-13.

12. H. L. A. Hart, "Are There Any Natural Rights?" *Philosophical Review* 64 (1955): 175-91.

13. J. Locke, *Two Treatises of Government* (Cambridge: Cambridge University Press, 1967), p. 289 (II, ii, 6).

14. *Ibid*, p. 318 (II, v, 47).

15. *Ibid*, pp. 188–89 (I, iv, 42-43).

16. *Anarchy, State and Utopia*, pp. 175-76.

17. *The Philosophy of Right*, p. 259.

18. *Principles of Political Economy*, p. 208.

19. *Ibid*, p. 233.

20. A. Ryan, *The Philosophy of John Stuart Mill* (London: Macmillan, 1970), pp. 213-30.

21. *Principles of Political Economy*, p. 233.

22. *Theory of Legislation*, pp. 119-22.

23. *Anarchy, State and Utopia*, p. 219.

24. James Mill, *An Essay on Government* (Indianapolis: Bobbs-Merrill, 1955), pp. 48-49.

25. *Theory of Legislation*, p. 109.

26. *Ibid*, p. 122.

27. *Anarchy, State and Utopia*, p. 213ff.

28. H. Reiss, ed., *Kant's Political Writings* (Cambridge: Cambridge University Press, 1970), pp. 147-48.

29. A. A. Berle and G. C. Means, *The Modern Corporation and Private Property*, rev. ed., (New York: 1968), pp. 293ff.

30. F. H. Lawson, *The Law of Property* (Oxford: The Clarendon Press, 1958), pp. 59ff.

31. *Anarchy, State and Utopia*, pp. 75-76.

32. *Kant's Political Writings*, p. 147.

33. J. S. Mill, *Utilitarianism, Liberty, Representative Government* (London: Dent, 1914), pp. 157-59.

34. *Anarchy, State and Utopia*, p. 206.

35. *Two Treatises on Government*, p. 306 (II, v. 28).

36. *The Law of Property*, p. 98.

37. J. P. Day, "Locke on Property," *Philosophical Quarterly* 16 (1966): 207-21.

38. *The Philosophy of Right*, pp. 40-41.

39. *Principles of Political Economy*, pp. 214ff.

40. R. Tuck, *Natural Rights Theories* (Cambridge: Cambridge University Press, 1979), pp. 78-79.

41. *Philosophy of Right*, pp. 52-54.

42. *Theory of Legislation*, pp. 202-3.

43. *Utilitarianism*, p. 157.

44. V. Haksar, *Liberty, Equality and Perfectionism* (Oxford: The Clarendon Press, 1979), pp. 253–55.

45. *Utilitarianism*, p. 158.

46. *Principles of Political Economy*, p. 233.

47. *Utilitarianism*, p. 11.

48. *Principles of Political Economy*, pp. 800ff.

49. *Ibid*, pp. 222–14.

50. J. S. Mill, *Essays on Economics and Society*, in *Collected Works* (1967), IV–V, pp. 463–98.

51. *Principles of Political Economy*, pp. 758–96.

52. *Essays on Economics and Society*, pp. 749–52.

53. J. Harris, "The Survival Lottery," *Philosophy* 50 (1975); 81-87.

54. P. Singer, "Utility and the Survival Lottery," *Philosophy* 52 (1977); 218–20.

55. *Kant's Political Writings*, p. 136.

56. J. Glover, *Causing Death and Saving Lives* (Harmondsworth: Penguin Books, 1977).

10

Persons and Property

Rolf Sartorius

My aim in this essay is to achieve a preliminary sorting out, within a
Lockean framework, of the basic principles that I believe must enter into
the construction of a comprehensive theory of private property rights.
The basic notion from which I begin is that as autonomous and responsible agents capable of entering into significant social relationships with
others we are entitled to political institutions which reflect the moral
right that each of us has to be treated as an individual with the capacity
to shape and pursue his or her own conception of a meaningful life. I
share the view of Charles Reich that "The institution called property
guards the troubled boundary between individual man and the
state. . . . In a society that chiefly values material well-being, the power
to control a particular portion of that well-being is the very foundation
of individuality."[1] "The troubled boundary" of which Reich speaks may
be understood as the line that separates the permissible from the impermissible use of coercion against the individual by the state. Although
not all moral rights and obligations, including those based upon entitlements to property, are enforceable, the domain of legitimate political
authority is limited to those that are.[2]

I might note at the outset that the approach I shall take throughout
is avowedly anti-utilitarian. Although consequentialist considerations
will enter in a variety of ways, the basic principles that I shall discuss
all support claims of right as claims that defeat counterclaims based
upon considerations concerning the promotion of utility except when
the consequences of satisfying those claims would be extremely severe.
It is not that utilitarians can not construct accounts of rights in this
sense. Rule-utilitarians[3] can in an obvious way, and I argued some years
ago that even act-utilitarians could support social norms which bar
direct appeals to utility in a manner that is perhaps not so obvious.[4] The

basic problem for any form of utilitarian theory no matter how cleverly constructed is that when it does yield the required principles of moral right it will do so for the wrong reasons.[5] For any form of utilitarian theory faces three absolutely central and, I believe, unanswerable objections, each of which must arise in its own way to any utilitarian theory of property rights. First, with whatever the maximization of utility is associated and whatever the notion of maximization (sum total or average utility), the maximand represents an aggregate measure that is totally insensitive to distributional considerations except insofar as they are causally relevant. Principles of property right are if nothing else independent moral constraints on permissible distributions of property and thus upon the welfare with which (as Reich notes) it is so closely associated in a society like our own. Second, any form of utilitarian theory must accord full face value to any and all sources of satisfaction, including what Bentham without any apparent embarrassment described as "pleasures of malevolence."[6] Ronald Dworkin may have gone to an extreme in attempting to build a theory of rights on a utilitarianism purified of such "external preferences," but he is surely correct in claiming that they ought to carry no weight whatsoever when utilitarian calculations are in order.[7] Among such preferences is envy, a utilitarian's accounting of which would lead him or her to adopt principles which would militate against distributions of property which are clearly morally unobjectionable.[8] Third, any form of utilitarian theory must reduce all forms of moral consideration to one common dimension such as preference-satisfaction or happiness in the sense that Bentham understood it. Problems of interpersonal utility comparisons aside, this represents both a big mistake and a little mistake. The big mistake, as Thomas Nagel has argued,[9] is the reductivist attempt to deny the significant differences in kind between the formally different dimensions — irreducibly "fragmented" on his view — upon which judgments of value are made. The *ultimate* significance of special personal relationships, and the rights and obligations that may surround them, must be denied by the utilitarian, for instance, which would lead him to deny that members of my own immediate family have any greater claim on my property than strangers who are in equal need of it. The little mistake, as Thomas Scanlon has argued,[10] is to assume that within the dimension of "utility" no distinctions are to be made between such things as urgent objective needs and strong subjective preferences. It is just such distinctions that must be made if any sense is to be made of the welfare rights for which we shall see there clearly is a place within a Lockean theory of private property.

H. L. A. Hart's classic "Prolegomenon to the Principles of Punishment" begins with a claim that in large part represents the basic strategy of my approach to what I shall argue is a genuine plurality of principles required to form a systematic theory of private property rights.

> There is . . . an analogy worth considering between the concept of punishment and that of property. . . . In both cases we are confronted by a complex institution presenting different inter-related features calling for separate . . . justification. In both cases failure to distinguish separate questions or attempting to answer them all by reference to a single principle ends in confusion. Thus in the case of property we should distinguish between the question of the *definition* of property, and question why and in what circumstances it is a *good* institution to maintain, and the questions in what ways individuals may become *entitled* to property and *how much* they should be allowed to acquire. These we may call questions of *Definition, General Justifying Aim,* and *Distribution* with the last subdivided into questions of *Title* and *Amount*. It is salutary to take some classical exposition of the idea of property, say Locke's . . . , and to observe how much darkness is spread by the use of a single notion (in this case 'the labour of (a man's) body and the work of his hands') to answer all these different questions which press upon us when we reflect on the institution of property.[11]

The single *notion* to which Hart alludes is what has come to be called Locke's labor *theory* of property, and the following two passages from Locke's *Second Treatise* have been described by Laslett as "perhaps the most influential statements he ever made."[12]

> Though the earth and all inferior creatures be common to all men, yet every man has a property in his own person; this nobody has any right to but himself. The labor of his body and the work of his hands, we may say are properly his. Whatsoever then he removes out of the state that nature has provided and left it in, he has mixed his labor with, and joined it to something that is his own, and thereby makes it his property. It being by him removed from the common state nature has placed it in, it has by this labor something annexed to it that excludes the common right of other men. For this labor being the unquestionable property of the laborer, no man but he can have a right to what that is once joined to, at least where there is enough and as good left for others. (section 27)

> It is labor indeed that put the difference of value on everything. . . . The improvement of labor makes the far greater part of value. . . . If we will rightly estimate things as they come

to our use and cast up the several expenses about them, what in them is purely owing to nature, and what to labor, we shall find that in most of them ninety-nine hundredths are wholly to be put on the account of labor. (section 40)

Hart is surely correct that one can take Locke to be answering a variety of different questions about private property in terms of the notion of an individual's labor. This indeed provides the basis for one standard interpretation of Locke according to which:

(a) Private, as distinct from communal, property is *defined* so as to make that which a person has private property rights in coincide with his person, the product of his labor, and what he has received by way of just transfer from others.

(b) The *general justifying aim* of a system of legal property rights is simply the protection of such preexisting moral ("natural") rights to property.

(c) The *distributive* questions concerning *title* and *amount* are to be answered in terms of labor as the basis of initial acquisition subject to the constraint that there be "enough and as good left for others." The right to transfer by gift or bequest or through exchange on the market might be seen on this view as flowing from the very definition of what it is to have a property right in something, including one's labor itself, the sale or gift of which to another gives the other a right to its product ("Thus the . . . turfs my servant has cut . . . become my property. . . ."[section 28])

With sufficient additions of detail, understood along such lines Locke's labor theory may be seen as providing the basis for a virtually unlimited right of capitalistic appropriation,[13] as well as a principled basis for labeling as impermissible (indeed, as a form of theft[14]) the redistributive programs of the modern welfare state. The entire account quite clearly depends upon coupling the labor theory of *entitlement* (section 27) with the labor theory of *value* (section 40), and either ignoring or giving insufficient heed to a number of the other things that Locke either says or implies about the nature and origins of private property. Once the labor theory of value is, as it must be, rejected, a suitably qualified version of the entitlement theory, based upon the entirely defensible notion that one has a right to the fruits of one's labors, conjoined with other Lockean conceptions not yet mentioned, provides the basis for a theory of property rights both quite different from and more plausible than that provided by the traditional interpretation. Although the position I shall sketch may be quite remote from that held by Locke himself, it draws so heavily upon what I take to be his basic insights as to be aptly characterized as "Lockean" in character. And it is surely no more of a departure from his views than the caricature contained in the traditional interpretation.

The difficulties with the labor theory of value are manifold, as indicated by the following list of counterexamples compiled by Nozick:

> found natural objects) valued above the labor necessary to get them); rare goods (letters from Napoleon) that cannot be reproduced in unlimited quantities; differences in value between identical objects at different places; differences skilled labor makes; changes caused by fluctuations in supply and demand; aged objects whose producing requires much time to pass (old wines). . . .[15]

Rejecting the labor theory is of course not to deny that the amount and kind of labor required to produce a thing is a factor that contributes to its market value. And neither is it to deny what the labor theory of entitlement affirms: that one has a right to the fruits of one's labors. But once the fruits of one's labors are no longer understood to include the value of the natural resources in fact owned and employed in production, the labor theory of entitlement no longer can be seen as providing a sufficient basis for a theory of property rights. At best, it will be able to play only a partial role in answering the central questions concerning general justifying aim and distribution in terms of title and amount. The theoretical gap left by rejection of the labor theory of value can, though, be filled in large part by an appeal to other conceptions that play a central role in Locke's account.

As I understand it, the guiding and overarching principle in Locke's theory of property is that of the right of life, "the fundamental law of nature being that all, as much as may be, should be preserved."[16] It is this to which Locke appeals to explain the limits on the right of the victors to acquire the property of the vanquished in a just war, as well as to vindicate the right of a man's wife and children to *inherit* a portion of his estate (a noteworthy constraint on the right of *bequest*).[17] It is this that is taken to dictate the acceptability of reasonable means for appropriating and employing the resources that are productive of the necessities of life at the very beginning of chapter V ("Of Property") of *The Second Treatise*, prior to the statement of the entitlement principle: "God, who has given the world to man in common, has also given them reason to make use of it to the best advantage of life and convenience." (section 26) And it is this that must be taken to underlie the much neglected redistributive principle of *The First Treatise*:

> God . . . has given no one . . . such a property . . . but that he has given his needy brother a right to the surplusage of his

goods. . . . As justice gives every man a title to the product of his honest industry . . . so charity gives every man a title to so much out of another's plenty, as will keep him from extreme want, where he has no means to subsist otherwise. (section 42)

Locke's remarks concerning the labor theory of entitlement in chapter V of *The Second Treatise* are relatively brief, the bulk of the discussion being devoted to a line of argument meant to rebut the position of those who would hold that it is wrongful for one to remove something from the commons without the consent of others. Without even pausing to note that the view "that God gave the world to Adam and his posterity in common" (section 25) would make the gaining of such consent impossible, Locke launches on a general argument strikingly similar to that found in Hume's and Bentham's discussions of private property. The argument would have been even more similar, of course, had Locke not believed that the labor theory of entitlement could take him a long way without appealing to general considerations concerning the protection of life and the promotion of welfare. Briefly, the argument is this.

The earth's resources are a common pool to be drawn on for mutual advantage, providing in large measure the means for the achievement of the *right*ful individual ends of the preservation of life and the pursuit of happiness. And they are to be used to this end in an efficient manner. This provides the grounds for prohibiting not only individual waste within a particular system of property rights (of which I take the spoilage limitation of section 46 to be but a special instance). Put more generally, it also provides a basis for each individual's claiming as a matter of moral right, part and parcel of the right to life itself, a right to participation within a just and efficient *system* for the exploitation of natural resources.[18] And that system is one of private rather than communal ownership, this because it provides the individual incentives required to bring forth the labor which for the most part accounts for the value that things have as they appear in the marketplace, typically greatly improved upon from the condition in which they are found in their natural state.

Such a system, it is argued, is not only efficient in the utilitarian sense of maximizing the sum total or per capita average of human satisfactions taken in the aggregate. Despite the great inequalities in possessions it is assumed it will generate, it is contended by Hume that like other *conventions* associated with rules of justice it is in the long-range common interest of *each*.[19] It is only reasonable, I believe, to take Hume to here be speaking of the situation, not of each particular individual, but of that of representative occupants of the socioeconomic strata to which a system of private property rights gives rise. Along these (Rawlsian)[20] lines, it is of the utmost significance to note that Bentham, Locke, and

Adam Smith all take pains to argue that a system of private property rights, with all the inequalities it generates, works to the advantage of *the least advantaged*. Having in section 40 of *The Second Treatise* argued that "the improvement of labor makes the far greater part of the value" of land, Locke goes on in section 41 to describe the system of communal property amongst the American Indians as one "rich in land and poor in all the comforts of life" due to the absence of the incentives to labor to which a system of private property rights gives rise. "And," he concludes, "a king of a large and fruitful territory there feeds, lodges, and is clad worse than a day-laborer in England." This passage is only slightly modified by Adam Smith in *The Wealth of Nations*: "The accommodation of an European prince does not always so much exceed that of an industrious and frugal peasant, as the accommodation of the latter exceeds that of many an African king. . . ."[21] Bentham, considering the objection to private property that "the laws of property are good for those who have property, and oppressive to those who have none," responds: "all things considered, the protection of the laws may contribute as much to the happiness of the cottage as to the security of the palace."[22]

The view that I find shared by the authors quoted above is not utilitarian, strict adherence to which would permit what the view under discussion prohibits — sacrifice of the least advantaged in the name of the promotion of the overall general welfare. Nor does it require that the inequalities that a system of private property rights generates be adjusted so as to *maximize* the advantage of the least advantaged. What it does require is that all, especially the least advantaged, be at least as well off as they would be under any system that presents itself as a realizable and morally acceptable alternative to a system of private property rights.[23] The principle in question, surely aptly described as a principle of *justice*, is closely related to the proviso that the initial acquisition of previously unowned resources leave "enough and as good for others." What the proviso must speak to is clearly not the distribution of land, virtually all of which in England was already owned by a very few in Locke's time, but rather the fruits of productive resources, including land, which provide the necessities of life and the means for the pursuit of happiness. Given Locke's belief in the great efficiency of a system of private ownership *and in its justice*, the proviso is more than satisfied, for not only are the least advantaged classes as well off as they would have been prior to the appropriation of most if not all of the land by the (industrious) few; they are *better* off.

The above skeleton may be fleshed out by amplifying upon the answers which it implies to the different questions about private property that Hart rightly urges us to distinguish.

1. Definition. Although Locke quite clearly thinks of *property* in terms of *things* that are in one's rightful possession, there is no reason to believe that he would have been opposed to the modern view that property rights are best understood as a complex bundle of liberties, claim rights, liabilities, powers, etc., over the possession, use, management, etc., of things as diverse as land, airspace, and the products of artistic enterprise.[24]

2. General Justifying Aim. Within the Lockean framework as I am interpreting it, the short answer to the question of what good is served by a system of private property rights is simply that, as with other legitimate legal institutions, it protects those moral rights that people have outside of and against government. With respect to property, I have claimed that these are two: (a) the right to the fruits of one's labor; and (b) the right to a just and efficient *system* of property rights as a "means" (as Locke phrases it in section 26 of *The Second Treatise*) to the preservation of life and the promotion of happiness.

Locke's labor theory of entitlement, as I understand it, provides some, but that a limited, basis for the complaint that taxation is theft. And the proviso that "there be enough and as good left for others," as I shall interpret it below, does indeed require some redistributive measures. But redistribution which goes beyond that required by the proviso and other defensible principles (such as the principle requiring provision of the means of minimal subsistence quoted from *The First Treatise*) may have the effect of undermining the incentive structure upon which the systematic justification (b) above) of the entire system of private property rests. This point, rightly emphasized by both Hume and Bentham,[25] implies that although no particular redistributive program may have this effect, the combined effect of an excessive number of such programs, coupled with the general insecurity created by government's being conceded the right to engage in redistribution for the sake of redistribution at all, may be so severe as to violate one's right to a just and efficient *system* of property rights.

3. Distribution: Title and Amount. Distributive principles may be classified according to whether or not they are concerned with the *initial* acquisition of unowned things or with the *transfer* of something owned by one person to another. I thus neglect here principles having to do with the ownership of things lost, abandoned, or last in the possession of those who die without leaving any heirs.

The only principle of initial acquisition that Locke seems to recognize is that which gives *title* to one who first "mixes" his labor with a previously unowned thing. With respect to *amount*, the labor theory of value implies that the value of one's property will, as it should, reflect the amount of labor expended in its appropriation and improvement.

Rejecting the labor theory of value, I assume that the labor theory of entitlement merely assures one of title to the fruits of one's labor. No normative conception of what value something should have on the market is presupposed. Indeed, I suspect that *any* notion of fair market value will turn out to be incoherent. But my interpretation of the labor theory of entitlement, unlike Lawrence Becker's recent explication of it in terms of the notion of what one deserves in return for one's socially valuable labors, requires no such notion.[26] Neither does it require an explanation of how one comes to have a right to something by "mixing" one's labor with it, an idea I find totally mysterious for a number of reasons, just two of which are the following. First, there is Nozick's question of why one doesn't simply lose one's labor rather than acquiring that which it is expended upon, just as one loses one's bottle of ink when one mixes it with the sea.[27] Second, as Richard Epstein has pointed out, the notion seems to be superfluous, for Locke's theory assumes that one's ownership of one's labor is established simply by one's being in possession of, and *thus* in ownership of, oneself. If possession is sufficient to establish self-ownership, why shouldn't it be sufficient to establish ownership of external things as well?[28]

My acceptance of the principle that one has a moral right to the fruits of one's labor comes simply to this: as an autonomous purposive agent one has a right to pursue any activity as long as in so doing one does not violate the rights of others. And surely others have no right to prohibit one from pursuing productive activities that involve the expenditure of one's own time and labor, physical or intellectual. What *I* produce is *mine*, and it is simply absurd to claim that I need other's permission to engage in innocent productive activities. As has been noted by others, such a principle of entitlement is not in itself sufficient to root title in those natural resources that are viewed as originally held in common; it reaches merely to the value-added-on product of one's labors.[29] But this, I believe, is not an unhappy result. For one need not believe that labor is responsible for virtually the entire value that things have, to believe that it is responsible in many instances for a *great part* of the value that things have. And in some cases, of course, such as intellectual, artistic, and athletic activities,[30] the labor theory of entitlement would result in virtually complete title with respect to the question of what proportion of the full market value of one's productive efforts one was entitled to. Few would suggest that there ought to be a "windfall" profits tax on the earnings of an entertainer or athlete who suddenly finds himself in great demand, a case quite unlike that of the ownership of scarce natural resources such as oil.

What of Becker's putative counterexamples to the principle that one is entitled to the fruits of one's labors?[31] I shall consider each of them briefly in turn. First, there is the suggestion that the labor theory of entitlement implies that parents own their children. Becker himself provides an adequate answer to this objection by pointing out that the entitlement theory is for Locke derivative from broader principles concerning the right to life and ownership of one's own person. Children have such *primary* rights and no principle understood as *derivative* can be fairly construed as implying the denial of them. Becker also rightly notes in this connection that a proper understanding of the primary rights from which the entitlement theory is derived explains Locke's view of how it is that (without one's own prior labors being involved) one can have a property right in one's own body.[32] This also explains the alienability of labor and accounts for why employees and those who provide services for others don't acquire rights to the *things* that are the products of their labor.[33] Second, there is Becker's claim that we do not generally believe that people have property rights in their ideas, citing the fact that patent and copyright will protect only *some* ideas and those only for a limited time.[34] Following Nozick's suggestion, I would reply that this does not impeach the entitlement theory but merely represents a (complicated) case of the application of the proviso that there be "enough and as good left for others" that accompanies it.[35]

I have admitted that the principle that one is entitled to the fruits of one's labors is not sufficient to explain the origin of private property rights in scarce natural resources and suggested that whatever their origin laboring on them does not generate a right to the full value of the final product. *If* one has a right to appropriate and work upon previously unowned land, for instance, the labor theory of entitlement implies only that one has a right to the harvest from the crops that one might plant on it. As Mill put it, "The essential principle of property being to assure to all persons what they have produced by their labour and accumulated by their abstinence, this principle cannot apply to what is not the produce of labour, the raw material of the earth."[36]

In order to explain initial acquisition of previously unowned resources of any value, one must move away from the letter at least of Locke's account in the direction of that provided by Hume and Bentham. That this is quite within the spirit of Locke's understanding of the origins of private property I have already argued. To recall that argument, consider again section 26 of *The Second Treatise*, which follows immediately upon the introductory section of the chapter on property:

> God, who has given the world to men in common, has also given them reason to make use of it to the best advantage of life and convenience. The earth and all that is therein is given to men

for the support and comfort of their being. . . . Being given for the use of men, there must of necessity be a means to appropriate them some way or other before they can be of any use or at all beneficial to any particular man.

The means to bring potentially productive resources into use are potentially quite diverse and limited only by considerations of efficiency, although the property rights to which any one of them gives rise may be constrained by the Lockean proviso and any other defensible redistributive principles. Highly pragmatic considerations such as security of title may be just as important in assessing potential means of establishing first title as is the overarching concern with establishing a system of private property rights that will provide the incentives to bring forth the efforts of individual industry. Hume sees original title as largely rooted in first possession, but on his view this method has no intrinsic moral claim on us whatsoever. Indeed, on Hume's view first possession as a means of establishing initial title is not simply *conventional*; it comes very close to being *arbitrary*, resting upon the "slightest" of "analogies"[37]—presumably one suggested by the psychological principle of association based upon the idea of contiguity in space or time.[38] Although the labor theory of original acquisition may appear less arbitrary, it loses that appearance when it is divorced from the labor theory of value and confined strictly to the products of one's labor rather than being applied to that which one has labored upon. Hume is correct, I believe, in suggesting that whatever systematic method of initial division of previously unowned things works most efficiently by way of producing the required incentive structure is the right one. First possession, first mixing of labor, equal division, division by lot—all are real moral possibilities no one of which can be laid claim to as a matter of natural right. All that can be claimed as a matter of right with respect to the ownership of valuable natural resources is a system of property rights that leads to their just and efficient employment. Any such system, I suspect, will, as does our own, reflect the operation of a variety of such principles, including the general principle that one has a right to the satisfaction of legitimate expectations based upon past practices concerning possession, initial or otherwise.

Unlike the highly conventional principles of initial acquisition, the operation of which within a given legal system may generate the expectations in question, the general principle that would require their satisfaction might be plausibly claimed to represent a matter of moral right. Such a principle would, of course, place considerable constraints upon what might otherwise be permissible forms of redistribution, a topic to which I shall turn next within the more general context of a consideration of principles of transfer. Given the importance of the point, let me make the transition to the topic of property distribution by means of transfer by quoting at length from Richard Epstein's remarkably perceptive discussion of the role that he believes the principle of first possession has played, and *thus* should continue to play, in the common law.

> Some weight should be attached to the rules under which a society in the past has organized its property institutions. Where those rules are respected there is no need, at great expense, to reshuffle entitlements amongst different individuals, even in the absence of any clear principle which indicates how the reshuffling should take place. There is no need, moreover, to attack the interests of those who have expended their labor and taken their risks on the expectation, reasonable to all concerned, that the rules under which they entered the game will be the rules under which that game will be played until its conclusion. These rules and these alone have the status of legal rules. . . .
>
> A repudiation of the first possession rule as a matter of philosophical principle calls into question all titles. It calls into question those which exist in the hands of the original possessors; it calls into question those who have purchased the title in question for good consideration, and those who have made improvements upon land acquired on the faith of the public representation that they could keep it for their own. It may be an unresolved intellectual mystery of how a mere assertion of right can, if often repeated and acknowledged, be sufficient to generate the right in question. As an institutional matter, however, it is impossible to conceive of any other system. . . .[39]

I shall discuss a number of principles under the general rubric of principles of transfer, concluding with a discussion of three distinct redistributive principles.

(a) Market Exchange. As did Locke, I believe that a system of voluntary free market exchange, externalities aside, is the only way of providing a noncoercive mechanism for the pursuit of those individual goals that depend upon exchange relations with others and that are of a character such that mutual benefit may be achieved with no one's rights being violated in the process. And I also believe it is efficient, not only in the sense of Pareto optimality employed by neoclassical economic theories of equilibria, but also in the sense that it provides a highly effective incentive structure for the bringing forth of innovative and socially productive labor. Although government interference with a free market may be required to prevent certain kinds of externalities, it should also be noted, following Demsetz,[40] that privatization of property rights may be called for precisely because it is an effective way of providing for the internalization of external diseconomies. Finally, insofar as the principle that one is entitled to the fruits of one's labor creates property rights, to that extent may one claim a right to enter into exchange relationships.

(b) Gift. Again, to the extent to which something is mine simply because I have made it, I have a right to do with it what I will as long as what I do with it does not violate the rights of others. And I do not violate the rights of others in driving down the market price of what they wish to sell by giving away what of it I own. Further good reason for a right of bequest as a form of intergenerational giving may be found in Demsetz's claim that a generalized concern on the part of testators for their heirs may to some extent prevent the imposition of externalities upon one generation by the one immediately preceding it.[41] If this view of a right of bequest is taken, it may be seen as at least derivative from the proviso that "there be enough and as good left for others" applied intergenerationally. Finally, there is Hume's not implausible claim that a right of bequest is an important part of the desired incentive structure.[42]

(c) Inheritance. *Bequest* is a form of giving; Locke seemed to believe (*The Second Treatise*, sections 72, 182–84, 190) that a man's wife and children have a right to *inherit* a substantial portion of his estate. Such a right would of course put considerable constraints not only upon the right of bequest but upon the right of the head of a family to dispose of his estate while he was living. Now I think it is quite clear that Locke believed that the right to inherit was quite closely tied to the right to the means of subsistence of those who are in a dependent position. But if this is the operative principle, it may under modern conditions justify far less than Locke thought it did. Given current employment opportunities for women, and the ability of children to fend for themselves past a certain age, a right in A to inherit a portion of B's estate might be said to exist only when A is not capable of providing for him/her self and B can be claimed to be responsible for A's incapacity.

(d) Rectification of Past Injustice. Compensation for past wrongs surely can require redistribution of property, and there seem to be no special difficulties of principle when compensation for damages among contemporaries is at issue. But when compensation for historical injustices such as slavery or the unjust taking of Indian lands is involved, a principle of rectification may run into square opposition from the kind of general reliance principle discussed by Epstein. I have nothing to add to the discussion of this important and perplexing topic beyond noting that a special case of the reliance principle may be a principle of:

(e) Adverse Acquisition. Adverse possession in the law of trespass, estoppel in contract, prospective overruling as a judicial procedure, and numerous other instances might be claimed to represent legal application of a general principle by means of which people may acquire rights even though acting wrongly or in a manner that perpetrates injustices they are not responsible for.

(f) Payment for Government Services. Compulsory taxation as a means of financing government services is a form of transfer that may be viewed as voluntary to the extent that the citizen may be taken to desire or to have implicitly agreed to their provision. Included here will be those services which represent the provision of public goods that will not be provided through the operation of private market mechanisms.[43] Financing them by compulsory taxation, as Hayek has noted, is morally problematic.

> It is not to be expected that there will ever be complete unanimity on the desirability of such services, and it is at least not obvious that coercing people to contribute to the achievement of ends in which they are not interested can be morally justified.[44]

I conclude my discussion of principles of transfer with three redistributive principles that Locke accepted.

(g) The Principle of Charity. This principle is described by Locke (*The First Treatise*, section 42) as giving each "a right . . . a title to so much out of another's plenty, as will keep him from extreme want. . . ." I know of no textual basis for resolving the question of what Locke really had in mind here. If the welfare rights in question are understood as enforceable by the state, they may obviously come into conflict with claims based upon the principle that one is entitled to the fruits of one's labors—what I have taken to be *the* fundamental property right enforceable by the state. There are a number of ways that one could go here, including a system that would limit the enforceability of the property rights of the affluent against the needy or require the affluent to give a certain percentage of their wealth or income to those in need but permit them to determine what form it shall take and to whom it shall be given. In light of my understanding of the principles that I shall discuss next, though, I am willing to bite the bullet and opt for a fairly extreme libertarian position which construes a right to charity as one that can not permissibly be enforced by the state. Those who have more than enough of the necessities of life on this view lie at best under an *imperfect* duty to render aid to those who are in need.

(h) Assuring the Justice of Capitalism. We have seen that Locke, followed by Hume, Bentham, and Adam Smith, believed that a system of private property rights benefits the least advantaged social classes as well as the successful capitalist. As Alan Ryan has put it, " . . . the labourer, along with society generally, benefits. . . . And this is the rationale of capitalism."[45] It is confidence in this that makes it possible to claim that the system is *just* as well as efficient. But unless one has an absolutely unshakable faith on this score in the operation of the invisible hand, it must be admitted that the redistribution of wealth might be required to assure that justice is achieved. As already noted, what is at issue here is the situation, *not* of particular individuals, but of the least advantaged *representative* person, who is to be made at least as well off as he or she would be under any alternative system of property rights that respects the principle that one is entitled to the fruits of one's labor. It is this latter qualification which disqualifies a system that satisfies Rawls's difference principle as a genuine alternative. In a Rawlsian system, in which inequalities are permissible only to the extent that they maximize the advantages of the least advantaged, natural ability and industry are treated as common pool resources like land rather than being viewed as a basis for unequal property rights. Under the appropriate conditions, this Lockean Principle of Justice, unlike the Principle of Charity, *would* legitimate (indeed, require) direct government involvement with the redistribution of wealth.

(i) The Lockean Proviso. Understood as an original limitation upon the right to appropriate natural resources, the condition that "there be enough and as good left for others" could not of course be literally satisfied by any system of private property rights. C. B. MacPherson has argued that the proviso plays no foundational role in Locke's theory but is rather derivative from the right of all to the necessities of life, its intent being satisfied if the entire system of property is just, that is, leaves the worst off at least as well off as they would be under a system of communal property.[46] And of course Locke thought it did much better than this, writing in section 37 of *The Second Treatise* that "he who appropriates land to himself by his labour, does not lessen but increase the common stock of mankind . . . [in] . . . the provisions serving to the support of humane life." The underlying assumption here must be that the resource base is sufficient to provide all with the necessities of life under a system of communal ownership. As is typical of writers in the Marxist tradition, MacPherson in fact makes that assumption.[47] But given the present press of overpopulation on agricultural resources at a global level, it is at least arguable that it is false, especially if it is required that any system of communal resource ownership respect the primary principle that individuals are entitled to the fruits of their labor. It may be that world hunger is the result of poverty (i.e., the lack of money to buy food on world markets) rather than insufficient agricultural productive capacity at the global level. But it may also be that any international political and economic reforms capable of eliminating the poverty and hunger in question would require coercive forms of redistribution of wealth that would clearly violate anything like a Lockean principle of entitlement to the fruits of one's labor.

Locke's view that God has given the earth "to mankind in common" (*The Second Treatise*, section 25), or any reasonable secular version thereof, would seem to require an equitable distribution of the wealth attributable to the exploitation of those resources which is permissible under a just and efficient system of property rights that respects the Lockean principle of entitlement. I here follow Peter Brown's interpretation of the Lockean proviso:

> People should have equal opportunity to enjoy the fruits of natural assets, *insofar as the equality of opportunity can be secured by a redistribution of the wealth flowing from the natural assets. Note that this does not imply equality or even equality of opportunity, but only that the wealth flowing from natural resources should be distributed in the most effective way to promote equality of opportunity.*[48]

With Brown, I understand the proviso to apply across national boundaries and, following Gregory Kavka, I understand it to apply intergenerationally.[49] Although I would vigorously reject Rawls's notion that inherited and socially acquired individual assets such as intelligence are to be treated as common pool resources for the purposes of the application of the proviso, I welcome Annette Baier's suggestion that it be understood to embrace those public goods that are part of a community's cultural heritage.[50] I take all of the obligations that the proviso generates to be enforceable obligations. Given my understanding of its spatio-temporal range of application, this raises some nice questions for political theory the discussion of which I shall not enter into here.

In conclusion, let me note that I believe that the acceptability of the account of private property rights sketched above must depend in large part upon how well it meshes with other accounts of what other kinds of institutions and social practices we have a right to in virtue of our status as autonomous and responsible social beings. Each such account will partially flesh out and thereby enrich the basic concept of human personhood that I take to lie in the background, and it is that concept as tentatively fixed at any given time by provisionally accepted accounts of some basic rights that will guide and inform the construction of accounts of yet other rights. The aim of the grand project that I am suggesting must eventually be carried out is to achieve a "vertical" integration of the account of particular basic rights with the basic concept of human personhood and a "horizontal" integration among the basic rights themselves, the overall result being a coherent and illuminating picture of human beings as free and responsible agents. For such other accounts that I believe complement my own account of private property rights in the manner required, I would recommend the following: Herbert Morris's argument that, as persons, we have a right to institutions in which we are punished rather than treated in response to our violation of important social rules;[51] Charles Fried's analysis of the right to privacy as providing the "moral capital" that must be spent to create and nourish relationships with others of love, friendship, trust, and respect;[52] Thomas Hill's account of the duty, to both oneself and others, to avoid being servile, which suggests a right to social practices and institutions that do not foster servility;[53] the discussions by F. A. Hayak and Lon Fuller of the rule of law, which suggest basic procedural rights to legal institutions of a particular sort;[54] Gerald Dworkin's and Joel Feinberg's account of the injustice involved in unjustified paternalistic intervention.[55]

NOTES

1. Charles Reich, "The New Property," *Yale Law Journal* 73, no. 5 (April 1964): 733.

2. Cf. Robert Nozick, *Philosophical Explanations* (Cambridge, Mass.: Harvard University Press, 1981), pp. 498–504, and Nozick, *Anarchy, State and Utopia* (New York: Basic Books, 1974), pp. 91–92.

3. I so interpret Ronald Dworkin, *Taking Rights Seriously* (Cambridge, Mass.: Harvard University Press, 1977). See Rolf Sartorius, "Dworkin on Rights and Utilitarianism," *Utah Law Review*, 1981, no. 2.

4. Rolf Sartorius, *Individual Conduct and Social Norms* (Encino, Calif.: Dickenson, 1975).

5. Cf., on the utilitarian's understanding of what, if anything, is wrong about slavery, John Rawls, "Justice As Fairness," *Philosophical Review* 67, no. 2 (April 1958): 187–89.

6. Jeremy Bentham, *The Principles of Morals and Legislation* (1789; reprint, New York: Hafner, 1948), p. 36.

7. Dworkin, *Taking Rights Seriously*, pp. 234–35, 276–77.

8. Note that Rawls, "Justice," characterizes his hypothetical agents in the original position as being free from envy.

9. Thomas Nagel, "The Fragmentation of Value," in T. Nagel, *Mortal Questions* (Cambridge: Cambridge University Press, 1979).

10. Thomas Scanlon, "Preference and Urgency," *Journal of Philosophy* 72 (1975).

11. H. L. A. Hart, "Prolegomenon to the Principles of Punishment," in Hart, *Punishment and Responsibility* (Oxford: Oxford University Press, 1968), pp. 3–4.

12. Peter Laslett, ed., *Locke's Two Treatises of Government* (New York: Mentor Books, 1965), p. 114.

13. C. B. MacPherson, *The Political Theory of Possessive Individualism* (Oxford: Oxford University Press, 1962), ch. 5.

14. Nozick, *Anarchy, State, and Utopia*, pp. 169–72.

15. *Ibid.*, p. 258.

16. *The Second Treatise*, sec. 183.

17. *Ibid.*

18. This is thus an instance of the general notion that, as persons, we have rights to institutions of certain sorts.

19. David Hume, *A Treatise of Human Nature* (1739), bk. III, pt. II, sec. 2.

20. See John Rawls, *A Theory of Justice* (Cambridge, Mass.: Harvard University Press, 1971), pp. 64f.

21. Adam Smith, *The Wealth of Nations* (1776; reprint, New York: Modern Library, 1952), p. 78.

22. Jeremy Bentham, *Theory of Legislation*, ed. C. K. Ogden (1931), p. 114.

23. The requirement that it be morally acceptable, and thus honor the principle that one is entitled to the fruits of one's labors, prevents it from requiring that Rawls's difference principle (Rawls, *A Theory of Justice*, pp. 82f.) be satisfied.

24. See Lawrence Becker, *Property Rights* (London: Routledge and Kegan Paul, 1977), ch. 2.

25. David Hume, *An Enquiry Concerning the Principles of Morals* (1751), sec. III, pt. II; Bentham, *Theory of Legislation*, pt. I, ch. 11.

26. Becker, *Property Rights*, pp. 49–56.

27. Nozick, *Anarchy, State, and Utopia*, pp. 174–75.

28. Richard A. Epstein, "Possession As The Root of Title," *Georgia Law Review* 13, no. 4 (Summer 1979):1227.

29. Although the distinction in question may be clear in principle, I must admit that I am not at all clear how it is to be applied in practice.

30. Cf. Nozick's Wilt Chamberlain example in *Anarchy, State, and Utopia*, ch. 7, esp. pp. 160–64.

31. Becker, *Property Rights*, pp. 46–47.

32. *Ibid.*, p. 39.

33. *Ibid.*, pp. 46–47.

34. *Ibid.*, p. 47.

35. Nozick, *Anarchy, State, and Utopia*, pp. 181–82.

36. J. S. Mill, *Principles of Political Economy*(1848; reprint, Middlesex, England: Penguin Books, 1970), bk. II, ch. 2, sec. 5.

37. Hume, *Enquiry*, sec. III, pt. II.

38. *Ibid.*

39. Epstein, "Possession," pp. 1241–42. A similar theme is sounded by Bentham, *Theory of Legislation*, pt. I, chs. 7 and 11.

40. Harold Demsetz, "Toward A Theory of Property Rights," *American Economic Review* 57, no. 2 (1967):348.

41. *Ibid.*, p. 355.

42. Hume, *Enquiry*, sec. III, pt. II.

43. For an extended discussion of public goods provision, see Rolf Sartorius, "The Limits of Libertarianism," in *Liberty and the Rule of Law*, ed. Robert L. Cunningham (College Station, Tex.: Texas A & M Press, 1979).

44. F. A. Hayek, *The Constitution of Liberty* (Chicago: University of Chicago Press, 1974), p. 144.

45. Alan Ryan, "Locke and the Dictatorship of the Bourgeoisie," *Political Studies* 13 (1965):224.

46. MacPherson, *Political Theory*, pp. 211–14.

47. C. B. MacPherson, "Natural Rights in Hobbes and Locke," in *Political Theory and the Rights of Man*, ed. D. D. Raphael (Bloomington, Ind.: Indiana University Press, 1967).

48. Peter G. Brown, "Food As National Property," in *Food Policy*, ed. Peter G. Brown and Henry Shue (New York: The Free Press, 1977), p. 74. Italics in original.

49. Gregory Kavka, "The Futurity Problem," in *Obligations to Future Generations*, ed. Brian Barry and R. I. Sikora (Philadelphia: Temple University Press, 1978), p. 200.

50. Annette Baier, "The Rights of Past and Future Persons," in *Responsibilities to Future Generations*, ed. Ernest Partridge (Buffalo, N.Y.: Prometheus Books, 1981).

51. Herbert Morris, "Persons and Punishment," *The Monist* 52, no. 4 (October 1968).

52. Charles Fried, *An Anatomy of Values* (Cambridge, Mass.: Harvard University Press, 1970), ch. 9.

53. Thomas E. Hill, Jr., "Servility and Self-Respect," *The Monist* 57, no. 1 (January 1973).

54. F. A. Hayek, *The Constitution of Liberty* (Chicago: University of Chicago Press, 1960), chs. 11 and 16; Lon Fuller, *The Morality of Law* (New Haven: Yale University Press, 1964).

55. Gerald Dworkin, "Paternalism," *The Monist* 56, no. 1 (January 1972); Joel Feinberg, "Legal Paternalism," *Canadian Journal of Philosophy* 1, (1971).

11

Rights and the Common Law

Charles Fried

I

The literature is rich with arguments that a satisfactory theory cannot make do on utilitarian propositions alone; (2) that rights are a crucial feature of a more adequate moral theory, and, of course; (3) that rights can neither be derived from, nor reduced to, considerations of utility.[1] I have elsewhere contributed to this literature[2] and have nothing to add here on these general themes. Indeed I am inclined to believe that those who are not convinced are unlikely to be moved by further abstract demonstrations. The bearing of this topic on law is evident. Rights are the proper subject of legal discourse, and so the derivation of rights must be of interest to legal thought.[3]

In recent years the dispute between utilitarians and rights-theorists as it concerns law has focused on the burgeoning field of law and economics. The attempt to show that legal rules can be explained in terms of economic efficiency—either normatively or descriptively—is just the modern day version of Bentham's attempt to subject those rules to the canons of utility. Once again the philosophical literature on this general topic is particularly rich.[4] In this essay I shall not seek to add to that literature at the level of general argument.[5] Rather in sections II to IV I shall deal with some quite concrete institutions, the basic common-law institutions of private law. My strategy will not be to show that utility theory and economic theory could not possibly account for these institutions, but rather to display them in sufficient detail that the utilitarian-economic claims will seem implausible. Though such a procedure cannot be dispositive, it should strengthen the force of the more abstract demonstrations. And if utility cannot satisfactorily account for the species legal rights, it cannot account for the genus of rights *tout court*.

In sections V and VI I change my tack and argue that the complexity of the basic institutions of private law and of the system of rights that they secure cannot be derived from any of the principal contemporary philosophical discussions of rights. I conclude with a suggestion about the nature of legal rights and of the mode of reasoning proper to their development.

II

There are three basic principles of private law: the contract or promise principle (let us call it K), the harm or tort principle (let us call it T), and the unjust enrichment or restitution principle (let us call it R). K holds that a person should keep her promises, and if she does not the law should place the beneficiary of a promise in the position in which the beneficiary would have been had the promise been kept. T holds that one who causes harm wrongfully should put the victim in as good a position as he would have been in had no harm been inflicted. R holds that when one person has been enriched unjustifiably at another's expense, the benefit should be returned.[6]

These three principles define a structure of relations between persons. T and R commit the law to the maintenance of a person's present system of rights and advantages, protecting those entitlements against involuntary diminishment, while K permits persons to make use of the entitlements so protected by implementing not only present dispositions of those entitlements but future dispositions as well.[7] And this immediately suggests that K is indeed a particularly important special case of a broader principle for which I have no single name, which is the principle allowing voluntary dispositions of one's entitlements. This principle would cover present gifts, as well as testamentary dispositions. I shall have little to say about the larger transactional or dispositive principle of which K is a special case, only because K is by far the most difficult instance of it.

The thesis I shall be developing holds that K, T, and R are—as any law student knows—incredibly complex subjects, principles with sub-principles, conflicting doctrines, priority rules, and the like. Over the centuries in the common law—and before that in the Roman law—jurists have engaged in the enterprise of elaborating these principles. It is my thesis that the elaboration of these principles cannot sensibly be viewed as an exercise in either economics or moral philosophy. Rather this has been a legal development, which has taken place according to what Lord Coke called "the artificial reason of the common law."

Consider R. Professor Dawson has shown how the German law has been particularly thorough in seeking to work out what it views as the great principle that no one should be enriched at another's expense.[8] Let us first contrast this "great principle" to T and K. The difference between T and R is R's focus on the defendant's enrichment. When a careless motorist injures a pedestrian the law gives little explicit attention to what the defendant got out of this "transaction." It focuses instead on the plaintiff's injuries. When one man punches another in the nose in a fit of anger, the law of assault does not inquire into the satisfaction that the assailant may have obtained, but rather is concerned to compensate the plaintiff's physical injury and his sense of outrage. The defendant's actions being wrongful in these cases, the law's attention is turned to making up for the harm that was suffered.

If, by contrast, I built a structure on your land in the reasonable but mistaken belief that the land is mine, the law will not inquire primarily into how much the structure cost me (what harm I have suffered) but rather whether you have been enriched by my mistaken action; and if I have been, it will compensate me in the amount of that benefit.[9] If by some error I discharge a debt that you owe to a third person, confusing you with another creditor of mine with the same name, for instance, once again the predicate for the relief I seek is not that you have done anything wrong (for you have done nothing at all) nor even that I have suffered a loss (at least that is not a *sufficient* predicate), but rather that you have been *enriched* by virtue of that loss.[10] If in my mistaken attempt to enrich you I had confided the money to an agent of mine who absconded, so that you never enjoyed any actual enrichment, this loss would be entirely my own.[11] (To be sure, if I did owe you the money and the same misfortune had befallen me, I would still owe you the money.) The first case would be treated rather like the last, if through my own foolishness or bad luck I had spent much more than is usual in building the structure on the land that was yours but I thought mine.[12]

This grand principle requires considerable qualification. If I build a hotel across the street from your restaurant as a consequence of which your restaurant prospers, when I might have prospered had I included a restaurant in my hotel, there is indeed a sense in which you have been enriched at my expense, but nobody imagines that I can claim any share in your profits. If you and I own service stations on opposite sides of a highway, and access to your station is greatly reduced when new interchanges are built, I may receive double the custom and so be enriched at your expense. Once again, there is nothing you can do about it. As is universally acknowledged, the predicate for recovery is that the enrichment be *unjustly* at the expense of the plaintiff. But what is this conception of injustice? Is it not the very function of the basic principles of private law, of K, T, and R, that these principles themselves spell out what constitutes justice or injustice? They are, as it were, analyses of the concept of justice in transactions, what Aristotle called commutative justice, justice in *synallagmata*.[13]

The same incompleteness of the R principle occurs in the concept of enrichment in cases in which we may assume that had there been enrichment it would have been unjust. For instance, imagine once again that, mistaking the property line, you have built a log cabin on my land in some remote portion of country. You built in the fall. Before I get to the land next spring the cabin is destroyed by lightning. Have I been enriched at all? It would be hard indeed to force me to pay out to you what might be considerable damages for a log cabin that I did not ask you to put on my land and that had burned to the ground before I ever knew it was there. The German law, as Dawson has shown, is assiduous in following out the implications of the concept of "enrichment" and holds that in a case such as this in which I am a wholly innocent enriched party (i.e., I did not compel you to build the cabin through duress, for instance, nor did I fail to insure it after I learned of its presence), there must be some actual accretion to the net asset value, as it were, of the defendant.[14]

Indeed the German law follows this idea through quite conscientiously. If an employer pays in error a former employee a pension in excess of that which is owed, the employee can resist a suit for restitution on the ground that he has spent the money on consumption. If he had spent the money on capital goods, perhaps the capital goods might be returned. If they had depreciated, the German law would seriously consider the claim that the employee had only been enriched in the amount of the depreciated value of the capital goods. And as for consumption goods, the question would be asked whether the consumption is consumption that the employee would have engaged in anyway, so that the employer's overpayment merely freed up other resources, with the resulting increase to the employee's net asset value after all.[15] As Dawson argues, the twists and turns of this notion of "erasable" enrichment can be quite dizzying, involving the most metaphysical speculations. The Anglo-American law in such cases take s much cruder line with the beneficiary. It will entertain the claim of "change of position," but only in rather limited, specified cases.[16] (For instance, when a creditor-defendant releases the debt of her true debtor because she believes herself to have been satisfied by the mistaken payment on the part of the plaintiff, this "change of position" will protect the defendant from a restitution claim by the plaintiff.)[17]

There are a number of situations, however, in which the Anglo-

American law digs in its heels quite determinedly. For instance, in the case of a contract frustrated through supervening impossibility. Thus, when a mover had moved pursuant to contract a structure halfway to its new location and the contract is discharged because a fire destroyed the structure, the Massachusetts court held the owner liable to pay for so much of the work as had already been done.[18] That the defendant had not at the end of the day been enriched in a balance sheet sense was irrelevant. Or when medical services are rendered to an incompetent, the fact that the patient does not regain consciousness before death hardly serves as a defense to a restitutionary claim on the part of those who supplied medical attention.[19]

III

It is not my purpose to argue that these features of the Anglo-American law of restitution cannot be explained or rationalized, only to point out how much rationalization is necessary, how many stops there are along the way; that it is not in other words a simple nonstop journey from the "great" principle of unjust enrichment to the conclusion in these cases. If a single principle like R generates untold complexities in its application, there are even greater impediments to a simple structuring of the whole common law of transactions. Consider the possibility that the triune structure I have proposed is not too simple but indeed too complex. Might it not be argued that each of the three principles might somehow or another be reduced to the other, so that they are all merely examples of one principle?

For instance might we not see tort as an example of unjust enrichment, T becoming R? The argument would go this way: the careless motorist of my example does in fact appropriate a value to himself by expending (I am using my terms with care) insufficient care along the way.[20] Indeed, the economic analysis makes us sharply aware of this possibility, for it shows that in large-scale enterprises care costs money, care represents opportunities foregone,[21] and thus injuries brought about through lack of care are instances of the defendant's enrichment at the plaintiff's expense after all. The point occurs also in the familiar analysis of negligence, in which the court is asked to compare the probability of harm with the benefit to the defendant and the cost of avoiding the harm[22] — surely a calculus that compares the defendant's enrichment to the plaintiff's loss.

Now it may be a defect of this analysis that it assumes rationality to an excessive degree. Often the defendant gains nothing at all from his careless conduct, nor would it have cost him anything to avoid it. But this objection hardly short-circuits a traditional R analysis, for it is analogous to the argument that the defendant was not "really" enriched because through his own fault or inattention he failed to benefit when others might have. The pensioner who has spent his pension on riotous living that he otherwise could not have afforded may have a defense to an unjust enrichment suit by the employer in German law, but he surely would have none in Anglo-American law. And even in German law if he should have known that he received the money only because of the plaintiff's mistake, then he is wholly deprived of the benefit of the "erasure" doctrine.[23] But should not a careless motorist at least be charged with responsibility of the same order for the "custody" of the good he appropriates—in this case the diminished care lavished upon the plaintiff?

The way in which R and T may be made to coalesce can be seen as an illustration of the difference between the economic conception of cost and the more commonsensical notions of harm or enrichment, or enrichment at another's expense. For the economist generalizes the notion of cost to include the notion of an opportunity cost, and thus the term expands to include all conceivable benefits or detriments along a single dimension, as it were. Cost is simply the segment of the line to the left of the zero point, that is, the negative segment, and opportunity costs are rightward movements foregone. Symmetrical with the concept of an opportunity cost would be the term (that I am just now making up) of an opportunity benefit: an opportunity benefit is something that saves a person an expenditure she would otherwise have to make. For instance, if the owner of some property adjacent to mine paves a right of way we both share in order to improve access to her property, I am saved that expenditure and obtain improved access to my land. Or if my neighbor installs powerful security lights on his property, thereby also lighting a portion of my property, I am similarly benefited. What the economist does is to calculate the net increment or decrement to my asset value (including the increase or decrease of liabilities I may have) as a result of the transaction in issue. Legal thinking, by contrast, is a good bit lumpier, more discontinuous. Not every opportunity cost is viewed as a detriment; not every expenditure saved is viewed as a benefit. This lumpiness has a number of sources.

First, the law asks not simply whether a party has suffered a detriment (cost *or* opportunity cost) but whether the deprivation was an advantage to which there was an *entitlement*, a right. Thus the plaintiffs in my hotel and service station examples may have suffered detriments, but they have lost nothing to which they were entitled.[24]

Second, the law is concerned with the *faultiness* or wrongfulness of the defendant's conduct quite beyond and apart from the question whether the defendant has appropriated a value to himself. So, in the hotel and service station examples again, the fortunate parties are liable for nothing, in part because they did nothing wrong. Nor is this point simply the obverse of the previous one, that the losing parties have no entitlement to the advantages they lost. For there are cases in which one might readily agree that a plaintiff had a right to an entitlement, say, to the safety of her person or the security of her property, and yet if she suffered injury or loss through an action that would be considered innocent there is no occasion for redress. This is illustrated in the ordinary negligence action, in which an innocent plaintiff sues a defendant who may have caused him harm but did so without fault.[25]

The point is illustrated in more complex situations as well. A defendant has obtained a benefit in a way that the law considers faulty—for instance, by making a contract that he then breaches, or perhaps simply with the knowledge that the benefit has been conferred on him by mistake, or perhaps by means of duress exerted on another. If the defendant then loses or dissipates the benefit (if the log cabin in my example is destroyed by fire, or a payment is dissipated on extraneous luxuries), this "change of position" would not relieve a defendant of the duty to make restitution even in German law.

Third, there is the concept of *responsibility*, which combines aspects of the previous concepts with ideas about causation, ideas that are quite peculiar to the law. Thus, for instance, Professor Dawson points out that the Anglo-American law of unjust enrichment is much less concerned than is the German law with the question of whether a defendant had suffered a real accretion to his net asset value at the end of the day. If even an innocent enriched party loses or dissipates the property—if a horse bought with the money breaks its leg and must be destroyed—yet this will not absolve the defendant from the obligation to make restitution. The reason that Dawson gives is that after a certain point—after the defendant accepts the money, for instance—what the defendant does with it becomes *his* responsibility, not the plaintiff's, and he cannot shift that responsibility to others.[26]

Dawson makes the strongest case for this concept of responsibility in recalling the famous Massachusetts case of *Vickery v. Ritchie*, the Turkish Bathhouse Case,[27] in which, through a fault of neither a builder nor owner, but of a crooked architect, the builder built a bathhouse believing he would be entitled to a much larger payment than the owner thought he had contracted for.

> The decision to construct a building at the location was the owner's decision, the building he had asked the plaintiff to build had been

built in accordance with his request and with an expectation on both sides of payment. When they failed to regulate by their own agreement the price to be paid, with neither party remiss in the bargaining process, the owner most certainly still must pay and there was no reason whatever as the court said, why the amount he must pay should depend on "the profit or loss to the owner, arising from his wisdom or folly." He should pay the value of the human and material resources that had been expended in accordance with this request. . . .

Under German law, it should be noted, the outcome in the Bathhouse Case would almost certainly have been different. . . . Any enrichment produced by the performance rendered would have been received without knowledge that its retention was unjustified so that under the German Code the owner would be obliged to restore no more than his net gain. This would probably be taken to be the value added to the owner's real estate. So because of the owner's "innocence" the builder would have to assume the loss on the investment that was due to the reluctance of Boston residents to take Turkish Baths. . . .[28]

This notion of responsibility combines ideas of fault and entitlement. Thus the restaurant is not responsible for the opportunity cost to the hotel, which is the benefit the hotel would have reaped had it included a restaurant. (Note the excessively counterfactual nature of some of these opportunity-cost analyses.) In the same way a competitor is not responsible for another's loss in fair competition, because she is entitled to compete, and competing is not a wrongful action. (Note how the concept of property is a specific case of entitlement, which blocks the easy passage from tort to restitution and back again, preventing the homogenization of all of these concepts along the single dimension of net benefit and cost, including opportunity.)

IV

Thus concepts such as entitlement, fault, property, responsibility make legal concepts insoluble in the medium of economic discourse. This insolubility is demonstrated further as one considers the distinction between the promise principle (K) on one hand, and T and R on the other.

It has seemed to some (particularly Grant Gilmore) that K may after all be made to dissolve into T.[29] The story goes like this. A promisee is harmed when his expectation is disappointed. If his loss is a reliance loss, that is, if he is worse off as a result of the disappointment than if he had not entered the transaction at all, then the T principle suggests compensation. But let us suppose he has not had a reliance loss, but only an expectation of profit that he does not realize. By the reasoning that turns T into R, we might say that he has suffered an opportunity cost, in the sense that he has been deprived of an hypothetical or counterfactual benefit. This counterfactual reasoning can be made a good bit less hypothetical, moreover, if we take into account the fact that had the plaintiff not made this contract for this benefit, he might have made another equally profitable one.

And in general, does not the promisor by breaking her promise for some reason of her own, appropriate a benefit that rightly belongs to the plaintiff, and thus enrich herself at the plaintiff's benefit? The seller who fails to deliver in order to make a larger profit elsewhere might on this analysis be seen as really selling another person's goods and profiting by this piece of dishonesty. This would be analogous to the case of the tort defendant who deliberately chooses to forego precautions or to profit by imposing a risk on the plaintiff. As we saw in that case, one might well characterize the defendant as profiting at the injured plaintiff's expense. And if it is said that the promisor might have failed to perform, not for calculating reasons, but through simple mismanagement of her own affairs, then this is analogous to the careless or inadvertent tort defendant, who also may enjoy no accretion to his net asset value by virtue of his breach of duty.

But here again there is a lumpiness in legal concepts that cannot be resolved into a clear broth of economics. First, the promisee suffers harm only insofar as his reliance is justified. The mere fact that A relies on B and is disappointed hardly makes B responsible for A's loss all by itself. Something more must be alleged in order to make B responsible. A moment's reflection will show that not even B's knowledge that A is relying should do the trick without more, because then B's freedom of action would be at the mercy of every instance in which the A's of this world gave notice that they were relying on the B's: am I really bound to run along the beach between 9:00 and 10:00 every morning because my neighbor tells me that it is then she sends her children out to swim, relying on the fact that I will save them in the case of trouble? B must be *entitled* to rely, and a promise is one of the strongest sources of such an entitlement.

Second, the attempted dissolution of K into R when there is only a disappointed expectation of profit will not work. That argument depends on the claim that if the promisee had not made *this* advantageous contract, why, he would have made another. But that assumes that this other contract would have been performed. If this is merely a factual prediction, one wonders why this alone should make the promisor responsible. Had my neighbor not relied on me she might have hired a companion for her children—true, but that assumes that she was entitled to rely on me. And if the assumption that the promisee might have profited by an available alternative contract is *not* a factual assumption (actually counterfactual) but a normative one, the argument plainly begs the question: Why would the alternative contract have resulted in any securer advantage than the first contract? If the first contract is not itself sufficient to create an entitlement to its benefit, then a second, alternative contract can create no more secure entitlement.

One cannot, I contend, without residue dissolve K into either T or R. The resulting broth will be lumpy.

The lumpiness is even more pronounced in the opposite direction, for one cannot even begin to dissolve T and R into K. How conceivably would you derive the obligation to compensate for harm done or the obligation to restore a benefit obtained at another's expense from the obligation to perform a promise? That last obligation (K) depends on a discrete, conscious action, indeed in the central case a consensual, bilateral action. How would you tell the story? The economist might have a proposal. Might we not view a traffic accident as taking place pursuant to an "implicit" agreement by the parties to this "transaction": the truck, say, might have calculated the hazards in the situation as might the automobile. Having calculated them and chosen to go forward on the basis of these calculations, each party may be taken to have agreed to the foreseeable risks, with the result that the losses are distributed on the basis of this implicit agreement. Nor does it matter that there was no agreement, because the economist would say that, both parties being rational, we may imply an agreement to whatever arrangement would be most efficient for all concerned in the long run. And this is exactly how the economists do, after all, analyze tort cases, when they allocate burdens and benefits to comport with that result that would have been agreed to had efficient markets been operating.[30]

As has been frequently pointed out, such an analysis requires a point of departure in which some distribution of entitlements and expectations is fixed. It is from this distribution that the parties may then be taken to bargain.[31] And this, of course, is just my previous point about entitlements all over again. Moreover, this dissolution would only work if hypothetical contracts and real contracts were equivalent, but they are not. Although there is some heuristic value in asking what contracts a person would have made under certain circumstances, it is bizarre to assume that this hypothetical notion prevails, while real contracts are a secondary notion. Surely, when competent parties make a real contract this overwhelms any argument about what rational parties would have done in a hypothetical situation just like theirs. Or does it? Might the economist say "No, indeed it does not." When the real contract diverges significantly from the hypothetical contract this is sufficient to raise doubts about the competence of the parties, and the hypothetical contract is what should govern. But since the economist is possessed of no conception of rationality besides that revealed by actual behavior, it is not clear how in the end the economist can escape ultimate reference to actual contracts.

What this last bit of lumpiness shows is that just as T and R are distinct concepts, so K is distinct from both of them; and indeed T and R are closer to each other than is K to either of them. T and R establish foundations for free exchanges, and K then enforces those free exchanges that take place upon those foundations.

V

Philosophical analysis had disclosed not only that there are value premises implicit in economic analysis, but more profoundly that economic analysis requires a rather thick foundation of value structures to go forward at all. This is a largely negative contribution, puncturing the bumptious pretensions of upstart social science to have found, in Austin's words, "the key to the science of jurisprudence." Can philosophy make a positive contribution? Some academic exponents of the rights thesis have seemed to suggest that not only can it make such a contribution, but that it really should rule the roost. As I indicated at the outset, I have great doubts about this claim.

What has even the most richly elaborated philosophical argumentation contributed to the science of law? (I put aside utilitarian philosophy, since I believe it is just the economic analysis of law in an older, more general avatar.) Consider, for instance, John Rawls's contribution.[32] Certainly no recent philosopher can match Rawls for the detailed specificity of his proposals. Yet he leaves the issues we are concerned with almost wholly untouched. His proposals bear on the structure of legal institutions — private legal institutions — only in the following general ways: he would hold that legal institutions must permit maximum political liberty and liberty of conscience, must permit fair equality of opportunity, and must be consistent with the maximin distribution of income and wealth. The last point, it might be thought, has the most direct bearing, but it is there that Rawls steps aside all together. For he argues, as I think he should, that distribution should be the special and explicit concern of a tax and welfare system, which accomplishes transfers against the

background of a functioning set of institutions (presumably the institutions of the market).[33] To put the matter differently, Rawls assumes
that it is the law that will define what are the components of income and
wealth, and that tax and welfare institutions (as in the classical welfare
state) will redistribute funds rather than general entitlements. One
might try to run an argument from Rawls's espousal of the rule of law,[34]
the liberty of the person, and fair equality of opportunity;[35] but that
argument would require additional substantial premises about the connection between institutions of property and liberty of contract, and the
overall conditions of liberty and opportunity. I do not suggest that such
arguments cannot be made, nor that I would be out of sympathy with
them once they were made—only that the philosopher in question here
does not supply the system of premises necessary to make them.

A more explicit concern with legal structures occurs—as one should
expect—in the work of Ronald Dworkin. But his governing principle of
equal concern and respect[36] hardly has more detailed, direct bearing on
questions of private law than do Rawls's principles of justice. We can get
more out of Dworkin's insistence that it is the role of judges to discover
and enforce rights, rather than to make policy.[37] For this requires the ef-
fort to explain how a set of rights might be found to exist in the domain
of private law. Does the principle of equal concern and respect then
generate answers to questions such as whether there is a right to restitution against the owner of the cabin that burned down before it was
discovered, or the payee of the pension who spent excess payments on
luxuries? Certainly both German law, which finds that ordering restitution would be unfair to the defendant, and Professor Dawson, who
holds that some at least of these losses should not be the plaintiff's
responsibility, are making arguments of fairness. They are not making
policy judgments of a kind that Dworkin holds are inappropriate for the
courts.

Dworkin concedes that many court decisions defining rights seem to
rest on policy judgments after all. The choice of liability rules in tort, for
instance, may be determined in part by economic considerations. The
great difference between a legislative or policy judgment and a court
judgment, he argues, is that courts should make such policy decisions
only prospectively.[38] Insofar as there is an issue of the preexisting rights
of the parties, it would be an injustice to defeat these rights and expectations by recourse to policy arguments. Indeed, even maximizing utility
(wealth) or achieving economic efficiency is *a* component of what
fairness requires, in the sense that it would be an unfair imposition for
somebody to insist on holding onto an advantage in the face of a potential great benefit to many others.[39] Thus Dworkin's argument is nuanced

and complex, and yet it does not come close to allowing us to move from his philosophical principles to the solution of legal problems at the level of detail I have considered in the previous sections.

A most important and suggestive recent philosophical contribution to a theory of private law comes from the work of Hayek and Nozick. Hayek treats the subject of the common law explicitly and at length. The rationality of the common law for him, is not any single person's explicit, instrumental rationality. It is an emergent rationality, which grows out of many small-scale actors (i.e., the judges) making deliberately limited decisions.[40] The picture is of common-law judges deciding "according to the law" rather than according to some grand economic or philosophical scheme. From the accretion of these myriad small decisions comes a healthily vital, continuously adjusting overall system. No doubt, the emergent rationality of the common law is in Hayek's mind related to the emergent rationality of the market, in which also no single system of actors (no bureaucracy, no central planner) aims at a result, and yet growth, flexibility, innovation emerge from countless small-scale decisions.[41]

Hayek is somewhat mysterious about just how it is that individual judges should be making their individual decisions on particular occasions. The best Hayek can do is to refer to precedent.[42] The individual judge does not seek to discover a great principle of justice and then apply it to the particular case, but rather seeks the nearest precedents to cover this case, thereby creating new precedents. It should be noted that Dworkin too is a great exponent of precedent; to him it is the job of the judge to mete out equal treatment, to treat like cases alike, and this means to treat the case before her in the same way that other similar cases have been treated in the past, analogously to these analogous cases.[43] Although this emphasis on precedent certainly gives the judges something different and special to do—they are neither economic planners nor philosophers on Hayek's view—it leaves open two crucial questions: First, what's so great about precedent? Second, is precedent a method at all; does precedent constrain; can anything be said about how prior cases control a new case?

Nozick's contribution is at a higher level than generality. In *Anarchy, State and Utopia*, Nozick makes the important distinction between end-state or pattern theories of justice and entitlement theories.[44] The former are all theories that assume a judgment about what the "best" disposition of resources, outcomes, indeed the overall configuration of society, should be, thereby making it a matter of justice or morality to come as close as possible to the desired goal. Efficiency theories are one example of such end-state or pattern theories, but so are efficiency theories constrained by distributive notions such as equality. I would not want to endorse all aspects of Nozick's system. (Those who are familiar with my writings know that I am no libertarian.[45]) It is, rather, the general formal point that interests me.[46] For Nozick—in contrasting entitlement to pattern theories—denies in *principle* the propriety of the law's conceiving its function to be the accomplishment of a particular end result or situation. And Hayek makes the same point.

Both authors emphasize the law as a framework in which individuals seek to accomplish a variety of their ends, and the law should not take responsibility for all the configurations arising from such individual efforts. Hayek's general conception is that of the "private sphere," which it is the overriding function of law to protect.[47] The law of property, torts, and I would suppose restitution, assure the integrity of the private sphere from unconsented-to intrusions, while the law of contract enforces voluntary dispositions between and across private spheres.[48] The economist, it would seem, does make the law take responsibility for final configurations—at least in principle—and so, it would seem, would some philosophers. What Nozick and Hayek propose is a system of concepts by which the law quite explicitly eschews any such responsibility even in principle, adopting as its role, rather the maintenance of a structure within which individuals might pursue a variety of individual aims.

Nozick's proposal suffers from indeterminacies analogous to Hayek's. Only a philosopher would imagine that the general notion of protecting individuals against unconsented-to infringements of their holdings is a conception sufficient to generate a body of law. Recall again the congeries of perplexing cases I laid before you at the outset of this article. Surely, Nozick's conception does not assist in resolving these cases. Nor, of course, does Hayek's allied notion of a "private sphere." In both cases, the general principles seem to be simply overwhelmed by the complexity of detail in actual life. For it is the task of the law not simply to recognize wrongful intrusions on the private spheres of individuals, but also to define those private spheres. Indeed, by identifying an intrusion on the part of A, the extent of A's private sphere is diminished while B's private sphere is enlarged.[49]

While philosophy may convince of the need to recognize a private sphere and may convince also of the impropriety of collective action that makes the existence of such private spheres wholly illusory, this conclusion is far too general. There remain the questions regarding the definition of the private sphere, the definition of the details of what constitute improper impositions across private boundaries and what constitute appropriate remedial steps. In other words there remain all the details of defining entitlements, fault, and responsibility. Philosophy can go as far as to argue that there must be law to identify and enforce these conceptions, and perhaps to exclude inappropriate end-state theories as a basis for such conceptions. But after that the law seems to be on its own.

VI

Philosophy—political theory—can tell us that a just regime, a regime of liberty, is one in which persons have rights. I would go further. In a regime of liberty the large part, the very texture of the citizens' situation, should be woven of substantive rights. Further still, philosophy may be able to tell us in a general way what some of these rights should be. An individual should have a right to the integrity of his person against intentional infringements.[50] Not only his body, his person, should be his as of right, but in some sense his talents, his efforts, the emanations of that person.[51] And the zone around the person should be wide enough that he has some sense of being able to move about at his discretion—in other words, a right to privacy.[52] And I am sure there is more. But philosophy cannot possibly determine the exact shape and extent of such rights. Philosophy can make the argument that some such rights exist. It can even spell out to some degree what it means for an interest to be treated as a right at all—how giving a person a right to this or that works logically against competing claims. But it is preposterous to imagine that philosophy can tell us whether there should be a right to privacy in a public telephone booth or in a department store dressing room,[53] whether the imperative that property rights be respected includes the right of ancient lights or the use of percolating waters.[54]

Consider again the problem of unjust enrichment. There may indeed be a grant principle that no one should be enriched at another's expense—Aristotle certainly thought so.[55] I suppose that if one child receives a legacy that by changed circumstances greatly reduces the inheritance of her brother or mother, decency may require that she relinquish a portion. As we have seen, however, to implement this principle in law requires the elaboration of a large number of other notions. Was the defendant truly enriched? If she was not, was it the plaintiff's fault or had the defendant taken charge of the benefit in such a way as to assume responsibility for it? And was the enrichment unjust? That is, was the defendant entitled to the benefit or at least entitled to ignore the interests of the plaintiff in appropriating it? From the general philosophical position that there should be a regime of secure entitlements (rights) and that such a regime should extend to control of at least some significant range of external resources, we may infer among other things: that defendants must be free to some extent to exploit the resources in which they have rights (property), even if this results in a loss of advantage to others; and that this same conception of property should offer some measure of protection to a plaintiff against involuntary transfer to others of some of the advantages associated with that property. Yet philosophy cannot, no more than economics, spell out exactly what the extent of the plaintiff's protection or the defendant's freedom of action should be: it can tell us only that there must be determinate answers to these questions that respect the rights of the parties—answers that do not subordinate the parties' interests to the general good. But that is just what the gradual elaboration of a body of law by precedent and analogy accomplishes.

Consider another example from the law of torts. Moral philosophy may tell us that a person should be responsible for harm wrongfully caused to the protected interests of another, and metaphysics may illuminate the analysis of the concept of cause;[56] but philosophy cannot determine the answer to questions such as when a necessary condition is so remote from an effect as no longer to count as a basis for responsibility, or when the intervention of extraneous forces cuts off responsibility for a result. Yet if the rights protected are to be truly determinate, then there must be determinate answers to these questions. Once again, the law, built up by the slow accretion of precedents under legal rubrics such as proximate and intervening cause, supplies that determinacy.[57] It is this body of law that allows us to say that if a plaintiff has once reached a place of safety, the defendant is no longer responsible for an ultimate harm, even if it is just the kind of harm the defendant unreasonably chanced creating and even if the defendant's act was a necessary condition of that harm. This should not disturb us: after all if I hurl a brick at a window we can all agree that I caused it to break, even though we may know nothing of the laws of physics regarding forces and tensile strength that might underlie such a conclusion.[58]

A final example. General principles support the evident point that in none of these cases should the state order a compensatory transfer of funds from a defendant to a plaintiff unless the plaintiff proves the elements of his claim to an impartial agency. But what is to be the composition of such an agency? If it can be shown that in a particular case a judge might more intelligently weigh a claim than a jury, is that entirely sufficient to defeat the defendant's right to a jury trial? And by what evidence is the claim to be made out? Philosophy is also much interested in the general concepts of evidence and justified belief. Statistics considers when a conclusion is supported and to what degree. Perhaps an individual juror should pay some attention to statistical principles, but when should the decision of a body of jurors be overridden? When is the chance of a misunderstanding so great that relevant evidence should be kept from jurors? If the answers to these questions were wholly determinate as a matter of philosophy and statistics, why should not all issues be determined by experts in these disciplines? Obviously, democratic participation in important state functions, the appearance of fairness, and administrative ease come into this matter of proving claims. But how these considerations interact with each other and with the epistemological principles regarding proof is a question neither of philosophy, nor of political theory, nor of statistics, but of law.[59]

So philosophy can illuminate concepts such as cause, will, intention, —concepts that play a crucial role in relation to fault and responsibility. It can tell us why fault and responsibility have the general significance they do in a legal system. But philosophy stops short of being able to tell us how far we should go in seeking to satisfy ourselves of a person's real intentions in a particular legal context. Nor can it say who should make such determinations, in what procedure, in how many days.

The picture I have, then, is of philosophy proposing an elaborate structure of arguments and considerations that descend from on high but stop some twenty feet above the ground. It is the peculiar task of law to complete this structure of ideals and values, to bring it down to earth; and to complete it so that it is firmly and concretely seated, so that it shelters real human beings against the storms of passion and conflict. Now that last twenty feet may not be the most glamorous part of the building—it is the part where the plumbing and utilities are housed. But it is an indispensable part. The lofty philosophical edifice does not *determine* what the last twenty feet are, yet if the legal foundation is to support the whole, then ideals and values must constrain, limit, inform, and inspire the foundation—but no more. The law really is an independent, distinct part of the structure of value.[60]

So what is it that lawyers and judges know that philosophers and economists do not? The answer is simple: the law. They are the masters of "the artificial reason of the common law." There really is a distinct and special subject matter for our profession. And there is a distinct method down there in that last twenty feet. It is the method of analogy, of precedent. Analogy and precedent are the stuff of the law because they are all the reasoning we can have when general philosophical structures and deductive reasoning give out, when these more determinate modes of reasoning are overwhelmed by the mass of particular details.[61] Analogy is the application of a trained, disciplined intuition when the manifold of particulars is too extensive to allow our minds to work on it deductively. This is not a denial of reason; on the contrary it is a civilized attempt to stretch reason as far as it will go. The law is to philosophy, then, as medicine is to biology and chemistry. The discipline of analogy fills in the gaps left by more general theory, gaps that must be filled because choices must be made, actions taken.

Philosophy, to be sure, has the last word. The argument I have been making is after all a philosophical argument. A judge who accepts my strictures will have to interpret and apply them, and that means interpreting and applying a philosophical argument. In this sense the judge is a moral philosopher and the law is a topic within moral philosophy. It is, however, a very special topic, with methods and constraints peculiar to itself. That is because no (other) branch of moral philosophy is as concerned with the public determination and enforcement of rights on the level of particular cases. The closest moral philosophy has come to the forms and methods peculiar to law has been in some religiously based systems of moral theorizing, such as the Talmudic and Thomistic systems. To the extent that these systems are addressed to the consciences of the faithful (as in the penitential literature), they show a far greater willingness to recur to first principles than is appropriate to law. When they assume the function of public judgment with public—sometimes even coercive—consequences (as in the case of adjudications as to the validity of marriages), the characteristics I here ascribe to law become strikingly prominent. Indeed they become just specialized systems of law. And that is my point. The law's rationality is a rationality apart. Is that a scandal? Why? We can teach it and students can learn it. We can recognize better and worse examples of it. When we say of a judge or lawyer that she is learned in the law, we assume that there is a body of knowledge to be learned in, and that such learning increases wisdom, judgment, and justice.

NOTES

1. See, e.g., David Lyons, *Forms and Limits of Utilitarianism* (1965); John Rawls, *A Theory of Justice* § 5, 83–85 (1971); "Two Concepts of Rules," 64 *Philosophical Review* 3 (1964); Robert Nozick, *Anarchy, State and Utopia* 28–29 (1974). For contrary views, see Brandt, "Towards a Credible Form of Utilitarianism," in Baruch Brody, *Moral Rules and Particular Circumstances* (1971). Donald Regan, *Utilitarianism and Cooperation* (1980).

2. *Right and Wrong*, pt. II (1978).

3. An earlier version of this essay was delivered as the Orgain Lecture at the University of Texas Law School, February 3, 1982, and published in University of Texas Law Review. Research for this article was supported by the Harvard Law School Research Program and The John M. Olin Foundation. The style followed in the notes is that of the *Harvard Law Review*.

4. For two excellent recent surveys, see the symposia in vol. 9 J. Legal Stud. (1980) and 8 Hofstra L. Rev. (1980).

5. I have stated my view in *Right and Wrong* 86–107 (1978).

6. See generally Robert Goff and Gareth Jones, *The Law of Restitution* 11 (2d ed., 1978);

George Palmer, *The Law of Restitution* 5 (1978); American Law Institute, Restatement of Restitution § 1 (1937). See also Gardner, "An Inquiry into The Principles of the Law of Contracts," 46 Harv. L. Rev. 1 (1932).

7. See generally, Charles Fried, *Contract as Promise: A Theory of Contractual Obligation*, ch. 2 (1981).

8. "Erasable Enrichment in German Law," 61 Boston Univ. L. Rev. 271 (1981).

9. See Palmer, supra note 6, § 10.9; Dawson, "Restitution Without Enrichment," 61 Boston Univ. L. Rev. 563, 609 (1981): ". . . the improver can be reimbursed for not more than his cost and, if that is higher, for not more than the gain that he mistakenly conferred. . . ."

10. See generally Palmer, supra note 6, § 17.2.

11. See Dawson, supra note 9, pp. 567–76.

12. Ibid., 594–597.

13. *Nicomachean Ethics*, bk. V, iv–v; see also Epstein, "Nuisance Law: Corrective Justice and Its Utilitarian Constraints," 8 J. Legal Studies 49 (1979); Posner, "The Concept of Corrective Justice in Recent Theories of Tort Law," 10 J. Legal Studies 187 (1981).

14. Supra note 8.

15. Id. at 286.

16. Id. at 288; supra note 9, 568–576.

17. Dawson, supra note 9, at 570.

18. 357 Angus v. Scully, 176 Mass. 357, 57 N.E. 674 (1900).

19. *In re* Crisan Estate, 362 Mich. 569, 107 N.W.2d 907 (1961).

20. See generally, Charles Fried, *An Anatomy of Values*, ch. 11 (1970); Friedmann, "Restitution of Benefits Obtained Through the Appropriation of Property or the Commission of a Wrong," 80 Colum. L. Rev. 504 (1980).

21. See generally, Guido Calabresi, *The Cost of Accidents* (1970).

22. United States v. Carroll Towing Co., 159 F.2d 169 (2d Cir. 1947).

23. See Dawson, supra note 8.

24. See generally Fried, supra note 3, 134–139.

25. See Brown v. Kendall, 60 Mass. (6 Cush.) 292 (1850).

26. Supra note 8, 285, 306; supra note 9, 597.

27. 202 Mass. 247, 88 N.E. 835 (1909).

28. Supra note 9, 596–597.

29. Grant Gilmore, *The Death of Contract* (1974).

30. See, e.g., Calabresi, *The Cost of Accidents* (1970); Posner, *Economic Analysis of Law* (2nd ed., 1977).

31. See, e.g., Fried, supra note 3; Kennedy and Michelman, "Are Property and Contract Efficient?" 8 Hofstra L. Rev. 711 (1980).

32. A Theory of Justice (1971).

33. Id. §§ 42–43.

34. Id. § 38.

35. Id., at 73, 201–205.

36. Ronald Dworkin, *Taking Rights Seriously* 180–183, 272–278 (rev. ed., 1978).

37. Id. at ch. 4.

38. Id. at 304.

39. Id. at 306–307.

40. Friedrich A. Hayek, *Law, Legislation and Liberty*, vol. 1: *Rules and Order*, chs. 4 and 5 (1973).

41. Friedrich A. Hayek, *The Constitution of Liberty*, chs. 2, 4, 15 (1960).

42. Supra note 40, pp. 85–88; supra note 41, pp. 61–62.

43. Supra note 36, at 110–115.

44. Supra note 2, at 150–164 (1974).

45. Charles Fried, supra note 3, ch. 5; "Is Liberty Possible?" *The Tanner Lectures on Human Values*, vol. 3 (Utah Univ. and Cambridge Univ. Presses, Salt Lake City and Cambridge, Eng., 1982).

46. Supra note 3, at 160–163.

47. Supra note 41, at 21.

48. See Fried, supra note 7; Fried, "Is Liberty Possible?" supra note 45.

49. See Fried, supra note 45.

50. See Fried, supra note 3, 32–34, 134–139.

51. Id. at 139–147.

52. Fried, *An Anatomy of Values*, ch. 9 (1970).

53. See generally Katz v. United States, 389 U.S. 347, 19 L. Ed. 2d 576 (1967) (telephone booth); United States v. Shelby, 573 F.2d 451 (5th Cir. 1978) (garbage can).

54. See generally Fried, *Contract as Promise* 99–103 (1981); "Is Liberty Possible?" supra note 45.

55. See notes 6, 13 supra.

56. See, e.g., G. E. M. Anscombe, "Causality and Determination," *in Collected Philosophical Papers*, vol. II (1981); Davidson, "Causal Relations," 64 J. Phil. 691 (1967); J. L. Mackie, *The Cement of the Universe* (1974); *The Encyclopedia of Philosophy*, vol. 1 *s.v.* "Causation" (1967).

57. See generally H. L. A. Hart and A. M. Honore, *Causation in the Law* (1959).

58. See Davidson, supra note 56.

59. See Fried, *An Anatomy of Values* 125–132 (1970); Tribe, "Trial by Mathematics: Precision and Ritual in the Legal Process," 84 Harv. L. Rev. 1329 (1971).

60. Cf. the discussion of prudence in Aquinas, *Summa Theologica* II–II qu. 47–51. See generally Nicolai Hartmann, *Ethik* (3 ed., 1926), for an interesting, suggestive, but I believe rather confused set of proposals regarding priorities and relations between types of norms.

61. Cf. Edward Levi, *An Introduction to Legal Reasoning*, ch. 1 (1948); James Murray, "Reasoning by Analogy" 29 U.C.L.A. L. Rev. 833 (1982).

Contributors

R. G. Frey, Senior Lecturer in Philosophy, University of Liverpool

Charles Fried, Carter Professor of General Jurisprudence, Harvard Law School

James Griffin, Fellow in Philosophy, Keble College, Oxford

R. M. Hare, White's Professor Emeritus of Moral Philosophy, Oxford; Research Professor, University of Florida

H. J. McCloskey, Professor of Philosophy, La Trobe University

J. L. Mackie, Former Reader in Philosophy and Fellow of University College, Oxford

Jan Narveson, Professor of Philosophy, University of Waterloo

Joseph Raz, Fellow in Law, Balliol College, Oxford

Alan Ryan, Reader in Politics and Fellow of New College, Oxford

Rolf Sartorius, Professor of Philosophy, University of Minnesota

L. W. Sumner, Professor of Philosophy, University of Toronto

Index

Index